Comparative Literature

Bapsi Sidhwa and Bharati Mukherjee

Comparative Literature

Bapsi Sidhwa and Bharati Mukherjee

A. Kalidass • J Samuel Kirubahar

AUTHORSPRESS

Worldwide Circulation through Authorspress Global Network
First Published (enlarged) 2012
by
Authorspress

Editorial
Q-2A Hauz Khas Enclave
New Delhi-110 016

Marketing
E-35/103, Jawahar Park
Laxmi Nagar, Delhi-110 092

e-mails: authorspress@rediffmail.com; authorspress@hotmail.com
Website: www.authorspressbooks.com

Comparative Literature: Bapsi Sidhwa and Bharati Mukherjee
ISBN 978-81-7273-668-2

Printed in India at Tarun Offset, Delhi.

Preface

> Everywhere there is connection, everywhere there is illustration. No single event, no single literature is adequately comprehended in relation to other events, to other literatures.
>
> (Matthew Arnold, Inaugural Lecture, Oxford, 1857)

Comparative literature is basically a Western concept in the European context. It began with the strong conviction that the wider divergence of literatures of the world under narrow lingual, national and regional framework could be transcended by drawing together the elements apparently various but essentially common. Matthew Arnold, in May 1848, felt a need to have a comparative approach in literature. However, George Saintsbury pointed out that before Arnold Henry Hallam had attempted to apply comparative approach to the study of French and English literatures. The development of comparative literary study as an academic discipline began with the Chair for Comparative Studies in 1871 and 1879 (E.S. Shaffer. N.P. and Weisstein 221).

Comparative literature is a complex and common discipline which involves the literary technique of comparison. Comparison in literature is made into comparative through the technical use of comparison of themes, genre, and movements and trends of a minimal pair of two literatures going beyond the confines of one country and through translation. It, in short, transports literary materials from one language / nation into another. The study necessarily involves the comparison of one literature with another / others. It is a way of looking at or into a literary response concerning national and international literatures, both Occidental and Oriental, not for enhancing the superiority or inferiority of any individual literature but for enhancing the total understanding of literature in mutual terms.

Comparative literature has been accepted as a distinct discipline. It studies the literature across cultural, national, and regional barriers. A comparison should be strongly based at either end. It needs a comprehensive knowledge of two literatures and their different traditions and outlooks. In *Introduction to the Study of Comparative Literature,* it is defined as "a study in terms of comparisons and contrasts of similarities and dissimilarities of literatures and cultures and countries more than one in order to contribute to the mutual appreciation of literary experiences of various people" (Subramanian et. al. 8). A comparatist adopts various approaches in his/her investigation. A study in comparative literature leads to a more comprehensive and adequate understanding of the works of art.

Bapsi Sidhwa (1939 -) and Bharati Mukherjee (1940 -) are the novelists of Pakistani and Indian diaspora. Their creative odyssey kept them identical in exploring the complexities of their choicest theme of expatriate and immigrant experience with journey as a quest motif. Their protagonists are all women who are lonely as an island in an alien land to assimilate or negate the values of the alien culture with physical and psychological violence. A review of the existing scholarship demonstrates that both Sidhwa and Mukherjee are comparable as they uniformly examine the expatriate and immigrant experience in their protagonists' quest for identity. R.K. Dhawan has brought out a volume on Sidhwa under the title *The Novels of Bapsi Sidhwa* (1990). In it, many of the research articles focus attention on Sidhwa's concern related to expatriate experience, immigration hazards, Parsi identity, women in the society, sexual violence and so on. Emmanuel S. Nelson's *Bharati Mukherjee: Critical Perspectives* (1993), is a collection of perceptive essays on Mukherjee's works. It excludes Mukherjee's latest works—*The Holder of the World* (1993) *Leave It To Me* (1977), *Desirable Daughters* (2002), and

The Tree Bride (2004), and mostly concentrates on her famous works *Wife* (1975) and *Jasmine* (1989). Fakrul Alam's book *Bharati Mukherjee* (1996) examines her works from the focal point of an exile's perspective related to the themes like aloofness of expatriation, exuberance of imagination and hunger for connectedness. Following the pattern set by these two early researchers, Nagendra Kumar in *The Fiction of Bharati Mukherjee: A Cultural Perspective* (2001) traces the phases of expatriation, transition and immigration. Hence, a review of the existing critical scholarship demonstrates that Sidhwa and Mukherjee are comparable as they share a similar perception related to women and their confrontation to adjust/assimilate/negate the alien culture in the phases of expatriation and immigration.

By making a survey of related literatures related to comparative approach between Sidhwa and Mukherjee, it is understood that no research has been so far undertaken to bring out the relative merits and uniformly shared thoughts among these writers under a stream of comparative approach. Hence, the choice of the authors was mainly to understand and explore possibilities of comparable / analogical grounds between these authors. It was also felt that the comparative approach between Indian-born and American-settled and Pakistani-born and American-settled would add extra dimension to the critical perspective and would serve to bridge the assimiliation and perception of Indian and Pakistani immigrants' struggle for existence in alien cultures /societies. Sidhwa's and Mukherjee's novels uniformly explore important issues such as displaced immigrant women, troubled marriages, the quest for identity in an alien culture, the clash between Indian and American values, sex and its violence, crafts (wo)menship and so on.

The present research on Sidhwa and Mukherjee under the title *Bapsi Sidhwa and Bharati Mukherjee: A Comparative Study* traces, analyses, and criticises comparable elements between these Third World, expatriate, immigrant and diasporic writers. It also examines the contrastive features that these two writers have in order to illuminate their individual genius as comparative studies not only include comparable /

analogical elements but also contrastive elements / features too. It is limited only to the novels written by Sidhwa and Mukherjee; however, when the critical argument demands consideration of other works like short stories and non-fiction, they are referred to in the course of the critical analysis of their works. The study may be taken as an inquiry into the status of women within their culture and also in (an) alien culture(s). The study subjects women to the state of centre and periphery, assimilation and dissimilation, absorption and negation and so on. However, the study also justifies its stand for not referring to male counterparts as they are marginalised in the works of art by Sidhwa and Mukherjee. Male counterparts are mainly presented as egocentric, domineering, materialistic, lusty, greedy and jealous.

The thesis on Sidhwa and Mukherjee is divided into six chapters:

Chapter I "Introduction" introduces the socio-cultural background of these two expatriate and immigrant novelists and highlights the possibility of comparison by making a review of existing scholarship on these writers. It also gives a short summary of the novels chosen for study for better understanding of the critical argument presented in the text / thesis.

The second chapter identifies Sidhwa's and Mukherjee's women characters as expatriates and immigrants and further focuses attention on the problems related to their stand as expatriates and immigrants in an alien land / culture. It enforces expatriation and immigration as a journey to carve out an identity of their own in which some character's like Zaitoon, Carol, Feroza, Tara, and Jasmine succeed either by rejecting the alien culture (Zaitoon and Carol) or by assimilating the alien culture (Tara and Jasmine).

The third chapter reveals the harsh reality that women are treated as sexual objects in America, India and Pakistan. They are also brutally victimized in their quest for excellence and womanhood. Their journeys are undertaken in search of fulfillment and self-expression. In fact, the sexual violence orbiterated on their body asserts the fact that female body has become a territory.

The Fourth chapter examines the difficulties of passage in and out of Pakistan and India to America, and points at bridges that cannot be built between cultures. It further asserts that some of Sidhwa's and Mukherjee's women find their ethnic and American identities with self, with tradition and with the wonders and horrors of a new culture with growing aspirations, hopes and desires which other characters are not able to do so.

The Fifth chapter is mainly intrinsic in approach as it examines the narrative technique, point of view, humour, irony, satire, allegory and so on.

The last chapter sums up the findings of the research by making comparison/analogies between these two women novelists—Bapsi Sidhwa and Bharati Mukherjee.

Dr. A Kalidass & Dr. J. Samuel Kirubahar

Acknowledgement

I owe a great deal to many persons for the valuable help they have rendered to me in the preparation of this book on Bapsi Sidhwa and Bharati Mukherjee.

I remain grateful to my guide and supervisor, Dr. J. Samuel Kirubahar, who is always fondly called as Big-Brother, for having initiated and motivated me to pursue research in Comparative Literature. It is he who inspired me to read the fictions of Bapsi Sidhwa and Bharati Mukherjee on the basis of comparison. He was maganimous enough to be my guide and supervisor and, in fact, guided me properly by providing necessary critical insights, which have sharpened my intellect by spending his valuable time, not for hours, but days together at his home and in the Research Centre in English, VHNSN College, Virudhunagar, to bring out this book. In fact, I cannot adequately express my sense of gratitude to my guide and supervisor who always remained generous in going through and commenting on the subject matter chosen for study. It is his keen interest and sustained help that favoured me a lot to complete this book.

I remember my teachers, Dr. V. Sachithanandan, Dr. K. Chellappan, Dr. N. Subramanian, Dr. D. Parameswari, at the Department of English and Comparative Literature, Madurai-Kamaraj University, who trained me in a new discipline called Comparative Literature after my Post-Graduation from VHNSN College, Virudhunagar.

I remain thankful to Dr. S. Kanakaraj, Professor and Head, Department of English, Directorate of Distance Education, Madurai-Kamaraj University, for his constant encouragement and intellectual help in completing this critical work.

My gratitude also goes to Dr. A. Mohan Kumar, Reader and Head, Research Centre in English, VHNSN College, Virudhunagar, for his immense motivation, inspiration, and all possible support without which it would not have been possible to complete this academic endeavour.

My sincere thanks goes to Prof. P.J. Joseph, Head (Rtd.), Department of English, VHNSN College, Virudhunagar, who encouraged me to register for doctoral research at Madurai-Kamaraj University. It is he who instilled in me a confidence to pursue scholarly research in the field of Comparative Literature.

I cannot forget the help of my well-wisher, Mr. A.K. Muthusamy, who has recently submitted a thesis on Naipaul and Arun Joshi, under a comparative stream, who remained always behind the progress of this work and made frequent enquiries about the progress of it.

I remain greatly indebted to Prof. N. Krishnamoorthy, Retired Head, Department of English, VHNSN College, Virudhunagar, for his unfailing help, constant encouragement and affection.

I am in special debt to my College Secretary and Correspondent, and members of the Management Board of the College for their magnanimity in having allowed me to do research as a part-time registrant amidst my tight curricular and extra-curricular activities.

I am greatly indebted to Dr. P. Sundarapandian, Principal, VHNSN College, Virudhunagar for his valuable support in publishing this book.

I remain equally thankful to Dr. S. Manickavel, Principal (Rtd), VHNSN College, Virudhunagar, and to Dr. A. Shanmugasundaram, Self-Finance Courses Director, for their competent advice from time to time.

I thank Dr. N. Anandham, Retired Principal, VHNSN College, Virudhunagar, Dr. Jeyaraman, Retired Head, Prof. P. Devandran, VHNSN College, Virudhunagar for their valuable support to complete this book.

I must really thank my fellow teaching staff at the Research Centre in English, VHNSN College, Virudhunagar, for their keen interest and timely help in proof-reading pages after pages with so much of patience and endurance.

I am extremely grateful to Prof. S. Kirubakaran, Vinayaga Missions University Engineering College, Salem, for his useful suggestions in preparing this book.

I remain grateful to University Grants Commission (UGC) for the financial support to procure books on Sidhwa and Mukherjee in the form of X Plan financial assistance to the Research Centre in English, VHNSN College, Virudhunagar.

I am also richly indebted to my father, mother, wife and daughter who constantly encouraged me in my research, especially, my wife, who has helped me in shaping this book.

I express my sense of gratitude to the librarians and staff members of the National Library at Kolkatta, British Council Library at Chennai, American Studies Research Centre (ASRC) at Hyderabad and Chennai, Library at Dhavanyaloka, Mysore, SCILET Library, The American College Library, Madurai, Post-Graduate Department Library, VHNSN College, Virudhunagar, and so on for having provided me the necessary primary and secondary source materials and for their pleasing and cordial approach whenever I approached them for source materials.

I fondly remember the pains taken by Selvi. M. Kokila, Computer Assistant, in bringing out the manuscript within a stipulated time by typing and executing the task to shape the work.

I am grateful to all those who have directly or indirectly helped me to complete this book on Sidhwa and Mukherjee for which I have drawn on the insights of numerous researchers on Sidhwa and Mukherjee, and which I have acknowledged wherever possible.

I remain indebted to Mr. Sudarshan Kcherry, Managing Director, GNOSIS, New Delhi, for bringing out this book. In fact, it is his encouragement that made me make this venture to publish in GNOSIS, New Delhi.

I bow in reverence to the Almighty God for His graces and bounties.

A. Kalidass

Abbreviations Used

Bapsi Sidhwa

The Crow Eaters (1980)	*Crow Eaters*	*CE*
The Pakistani Bride (1983)	*Bride*	*PB*
Ice-Candy-Man (or) Cracking India (1988)	*Candy-Man*	*ICM*
An American Brat (1994)	*Brat*	*B*

Bharati Mukherjee

The Tiger's Daughter (1971)	*Daughter*	*T*
Wife (1975)	*Wife*	*W*
Days and Nights in Calcutta (1977)	*Days and Nights*	*DNC*
Darkness (1985)	*Dark*	*D*
The Middleman and Other Stories (1988)	*Middleman*	*MS*
Jasmine (1989)	*Jasmine*	*J*
The Holder of the World (1993)	*Holder*	*HW*
Leave It To Me (1997)	*Leave*	*LM*
Desirable Daughters (2002)	*Daughters*	*DD*
The Tree Bride (2004)	*Tree Bride*	*TD*

Contents

1

Introduction

> We should begin by acknowledging that the map of the world has no divinely or dogmatically sanctioned spaces, essences, or privileges [....] what matters a great deal more than the stable identity kept current in official discourse is the contestatory force of an interpretative method whose material is the disparate, but intertwined and interdependent, and above all, overlapping streams of historical experience.
>
> (Said, *Culture and Imperialism* 311-312)

Literature is a powerful tool in the hands of creative writers to modulate and change the societal framework. It reveals principally three sets of relationship: human being in relation to the universe, individual in relation to society, and man in relation to woman. The primary motivation of the novel has always been a projection of a social situation and the reflection of social consciousness. In other words, the novel may be considered a document of social criticism. It tends to reflect the contingent reality in an artistic fashion.

Literature, being a subsystem of a given culture, offers an illustration or exemplification of some general pattern or syndrome. Minority discourse is characterized not only by an urge to adopt and assimilate but also by a culture of protest and resistance. Culture is not merely an organizational principle holding together the members of a community. It is also a means of establishing its separateness from and resistance to other communities.

Fiction in English, written by both native and non-native speakers, has acquired a prestigious position all over the world.

Fiction embodies ideas and experiences of human being in a subtlest way. Especially, fiction by women writers, provides insights, a wealth of understanding, a reservoir of meanings and above all a basis for discussion as they always oppose / challenge patriarchal domination. It is to be accepted that woman being equally potent of other 'self' of man and her outlook being essentially different from that of man, her work is complementary and supplementary to the man's. Women began to register their protest against the established standards and customary values. In fact, of all the different phases in literature in English, 'Women's movement' passes through and reaches a climate which may be described as the phase of discovery where their attention turns inward. They are in search of identity which is reflected in the writings of the contemporary women novelists.

The rise of Indian women novelists may be traced back to the last quarter of the nineteenth century which threw up a number of women writers of fiction in English. Ramamurthi in *The Rise of the Indian Novel in English* observes:

> [...] these writers make an interesting study from at least two points of view: the very emergence of women writing in English during the period was of great significance, for their works, scanty in output as they were, were qualitatively superior to those of many others who wrote before and after them. This claim should be accepted as perfectly justified at least in respect of a few writers like Toru Dutt, Mrs.Ghosal, Sorabji Cornelia and Krupabai Sathianathan.
>
> (66)

The works of these writers reflect the obstacles faced by women, the disadvantages they suffered from, and the cruel tentacles of customs, superstition and other social maladies they were entangled in. Mostly, they were and are still autobiographical in nature by artistically mirroring social problems. In fact, literature by women becomes an instrument of social reform.

Language, music, culture, social milieu, beliefs and problems are the same both in India and Pakistan. The only difference of opinion is on political issues. People on both the sides share the same joys and sorrows. They have same dreams and aspirations. Only names of places have changed in the narratives of Indian and Pakistani writers. Writers like Manohar Malganokar, Arun Joshi, Anita Desai, Khushwant Singh, Bhabani Bhattacharya, Raja Rao, R.K. Narayan, Vikram Seth, Bharati Mukherjee and Arundhati Roy do not seem new and foreign to the readers in Pakistan. Similarly, writers like Sadat Hassan Manto, Bapsi Sidhwa and Attia Hosain are not unknown in India, because they share the same concerns, tragic or pleasant.

Hashmi in "Prolegomena to the Study of Pakistani English and Pakistani Literature in English" says that "the quality of the writing in Pakistan is best described by a literature which has outstripped its colonial origins and evolved a new personal identity of its own" (6). Though the novel has not been a particular popular genre with Pakistan creative writers, the presence of novelists like Ahmed Ali and Zultikar Ghose indicates its standard. It was Sidhwa who gave a distinct identity to Pakistani novel in English.

The Parsees are of an ethno-religious minority in India, living mostly in the west coast of the subcontinent, especially in Bombay. In Pakistan, most Parsees reside in Karachi and Lahore. They are of Persian descent; the word 'Parsee' means a native of 'Pars' or 'Fars', an ancient Persian province, now in southern Iran. They left their homeland over 1,200 years ago to save their religion, the teachings of Zoroaster, from being Islamized by the invading Arabians. They are the followers of the Prophet Zarathustra. Their religion is known as Zoroastrianism. It was founded around 2,000 B.C. Its essence is to be found in the five Gathasar Divine songs of Zarathustra.

The Parsees have the feeling of group identity and active participation in the social, cultural, and economic life of both India and Pakistan. Their religion was founded by the prophet Zoroaster, a monotheist with the sole God Ahura Mazda (wise Lord) being the Creator as well as the judge on the day of the Last Judgment. Ahura Mazda rules over the good spirits (Spenta Mainyu) created by him, which are opposed in the world by the evil spirits (Angra Mainyu). The ethics in

Zoroastrianism demand active defence of the good, which explicitly includes truthfulness, righteousness, and charity. Earthly renunciation and asceticism are condemned by Zoroaster because they indirectly support the evil in its battle.

When India was fighting against colonial rule, not much creative writing was done by the Parsees. The Parsees, such as Phirozshah Mehta and Dadabhoy Naoroji, have written some non-fiction. The future of the Parsi community has been so closely identified with the British during the colonial era, with the end of the Raj and the exodus to the West. Now, after decades of silence, that Parsi voice has been raised once again. The 1980s have seen the re-emergence of the Parsi writers as Bharucha in "Reflections in Broken Mirrors: Diverse Diasporas in Recent Parsi Fiction" regards:

> Not only have older writers, R.K. Narayan, Mulk Raj Anand and Raja Rao, produced significant new work but a host of new writers have appeared-Salman Rushdie, Amitav Ghosh, Upamanyu Chatterjee, Rohinton Mistry, Firdaus Kanga, Bapsi Sidhwa, Farrukh Dhondy, Dina Mehta and Boman Desai [...] However, the majority of the second-generation Parsi writers are in the area of fiction. (32)

Parsi writers have contributed a lot to Indian English Literature. They have been in the vanguard of creative writing in English by Indians. The Indian Parsi novelists have written on the way of life of their community. It is completely distinct from that of other Indians. The Parsi novelists have given meaningful indications of their way of life. Pathak in "Problematising the Minority Discourse: Inlets to the Parsi Sensibility" maintains that the "Parsi novelists have reflected through their works the dilemma of the minority community and its identity crisis" (95).

The Parsees have become the most Westernized of all Indian communities. This make them alienated from the Indian mainstream and also cut them off from their own Parsi roots. They are extremely small minority in India. In this situation, the Parsi community is making its glorious Persian past and its 1300-year-old Indian association. This assertion of Parsi identity is reflected in recent fiction by Parsees.

Parsi writers have contributed their might to literature. They have made an enduring mark in the literary arena. It is rightly pointed out by Mangayarkarasi in "Parsi Identity in Boman Desai's *The Memory of Elephants* and Bapsi Sidhwa's *The Crow Eaters* and *Ice-Candy Man*" as:

> The writers have undertaken the double responsibility of focusing on their social problems and also reiterating their identity. The Parsi story is filled with pathos because of their long delayed recognition and the emptiness of the promise made to this colonial elite whose fragile image is full of paradoxes and dilemmas.
>
> (177)

Parsi life is portrayed in Parsi novels. Zoroastrian ethos is also powerfully expressed in the Parsi novels. Narendrakumar, in "Parsee Writing: A Note", says that the Parsi novel voices:

> [...] the ambivalence, the nostalgia and the dilemma of the endangered Parsee community. In Parsee novel in English, the 'operative sensibility' is Zoroastrian. The Parsee novelists have forged a dialect which has a distinct ethnic character. [...]. The triumph of the Parsee novelists in the use of English language is largely due to westernization and exposure to English culture.
>
> (32)

The elite consciousness of Parsees has not been acknowledged by the new rulers of India. Now, Parsees are trying to reorient and assimilate themselves into the Indian mainstream. They are ready to adopt Indian culture and jettisoning their Parsi identity. It has ensured their separate preservation in the all-embracing Indian ethos. The current Parsi writers picture the problem of Parsi identity and the assimilation of Parsees into the Indian milieu or the immigrant experiences.

Sidhwa was born in Karachi in 1939. She was brought up and educated in Lahore. She had graduation from Lahore's Kinnaird College for women. Initially, she spent her life as a housewife and an active social worker. Her primary interests were women's rights and social investigation. In 1970, she had taken a part of women's delegation to Iran and Turkey. She had represented Punjab at the Asian Women's Conference in 1975. She actively involved herself in setting up the Destitute women's and children's Home in Lahore. She failed in her first marriage. As a resilient young woman, she started writing of loneliness and moreover as an isolated child, she had no alternative but to read copiously.

Sidhwa is a Pakistani English fiction writer. She was the recipient of Pakistan's highest honour in arts: Sitara-i-Imtiaz. She began her writing carrier at the age of 26 after visiting the Karakoram mountain area of Pakistan where she happened to listen to the story that she told in the mould of Zaitoon in *The Pakistani Bride* (1983) (titled also as *The Bride* in America). In fact, she wanted to make a short story out of what she listened to but in due course it became a novel. Through her first novel, she discovered a love for writing. *Bride* took four years to complete; she wrote it and then re-wrote it.

She wrote her first two novels in Pakistan when no one was publishing in English at that time. So, after receiving many rejections, she decided to self-publish and self-distribute *The Crow Eaters* (1980). Then in 1980, Britian's Jonathan Cape decided to publish it after receiving a copy of her self published *Crow Eaters.*

Her second novel *Crow Eaters* is a lively and humorous story about the Parsi community of Pakistan. The title of the book is a translation of a derogatory term used for Parsees who are stereotyped on being excessively loud and talkative.

It was her third novel, *Ice-Candy-Man* (1988), also known as *Cracking India,* that earned Sidhwa an international acclaim and acceptance as one of the most promising novelist in English from South Asia. Her novels have autobiographical elements. She based the parents' characters in *Crow Eaters* on her own parents. In *Candy-Man / Cracking*, the child protagonist, Lenny, is reminiscent of Sidhwa's own childhood.

Sidhwa is unique in her writings. Her range of settings, plots, themes, and characters make her one of the modern Commonwealth novelists. Allen in "Reading the Body Politic in Bapsi Sidhwa's Novels: *The Crow Eaters, Ice-Candy Man* and *An American Brat*" states that the "novels of Bapsi Sidhwa are boisterous, slightly ribald and ingenuously irreverent" (69). She is fluent in several languages: English, Urdu, Gujarati and Punjabi. Anyhow, she has written only in English. She has no feelings of guilt about writing in English. In "Why do I Write?" she admits that for her "writing has become a natural condition of existence, and very often an act of joy. Of course it can be painful, slow, and difficult at times, but it is always a labour of love. When it ceases to be so, I'll give it up" (34).

Sidhwa's novels have aroused a variety of reactions. Her interests are immense. She cannot be easily categorized as just a comic writer or a Parsi novelist. In her novels, as Dhawan in 'Entrée; The Fiction of Bapsi Sidhwa" observes: "The themes vary – the partition crises, expatriate experience, the Parsi milieu, and social idiosyncrasies of this small minority community, the theme of marriage, women's problems, patterns of migration, the complexities of language and the art of story telling" (9). She writes about the life in her home territory in the earlier time. She has shown the Indo-Pakistan familiar surroundings with background history of Indian partition and independence. Dhawan in "Entrée: The Fiction of Bapsi Sidhwa", says:

> Her novel reflects the recent trend of globalization, the concept of the world as a global village and increasing movement of professionals ('brain drain') from the Third World to First World nations like the USA, England, Australia and Canada. As people move from one part of the world to another, national boundaries dissolve, the formation and maintenance of community takes on new dimensions.
>
> (22)

Jussawalla in "Navjote Ceremonies: The Location of Bapsi Sidhwa's Cultute" also says that Sidhwa's main theme "initiation and awakening into oneself as Indian or Pakistani is connected to the sub continental peoples and their land and religion is the essential theme of Bapsi Sidhwa's novels and this is what makes them so real and engaging to the reading public" (82). She has a unique individual voice in her writings. She is a distinctive Pakistani, yet she reflects Parsi ethos in her writings.

Afzal in "Indian Sub-Continent: Pakistani Writing in English: 1947 to the Present: A Survey" observes: "Most of her novels are written with a lawdy, irreverent attitude that acknowledges the comic in even the most serious of situations, and thus allows Sidhwa to see the humanity in all people, irrespective of caste and creed, and despite their short comings and at times, despite their cruelty" (59). She has very lucid views on the role of a writer in modern society. She strongly feels that a writer of fiction cannot really alter social reality or change the world, what she can do is only mirrorise the world and its harsh reality. She has been influenced by Charles Dickens, Leo Tolstoy and V.S. Naipaul. She has also been influenced by the Urdu writers like Mirza Ghalib, Alama Iqbal, Faiz Ahmed Faiz, and women poets like Zehra Nigar and Kishwar Naheed.

In the works of Sidhwa, borders act as important agents for the actions of her texts. It has been observed by Gravley in "Dangerous Crossings in Bapsi Sidhwa's *Ice-Candy-Man (Cracking India)* and *An American Brat*" as follows:

> These borders are not only the physical borders between countries and neighborhoods, but also the invisible borders placed between religious groups, between classes, between stages of development, and between women and men. These physical and psychic borders often represent limitations placed on the characters in their struggle for entry into the dominant social structure.
>
> (81)

Sidhwa has created her women characters in her novels as herself as in her real life. Her women characters are, observes Singh in "Buoyant Woman":

> Fairly beautiful, intelligent, modest but strong-willed, and courageous. Rebellion is not in their nature. They try to cope with parental, societal and cultural pressures in their life as much as they can but when they find their very life

> or identity in danger, they throw off all shackles and fight with full forces to foil the foul attempts of their adversary. Their tactics vary with the nature and strength of their opponent.
>
> (22)

Mukherjee, born in Calcutta, India, on July 27, 1940, is the daughter of Sudhir Lal and Bina Mukherjee. She grow up as an upper middle-class Brahmin girl of educated parents. She attended a convent school created for English girls. Remembering her experience at school she in "BANGLA: The Way Back, says:

> I was eight when I was initiated into bilingualism. At the school in Sloane Square, I spoke the English I heard around me. At home I spoke the Bangla I had in our Kolkatta house. My Bengal identity was not at all threatened by my growing fluency in the former colonizer's language. The shock came from suddenly seeing myself as a minority, a brown girl in a white school. I was still a member of the world's most elite linguistic club, but no body in school knew that.
>
> (20)

In 1959, she graduated in English Literature from Calcutta University. In 1961, she also got her master's degree from Baroda University. She came to the United States for postgraduate work. In September 1963, while attending workshop at the University of Iowa, she married Clark Blaise, Canadian-American writer. In 1966, Mukherjee completed her doctoral degree in English and Comparative Literature. She worked in many colleges and universities. Mukherjee won the Canada Arts council Award in 1973-74 and 1977, the Shastri Indo-Canadian Award in 1976-77 a Guggenheim Foundation Grant in 1978-79 and the National Book Critics Circle Award in 1988.

Mukherjee's work deals with Indians coming to terms with American, including Canadian experience, with an ongoing quest from expatriation to immigration. In her works, she is concerned with the life of South-Asian expatriates/ immigrants in USA. She is also concerned with the problem of acculturation and assimilation. Hers oeuvre comprises novels, short stories, non-fiction prose, sociopolitical commentaries and journal articles and interviews. She has emerged as an important Indian English fiction writer in the last decade. D'Souza in "Bharati Mukherjee" observes:

> A thread that runs through all Mukherjee's eight works of fiction is difference-cultural, religious, racial, sexual and economic class difference. In the contemporary world in which her fiction is set, various upheavals – crippling legacies of colonialism, migration, instances of discrimination and violence, encounters with cultural otherness.
>
> (180)

Nelson in "Introduction" says:

> As a Calcutta born writer who now calls the United States her home after having spent many bitter years in Canada, Bharati Mukherjee is part of a variety of rich literary traditions. Her works can certainly be read in the national context of Indian writing in English and in the international context of the literature of the Indian Diaspora.
>
> (ix)

Mukherjee has started writing from 1971, Her works are *The Tiger's Daughter* (1971), *Wife*, *Days and Nights in Calcutta* (non-fiction 1977), *Darkness* (short stories, 1985), *The Middleman and Other Stories* (short stories 1988), *Jasmine*, *The Holder of the World*, *Leave It To Me*, *Desirable Daughters* and *The Tree Bride*.

Mukherjee identified V.S Naipaul as her model in 1977. In *Days and Nights* she says:

> But for me, an accidental immigrant, the brave and appropriate model is not R.K. Narayan but V.S. Naipaul. In myself I detect a pale and immature reflection of Naipaul; it is he who has written most movingly about the pain and absurdity of art and exile, of 'third world art' and exile among the former colonizers; the tolerant

> incomprehension of hosts, the absolute impossibility of ever having a home, a '*desh*'.
>
> (299)

American dream figures prominently in all her fiction. But after her settlement in America, she covers many moods of expatriation like nostalgia, frustration and hope. The shift to America wrought a sea change in her personality and gave a new strength to her culture and literary aspiration.

Gabriel in "'Immigrant' or 'Post-colonial?' Towards a Poetics for Reading the Nation in Bharati Mukherjee's *The Tiger's Daughter*" says: "Articulation of her cultural and aesthetic concerns does formulate itself in terms that point to the potential divergence between the kinds of discursive and representational spaces occupied by the 'post colonial' and 'immigrant' writer" (89). In fact, her theme is not mainly the larger community's perception or oppression of Indian immigrants in Canada and the acceptance of them in the United States, but about individuals' yearnings to flee the world of bourgeois morality and middle-class superficiality in which they are trapped. Her work is about the ethos of the Indian community in North America. Her fiction truly reflects the temperament and mood of the present American society, as experienced by immigrants in America.

It is nearing three decades since Mukherjee has left India for the American continent. But the familial ties continue to bind her to the country of her birth. S.P.Swain in "Problems of Identity: A Study of Bharati Mukherjee's *Desirable Daughters*" observes that "Bharati Mukherjee looks at India from the perspective of Third world writer, an expatriate and an immigrant. India figures in her novel as a part of memory as a third world place, as a fragment of nostalgia" (129). She is at pains to emphasize that she is an American writer because of her own struggle with identity first as an exile from India, then as an Indian expatriate in Canada, and finally as an immigrant in the United States even though she has been greatly attached to Calcutta, since she has been born and brought up there. Sathupati in "Psychotic Violence of Dimple in *Wife*" affirms:

> In fact, Mukherjee had to come to terms with her own identity in an alien land, caught as she was between two conflicting cultures. Also, she had to contend with racial discrimination during the years she spent in Canada, precisely between 1972 and 1980. She managed to overcome both the crises and this brought her a sense of elation and confidence. Mukherjee's early experiences had a great bearing on her writing and outlook of life.
>
> (78)

Mukherjee has had various types of experience in life. As Devi in "Negotiating the Gap: Cross-Cultural Tensions in Bharati Mukherjee's Short Fiction" states: "Bharati Mukherjee, the Indian-born North American novelist uses language as a tool to give expressions to this perennial struggle on the part of third-world immigrants in their attempts to assimilate into North American lifestyle" (21). She can be defined as a writer who has lived through several phases of life, from as a colonial to later as a citizen in the United States. Myles in "Bharati Mukherjee" expresses:

> Bharati Mukherjee has successfully fused together her several experiences, life and background so to say, into a new kind of literature—the 'new immigrant' literature, the main thrust area in her novels being a description of the condition of the Asian immigrants in North America with particular reference to the changes taking place in South Asian women in a new world.
>
> (107)

As Mukherjee talks about an Indian immigrant community in America, Sidhwa in *Crow Eaters* celebrates the achievements of a tiny Parsi community in Pakistan and in America. It has survived migration without losing its cultural identity. The novel begins with an extended flashback. Freddy Junglewalla narrates the story of his early years to his seven children and some neighbouring kids. At the age of 24, Freddy embarked on a journey to Punjab with his wife and mother-in-law. He struggled many years with his mother-in-law for control over his household. He frightened his mother-in-law by setting fire to his shop, through a fraudulent insurance scheme. Later, he became rich and the master of his house. He strove hard and became rich and popular.

In the middle of the novel, his two daughters Hutoxy and Ruby were married off. The third daughter, Yasmin too got married later. His eldest son Yazdi fell in love with Rosy. But Rosy was forced into prostitution. Shockingly, Freddy himself slept with her. Yazdi was shattered and renounced the world, using his monthly allowance to help the poor and homeless. Finally, Billy, the youngest son, had to carry on Freddy's business. He married Tanya. The book ends on a hot day in June 1940, with Freddy's peaceful death at the age of 65. Thus the novel describes the social mobility of a Parsi family, the junglewallas, during the British Raj in the early twentieth century.

Her second novel, *Bride,* describes the struggle of an orphaned girl. The novel is based on a true story, narrated to Sidhwa. Zaitoon, a Punjabi girl is orphaned by Partition. She is adopted by Qasim, a tribesman. Social compulsions make him marry her back into his mountain tribes. Qasim knows she is unsuited to such a harsh life. She is married to Sakhi. She is almost raped by Sakhi on their first night of marriage. She rebels against her husband Sakhi. Her constant fear of She beating and sexual force make her decide to go away from Kohistan. During her flight, she is unable to escape the violence which prevails in the stark hills of Kohistan. The novel ends with her epic struggle to find the bridge and cross it. Her choice of freedom over slavery, her rejection of the oppressive and brutal tribal society, her courageous and heroic struggle for survival against impossible odds are a testimony to the fighting spirit of the weak. Sidhwa based *Bride* on an actual story she had heard about a Punjabi girl like Zaitoon who had entered into an arranged marriage with the Himalayan tribal man, attempted to escape, and after 14 days of wandering in the mountains was found by her husband; he cut off her head and threw her body into the river.

In her third novel, *Candy-Man,* Sidhwa describes Partition through the eyes of the young Lenny. Lenny is a Parsi girl who led a comfortable life before Partition. She narrates the events.

She is more conscious about the changing environment around her. The Muslim League motivates the Muslim community to raise a demand for a separate nation for the Muslim. The slogans of 'Pakistan Zindabad' are heard in the streets. This leads to the killing of innocent people on both the sides. The news of bloodshed spreads like wildfire. Dilnawaz, the Ice-Candy-Man, waits for his sisters on Lahore railway station. When the train arrives from Gurdaspur everyone is shocked as the train is loaded with mutilated bodies of Muslim passengers. The friendly Dilnawaz turns, and desires to kill the Hindus. He abducts his friend Shanta and takes her to Hira Mandir of Lahore, a locality of prostitutes.

The Ice-Candy-Man has loved Shanta from the core of his heart. But now she is a Hindu for him. Shanta is rescued. She reaches the relief camp at Amritsar. Meanwhile, the Parsi community remains neutral. Lenny's life becomes a nightmare. Ice-Candy-Man begins to roam about in the streets of Lahore to avenge the death of his Muslim friends. Finally, Lenny's godmother helps Shanta and other Hindu neighbours flee from the violence-stricken Lahore. The horrors of Partition are aptly depicted in this novel on Partition.

An American Brat (1993), Sidhwa's fourth novel, is the story of a young Parsi girl's Americanization. Feroza, the heroine, has been brought up in the small but prosperous Parsi community in Lahore. Zareen, her mother, feels that Feroza should go to the USA. Zareen thinks that travel will broaden her outlook. But once she has tasted the freedom of America, Feroza is unwilling to return to Pakistan. After a hard struggle, She completely assimilates the American lifestyle. She wants to marry a man outside the Parsi community. Zareen feels and warns her daughter that marrying a non-Parsi is a cultural suicide. Feroza does not care about her mother's advice. In the end, she realizes that she is irrevocably poised between two cultures. The novelist suggests that immigration is one of life's essential rhythms and that the losses it incurs are really gains in self-knowledge.

Mukherjee's first novel *Daughter* deals with the problems of expatriates. The novel is about Tara's return to her native

Calcutta from the States after seven years. Tara is surprised to find that she has changed in just seven years. She is forced to face the situation as the wife of an American. It amazes and disturbs her. During her visit to Darjeeling, she has to face ugly and violent incidents. It is too big for her bear the cultural-shock after her return from America. She is keenly aware of the indifference and smug maliciousness of her privileged circle of friends and family. She finds it difficult to relate herself to her family, city, and culture in general. At the end of the novel without taking leave of all, she leaves for America in a hurry. She is confronted with the strangeness of her own culture.

Tara is, a girl from the very upper class Camac Street of Calcutta with a corresponding upper class upbringing. She had been sent to Vassar for higher studies at the age of 16. Now she has come home for a holiday trip, to visit her parents after seven years, having married a white American sometime in the intervening seven years. The novel is about her experiences during this trip. Her old milieus, her family, her ideas of yore, seem to confront the 'American' Tara as it were. She finds herself a misfit in her parents' home, and among her lifelong friends. She wants to be happy but finds that she cannot be so, and realises that the state of happiness is never the outcome of strenuous exercise to bring it on. Political turbulence, poverty, over-population, corruption, hypocrisy—all the problems that plague Calcutta seem to make her emotionally insecure and unstable. She can never express her love for her husband David in her letters to him. She misses him a lot. She is homesick and this time 'home' is America for her. But she is not conscious about it. It is conveyed in the way in which Mukherjee shows how she weighs and balances all the aspects of her cocooned, ivory-tower existence in Calcutta and Darjeeling.

Tara is now an outsider looking at her own life, from outside. Her friends Sanjay, Pronob, Nilima and Reema are on the inside. This contrast in their attitudes to their lives and Tara's, is very subtly executed by the author. Tara is shown as being an Indian-American for she now looks at India with eyes of an American. So she finds herself marginalized on the psychological level. She had experienced a similar sort of syndrome once before when she had first landed in America. She had been desperately homesick, lonely, and desperate to belong—in fact she was in the typical position of an immigrant. This had made her hyper-sensitive and she finds herself being slighted when no such slight had been intended. Gradually, she blossoms into an independent person and she starts to think for herself, for independence is something which grows automatically when there are no props which one can lean on and be dependent. She to adjust to things which had been outside the purview of her previous idea of life as a whole. Bringing out the garbage, doing menial physical household work is one such adjustment. Far more difficult for her is adjusting to a husband who has often misunderstood her affections for her family as over-dependence, who is hostile to genealogies and cannot stand it when Tara mentions her forefathers or the many relatives she has in her extended family. So Tara is not very happy in her new home either. She has come to India without David maybe because she wanted to sort out this rather confusing melee of emotions and impulses that assail her. In India, she finds that David and her life in America seem rather far-away, unreal and this makes her naturally very insecure. She is literally, neither here nor there. She is misfit with her Calcutta milieu and she is always under stress in America trying to be correct, trying not to be a gauche immigrant, trying to be American.

Tara is intelligent, highly educated and capable of self-analysis. She is conscious of her instability, insecurity and unhappiness. That she is seduced by Tuntunwala is a different point. She had lacked the ability to take any action to stop him but she had been conscious of this inability too. This can be contrasted with Dimple Dasgupta, the chief protagonist of Mukherjee's later novel, *Wife*.

Mukherjee presents a very different sort of a woman in *Wife*. Dimple, like Tara, is on the periphery. She is a new immigrant too. But here the similarity ends. She comes from the middle class family of Calcutta with a very ordinary, lacklustre but easy and comfortable upbringing. She has never had to face any sort of crisis. She has never had to think seriously about anything in life. The difference with Tara is that Dimple is intellectually incapable of rising above this mundane inane existence. She seems to be plain, stupid and hardly representative of the class of girls she is supposed to typify. On the other hand, Tara is a very plausible character and one feels that one can meet such a person quite often.

Wife is recounted by an omniscient third-person narrator. The first part is set in Calcutta. It is centred on the dreams, fantasies and aspirations about the marriage of Dimple Dasgupta. She has married Amit Basu, a mechanical engineer. He has already applied for immigration to Canada and the US. The second part is set in the Queens' area of New York. There begins Dimple's adaptation to the American way of life. Again a disturbing gap between life's promises and actual experiences is highlighted. In the third part, the Basu couple moves into a subset flat in Manhattan. Dimple's ardently smooth domestic life seems to fall apart as she undergoes cultural shock and psychic dislocation. Her fantasy world feeds on television talk shows. The inner violence in her personality reaches a climax and she murders her husband. It signifies how an innocent, duty-conscious husband falls, a prey to the neurotic madness of his wife.

Wife is a novel about a Bengali girl called Dimple. She is eager to get married. In fact, her very existence can be described as a waiting – to enter into that blessed state of holy matrimony. A highly eligible groom is found for her. They get married and after a very short time, which can again be described as a waiting, they emigrate to the States. However, New York terrifies her. She has never seen such bigness before; the bigness is thrilling and a little scary as well. It is almost impossible for her to adjust to it. The admission of inadequacy has chilled the air. They are staying with another Bengali couple. Somehow she does not find the experience of being in America is all that pleasant. Her husband is aloof, worried (he had not found a job), she is doing chores all day, she is scared to go out alone so, she is in a tiny flat all day. They have no privacy. She is homesick. America is not confidence-inspiring.

She has gone into a meat shop to buy cheesecake and has a taste of American communalism. Comprehending all this is beyond her. She begins to have doubts. After a while, her husband finds employment and they move to a furnished flat vacated by some friends of their host.

Dimple is alone the entire day. It is almost like solitary confinement. She does not mix or try to mix with Americans. Her husband does not like it and has forbidden her. She is living in an area where there are no other Indians. So she sleeps through the day. She becomes lazy. She floats in and out of dreams. She does not even bother to get up and eat or dress or clean the house. She is aware of her condition for she thinks to herself that she has not expected her mind to be strained like this beyond endurance. She has not anticipated inertia, exhaustion, endless indecisiveness. In her mind, she is going over methods of suicide. She has found about nine methods to do this.

Some friends drop in. They are veritable Bengali even in New York. It is as if they are living in a ghetto called Ballygunge (a locality in South Calcutta). Some other acquaintances, Ira Mullick, Milt Glasser and Ira's friend Leni, drop in. They try to break her inhibitions, try to bring her out, normalize her and to a certain extent succeed. But her mind has become all confused. TV is her best friend. It gives and gives and never asks for anything. She confesses that she cannot keep up with them. She is scared of self-service elevators, of policemen, of gadgets and appliances. She does not want to wear Western clothes as she thinks she would be mistakenly taken for a Puerto Rican. She does not want to lose her identity but feels isolated, trapped, alienated and marginalized. The balance of her mind is going. She tries to stab her husband with a knife when he comes up from behind her in a playful gesture. This is an indication of her mental health. But nobody has paid any heed. She goes out for lunch with Milt Glasser, brings him up for a coffee and seduces him. She coolly keeps this side of her life a secret from her husband. She has managed to cast to the winds the immigrant values of caution and cunning. She is half-in-love with him. She seduces him and in the end she stabs and beheads her husband in a fit of maniac depression like Maya who has killed her husband Gautam in a fit of frenzy and madness in Anita Desai's *Cry, the Peacock*.

Mukherjee has concentrated on disillusionment in this novel. It seems that it is her mission to prove that to survive and to do well in the States, one must become American in one's thoughts and actions. It is no use being the same, it being on the psychological plane. Those who are incapable, break down like Dimple.

Mukherjee's *Jasmine* depicts the problems of the people emigrating to America with the dream of new life. As the American dream fascinates them, they undertake their hazardous journeys to America. They are all breaking their social, cultural and moral obligations. The novel describes the journey of the heroine, Jasmine, through hunger, ill treatment, violence, rape and murder.

Jyoti is the seventh child in a family of nine. She is told by an astrologer that she would become a widow like that of Maya who has been foretold by an albino astrologer that she would become a widow in *Cry, the Peacock*. She marries Prakash at the age of 14. Suddenly, he becomes the victim of the bullet of a Sikh terrorist. She becomes a widow at the age of 16. Her deceased husband's aim is migrating to the USA.

Jyoti finds her way to New York on forged papers. She adapts herself successfully to the illegal employments available to such immigrants. In the course of many transactions, she acquires many names. Each name indicates a new phase in her Americanization. The end of the novel leaves the readers with the picture of a woman still adjusting to America. She is with the child of one man and runs away with another man to pursue a new dream of happiness in America. In Mukherjee's terms, adaptability and change are to be celebrated. Jasmine becomes truly Americanized, not just in peripheral social or cultural mores but in a primal intensity of spirit. She finds peace neither in India nor in America, but in the American dream.

In the beginning of the novel, *Jasmine,* Jyoti, the young girl, is almost a picaro. She passes through life, going through experiences at a frantic pace. Her childhood in a Punjab village, her early teenage marriage to Prakash Vijh, her widowhood, her decision to go to America all alone and all that befall her that moment onwards, is almost Tom Jonesque. Hardly anything happens in *Daughter* and *Wife* but *Jasmine* is a long endless tale of happenings. It is almost a chain of lives. Her path through her new homeland weaves through a shifting American landscape, from Florida and the primitive brutality of the scarred Vietnam veteran to an India recreated with stifling insularity in Queens; to Manhattan's upper Westside and the exotic mystery of the self-assured young couple for whom she works. Then once again she shifts to Iowa and Bud Ripplemeyer, and right at the very end she once again is moving to California. It is coincidental that she is moving literally in the westerly direction. The point is that she seems to be perpetually on the move. She is in search of something which eludes her. The way Jasmine takes on mainstream USA. is a mixture of the humanistic individualism and medieval suppression of the individual's self. She judges her actions according to her own humanistic standards. She cannot be like her sisters and accept fate. She has to cock a snook at fate at every turn. She wants to reposition stars that control her destiny. This is humanism of a high order, indeed.

Transformation and migration are once more Mukherjee's two major themes in her next novel, *Holder*. Beigh Masters is the narrator born in New England. Her narrative has two threads. The first one is about her own twentieth century research on traces of a distant female relative from the seventeenth century. The second one is about the adventures of this seventeenth century character, Hannah Easton (1670-1750). The widowed Hannah undergoes many adventures, and finally comes back to New England where she is reunited with her mother, Rebecca Easton. A heart-rending love affair between the rebellious Hindu Raja and the New England Salem Bibi results in the birth of a black-eyed, black-haired daughter named Pearl Singh. Hannah's movement to the east is no accident nor is her role of an expatriate that of chance. Hannah's early life points most emphatically to a life of passion and feeling. Hannah as an expatriate can only embrace the new world in its entirety. It is a novel of expatriation, of a quest and a journey, not only to geographically diverse lands but to culturally variant societies which help question and abandon conventional moral and social values. Hannah's life succeeds in questioning and discovering new ways of defining reality in a world, which was essentially orthodox.

Mukherjee's, *Holder* is also a tale about dislocation and transformation arising when two cultures come into contact with each other. But here it is not the modern American world coming into clash with ideas belonging to the old country. Here the Puritan American Seventeenth and early Eighteenth century world is trying to come to terms with the Mughal Indian view of life. The story is mainly about Hannah Easton who was born in 1670 in Nipmuc Indian country some distance away from Salem. But though she was born in a Puritan age, she could hardly be described as one. Her father Edward Easton had come from England. He had been a Roundhead sympathizer and Charles II had just been restored. Perhaps he felt England was no place to stay for a person of his leanings. Or perhaps he had suddenly got fed up with his sedentary life as a clerk in Leadenhall and had just walked away from his old self to America, to be a pioneer farmer. His wife and daughter had done the same walk away from their old selves.

Rebecca Easton, Hannah's mother, had chosen to live with a Nipmuc, to abandon the white Puritan world to stop being a pious widow. She had abandoned her child and run away with her love, she had planned it in such a way that no stigma tainted her child. She herself had been thought to have been murdered. But the child had been old enough to remember. Her love for her mother did not diminish at all for she shared the same free spirit but the burden of secrecy did torment the child and the later adult.

Hannah Easton grew up in her foster family's household praying dutifully for humanity, gratitude and meekness. She married Gabriel Legge fully recognizing the fact that he was untrustworthy. Maybe she was unconsciously imitating her mother's behaviour – running off with a treacherous yet exotic alien. She kept diaries and they faithfully portray a woman who is passionately curious, who makes discovery in every branch of knowledge that she encounters (later in life she wrote movingly on sexual passion too). So when Gabriel asked her to accompany him to India leaving her affluence in Stepney she agreed. Her curiosity was robust and status-conscious she had never been. She was alert to novelty but her voyage was mental, interior. Getting there was important, but savouring the comparison with London or Salem, and watching her life being transformed, that was the pleasure. She did not hold India up by the lamp of England, or of Christianity. She did not fear the unknown or the unexplored. She judged the world from a single unassailable place. It might have been from a forest in Brookfield, before the expulsion from that New World Eden.

Circumstances then put themselves in top gear and Hannah's life started to change at a frantic pace in the year 1700. First, she left Gabriel on grounds of his unfaithfulness. Next, she saw his ship sinking and was saved from an angry mob only to be almost drowned when a bridge collapsed. She had been pulled out of the water by Jadav Singh, the Raja of Devgad, and soon she became his biwi. She was astute enough to analyze her position. She had separated from Legge because he had a biwi but in the end she became a biwi herself—carrying an illegitimate child. But she was in love for the first time in her life of 30 years. The intense person that she was, she could kill Morad Farah and take extreme steps like going to meet Emperor Aurangzeb to beg him not to fight against the Raja. In the end, she asked him to come back to America and be "a father" but the Raja found that to be a preposterous and extremely unhonourable course of action and banished her to the common women's room—she ceased to be his favourite. Hannah Easton came back to America, searched out her mother from a mental asylum, brought up her "black" daughter Pearl Singh and resolutely, fearlessly, stayed in Salem all her life—together with her mother's five half-Nipmuc children.

Mukherjee's *Leave* contains a prologue, followed by three parts and an epilogue. It is recounted by a first person narrator, Debby DiMartino. It is the tale of an adopted child in search of her biological mother and father. The prologue presents a village storyteller in Devigaon. In the first part, Debby DiMartino takes wing from her foster parents' home in upstate New York. She has a love affair with a Chinese-American, Frankie Fong. Then, she decides to move West in search of herself and of her biological parents. The second part is set in San Francisco. It presents Debby in her new incarnation as Devi Dee through all her encounters and adventures as she continues her search. In the third part, complex triangles of desire and violence overlap as a mysterious female writer. Ma Varuna herself reveals to be Devi Dee's Bio-Dad and takes the novel to its apocalyptic climax. In the epilogue, Devi Dee is alone on board the houseboat in the bay of San Francisco, after a mega-earthquake has struck.

Daughters is a fictionalised version of Mukherjee's article entitled "Two ways to belong" published in *New York Times* 22 September 1996 and its revised version entitled "The Road to Ballygunge" was published in *Half and Life* edited by Claudine Chiawei O'Hearn dated 1998. In this article, Mukherjee talks about how she and her sister Mira interact with the country of their choice.

Mukherjee's *Daughters* is a brilliantly woven story of three Calcutta Brahmin sisters, renowned for their beauty, brains, wealth and privileged position in their society. The novel begins with a mythical story. The story is about a pre-arranged marriage that goes wrong when the intended groom dies from a snake bite, even though worship has been made to the goddess of Snake, on his way to the wedding ceremony. The author tells the readers that in Hinduism a woman reaches nirvana through worshiping her husband as a God. A woman without a husband is not only a social outcast but doomed to be reincarnated. In order to save his beloved daughter, from this fate, her father marries her to a tree. Now married, she can wear vermillion in the parting of her hair and she will not be ostracized. Like her other two sisters, she is now married.

Mukherjee begins the novel *Daughters* by telling the story of "The Tree-Bride", which has a pervasive influence on the rest of the book. Jai Krishna Gangooly was a pleader at Dacca High Court. As a Bengali Brahmin, he was a staunch believer in Hindu culture. When Tara was five years old, he arranged her marriage. Just before the wedding the bridegroom's father increased his demands for the dowry. Refusing to be cowed into submission Jai Krishna took his daughter into a deep forest and married her to a tree, and thus Tara became known as Tree-Bride. But that was decades ago. Several generations down the line, Tara, the narrator, marries the best available man and goes to America, where her new husband, Bishwapriya Chatterjee, makes millions in the Silicon Valley. In due course, she gets a divorce and walks away with millions following the settlement. She lives independently with her son, Rabindra known as Rabi, and freely sleeps with Andy, her carpenter, as well as with friends of her ex-husband. In short, unlike her ancestors, she enjoys complete social, financial and sexual freedom. But the strange behaviour of her son and the emergence of Chris Dey claiming to be the son of her sister Padma begin to disrupt her safe haven. Naturally, she turns to her family and wants to be reconciled with her ex-husband, but an explosion destroys her house and wounds Bishwapriya very badly. In the end, Tara returns to Mishtigunj, where the Tree-Bride lived not for rest but to follow the Ganges to its source. The narrator and the Tree-Bride reach the same dead end, although through different routes.

Tree Bride, a sequel to *Daughters,* continues to follow the life of Tara Chatterjee. She is trying to reconcile with her husband, raise her son, and re-search her family history back in colonial India related to her great-great-aunt, Tara Lata Gangooly who was married to a tree when she was five after her fiancé had been killed. Thereafter, the *Tree Bride* had to spend her life as a resistance fighter against the British Raj. She also finds a woman whose British grandfather has a direct connection to the Tree Bride. She tries to find the connections and coincidences of her past and present. To understand her rich experience of revelations, *Daughters* and *Tree Bride* are meant to be read in succession.

It is through an extensive research, it is felt that Sidhwa can be compared to many authors. She may be compared to Charles Dickens. Her novel *Brat* is compared to Jhabvala's *Heat and Dust* as Feroza and Olivia are comparable in "Feroza in Bapsi Sidhaw's *An American Brat* and Olivia in Jhabvala's *Heat and Dust:* A Psychological Study" (Barche 46-55). Further, Yazdi of *Crow Eaters* is compared to Thom of Rudy Wiebe's *Peace Shall Destroy Many* as these novels deal with the theme of ethnicity in "Ethnic Identity in Rudy Wiebe's *Peace Shall Destroy Many* and Bapsi Sidhwa's *The Crow Eaters*" (Kapadia 121-133).

Brat is compared to Attia Hosain's *Sunlight on a Broken Column* as these novels deal with Hira Mandir or red light areas in the Indo-Pakistan sub-continent. Further, Yazdi of *Crow Eaters* may be compared to Noah Adler of Richler's *Son of a Smaller Hero.* Further, as *Crow Eaters* deals with an account of a way of life as a saga, it is comparable to *The Forsyte Saga* of Galsworthy. Further, partition novels of Manohar Malgonkar, Kushwant Singh and Chaman Nahal are compared to the partition novel(s) of Sidhwa. The violence portrayed in *Candy-Man* bears close resemblance to Amitav Ghosh's *The Shadow Lines* and the horror portrayed in the novel demands parallel to William Goldings *The Lord of the Flies.*

In fact, it is understood that Mukherjee has felt fascinated by Jane Austen and E.M. Forster. Her writings also resemble Bernard Malamud and Isaac Babel. She has a close literary kinship with Joseph Conrad. Gita Rajan in "Bharati Mukherjee (1940 -)" says that critics have compared Mukherjee to V.S.Naipaul, Anton Chekov, and Bernard Malamud (240). The subtlety of Mukherjee's analysis of human relations has led Victoria Carchidi to draw comparison between Mukherjee's work and that of Jane Austen. Further critics have affiliated Mukherjee to others.

Roshini Rustomji—Kerns places Mukherjee with Santha Rama Rao and Kamala Markandaya as South Indian women recreating in their writings, the lives of immigrants and expatriates. Kerns compared Santha Rama Rao's *Home to India* to Mukherjee's *Daughter* (655-665). F.A. Inamdar in "Immigrant Lives: Protagonists in *The Tiger's Daughter* and *Wife*" points out that Mukherjee's *Wife* thematically resembles Arun Joshi's *The Foreigner*. Inamdar also points out the thematic unity between *Wife* and *Free and Equal* of Lalita Candbhir as these novels dramatise the protagonist's search and frustration for employment. M.L. Bandit in *New Commonwealth Writing – A Critical Response* compared Margaret Lawrence's *The Diviners* and Mukherjee's *Daughter*. In it, Morage of *Diviners* is compared to Tara of *Daughter* under the concept of self and feminity. P. Budholia in "Dialectics of Culture / Acculturation in Bharati Mukherjee's *Jasmine* and Anita Desai's *Journey to Ithaca*" compares Mukherjee to Anita Desai (20-29). Gabrielle Watling in "Hybridity as Agency for the Post-Colonial Migrant; Bharati Mukherjee's *Jasmine* and Sara Suleni's *Meatless Days*" compares *Jasmine* and *Meatless Days* under the theme of migration and culture clash (60-70). In "Kamala Markandaya, Bharati Mukherjee, and the Indian Immigrant Experience" Emmanuel S. Nelson compares Markandaya's novel *The Nowhere Man* with Mukherjee's *Darkness*. P. Swain compares Sindi Oberoi of *The Foreigner* and Maya of *Cry, the Peacock* with Dimple in the research article "Dimple in *Wife:* A Study of Lacerated Self "(82-89). Dimple is also compared to Maya of Anita Desai's *Cry, the Peacock* by Jasbir Jain in "Foreignness of Spirit: The World of Bharati Mukherjee's Novels" (12-19). Further, S. Indira compares Bharati Mukherjee's *Wife* with Anita Desai's *Cry, the Peacock* in "Exploration of Inner Space: Anita Desai's *Cry, the Peacock* and Bharati Mukherjee's *Wife*" (59-65). S. Sujatha also made a comparative study of these novels under a head "The Theme of Disintegration: A Comparative Study of Anita Desai's *Cry, the Peacock* and Bharati Mukherjee's *Wife*" (45-49). Mukherjee's *Holder* bears resemblance to Nathaniel Hawthorne's *The Scarlet Letter* under Puritan theme and certain identical names like Pearl and Little Pearl.

Mukherjee's works look like the haphazard offerings of an energetic and prolific writer. But on closer scrutiny one can understand that Mukherjee's creativity is focused on a diasporic imagination with a razor-sharp precision. Gita Rajan in

"Bharati Mukherjee (1940 -)" observes: "The trope of diaspora, of dislocation transcends the rhetorical dimension of the text and becomes the material core of Mukherjee's narrativity" (240). In all her works, one can find autobiographical instances with an imprint of alternate selves in dislocated cultural topographies. However, current critical debate is focused on issues of postcoloniality and multiculturalism and the need to recognize and legitimize difference, particularly experiential difference. In, *Wife* and *Middleman,* Mukherjee seems to replicate the techniques of Charles Dickens, Thackeray or Hardy. In fact, Mukherjee's narratives function as ironic commentaries of contemporary culture and society. The critics also question her complete rejection of Canada for its overt racist politics as she situates her characters in America.

Both Sidhwa and Mukherjee are convinced that they are, as artists, destined to undertake the serious task of focusing the cultural crisis of their contemporary societies. Both writers belong to a social and literary transitional period in their countries. They are keenly sensitive to the changes in the mainstream of their cultures. So the primary aim of this research work entitled, *Bapsi Sidhwa and Bharati Mukherjee: A Comparative Study,* is to establish a close affinity between these two novelists, one a Pakistani and the other an Indo-Canadian-American. A comparative study of Sidhwa and Mukherjee is an evidence of the fact that these two writers belonging to two different cultures and nations could think of certain problems and depict a few situations, which could share some common features.

Works Cited

Afzal-Khan, Fawiza. "Indian Sub-Continent: Pakistani Writing in English: 1947 to the present: A Survey. *Wasafri.* No.21 (September, 1995), 58-61.

Allen, Diane. S. "Reading the Body Politic in Bapsi Sidhwa's Novels: *The Crow Eaters, Ice-Candy Man* and *An American Brat*". *South Asian Review.* Vol. 18. No. 15 (December, 1994): 69-80.

Barche, G D. "Feroza in Bapsi Sidhwa's *An American Brat* and Olivia in Jhabvala's *Heat and Dust*: A Psychological Study". *Parsi Fiction.* Vol. 2. Ed. Novy Kapadia. New Delhi: Prestige Books, 2001: 46-55.

Bharucha, E. Nilufer. "Reflections in Broken Mirrors: Diverse Diasporas in Recent Parsi Fiction". *Wasafiri.* No. 21 (September, 1995), 32-35.

Blaise, Clark and Bharati Mukherjee. *Days and Nights in Calcutta.* 1977. USA: First Hungry Mind Press Printing, 1995.

Budholia, O.P. "Dialectis of Culture / Acculturation in Bharati Mukherjee's *Jasmine* and Anita Desai's *Journey to Ithaca.*" *The Quest.* Vol.20. No.1 (June, 2006), 20-29.

Desai, Anita. *Cry, the Peacock.* Calcutta: Rupa and Co., 1980.

Devi, Itishree. "Negotiating the Gap: Cross-Cultural Tensions in Bharati Mukherjee's Short Fiction" *Revaluations.* Vol. 2. No.3 (Winter, 1996), 21-29.

Dhawan. R.K and Novy Kapadia. eds. "Entree: The Fiction of Bapsi Sidhwa". *The Novels of Bapsi Sidhwa:* 9-26.

D'Souza, Florence. "Bharati Mukherjee". *A Companion to Indian Fiction in English.* Ed. Pier Paolo Piciucco. New Delhi: Atlantic Publishers, 2004: 179-209.

Gabriel, Sharmani Patricia. "'Immigrant' or 'Postcolonial'? Towards a Poetics for Reading the Nation in Bharati Mukherjee's *The Tiger's Daughter*". *The Journal of Commonwealth Literature.* Vol.39. No.1 (2004), 85-103.

Gravley – Novello, Lori. "Dangerous Crossings in Bapsi Sidhwa's *Ice-Candy Man* (*Cracking India*) and *An American Brat*". *South Asian Review.* Vol. 18. No.15 (December, 1994), 81-93.

Hashmi, Alamgir. "Prolegomena to the Study of Pakistani English and Pakistani Literature in English." *New Literatures Review.* No.25 (Summer, 1993), 1-21.

Inamdar. F.A. "Immigrant Lives: Protagonists in Bharati Mukherjee's *The Tiger's Daughter* and *Wife*". *Indian Women Novelists.* Set I. Vol. V. Ed. R.K. Dhawan. New Delhi: Prestige Books, 1991, 187-196, also in *The Fiction of Bharati Mukherjee: A Critical Symposium.* Ed. R.K. Dhawan. New Delhi: Prestige Books, 1996:39-52.

Indira, S. "Exploration of Inner space: Anita Desai's *Cry, the Peacock* and Bharati Mukherjee's *Wife.*" *The Fiction of Bharati Mukherjee: A Critical Symposium.* Ed. R.K. Dhawan. New Delhi: Prestige Books, 1996, 59-65.

Jain, Jasbir. "Foreignness of Spirit: The World of Bharati Mukherjee's Novels". *Journal of Indian Writing in English.* Vol. 13. No. 2 (July, 1985), 12-19.

Jussawalla, Feroza. "Navjote Ceremonies: The Location Bapsi Sidhwa's Culture." *The Novels of Bapsi Sidhwa*: 80-87.

Kapadia, Novy. ed. "Ethnic Identity in Rudy Wiebe's *Peace Shall Destroy Many* and Bapsi Sidhwa's *The Crow Eaters*". *Perspectives on Canadian Fiction.* Ed. Sudhakar Pandey. New Delhi: Prestige Books, 1994, 121-133.

Kumar, Narendra V.L.V.N. "Parsi Writing a Note". *Parsee Novel.* Ed. V.L.V.N. Kumar Nagendra. New Delhi: Prestige Books, 2002, 27-33.

Mangayarkarasi, R. "Parsi Identity in Boman Desai's *The Memory of Elephants* and Bapsi Sidhwa's *The Crow Eaters* and *Ice-Candy-Man*". *Some Perspectives in Indian Writing in English.* Chennai: The Dept. of English, SDNBV College for Women, 2005, 177-190.

Mukherjee, Bharati. *The Tiger's Daughter.* 1971. New Delhi: Penguin, 1971.

________. *Wife.* 1975. New Delhi; Sterling Publishers, 1976.

Mukherjee, Bharati. *The Middle Man and Other Stories.* 1988. New Delhi: Prestige, 1989.

________. *Jasmine.* 1989. New Delhi: Viking, 1990.

________. *The Hindustan Times.* 9. Feb., 1990, 3.

________. *The Holder of the World.* 1993. New York: Fawcott Books, 1993.

________. *Leave It To Me.* 1997. New York: The Ballantine Publishing Group, 1999.

________. *Desirable Daughters.* 2002. New Delhi: Rekha Printers Pvt. Ltd., 2004.

________. *The Tree Bride.* 2004. New York: Hyberian Books, 2004.

________. "BANGLA: The Way Back". *The Genius of Language: Fifteen Writers Reflect on Their Mother Tongues.* Ed. Wendy Lesser. New York: Pantheon Books, 2004, 11-24.

Myles, Anita. "Bharati Mukherjee". *Feminism and the Post-Modern Indian Women Novelists in English.* New Delhi: Sarrup & Sons, 2006, 107-123.

Nelson, Emmanuel. S. "Kamala Markandaya, Bharati Mukherjee and the Indian Immigrant Experience". *Toronto South Asian Review.* 9. No. 2 (Winter, 1991), 1-9.

Nelson, Emmanuel. S. "Introduction". *Bharati Mukherjee: Critical Perspectives:* ix-xvii.

Pandit, M.L. *New Commonwealth Writing: A Critical Response.* New Delhi: Prestige Books, 1996.

Pathak. R.S. "Problematising the Minority Discourse: Inlets to the Parsi Sensibility". *Parsi Fiction.* Vol. I, 88-99.

Rajan, Gita. "Bharati Mukherjee (1940 -)". *Writers of the Indian Diaspora: A Bio-Bibilographical Critical Source.* Ed. Nelson Immanuel. Connecticut: Greenwood Press, 1993, 235-242.

Ramamurthy. K.S. *The Rise of the Indian Novel in English.* 6th ed. New Delhi: Sterling Publishers, 1987.

Rustomji-Kerns, Roshni. "Expatriates, Immigrants, and Literature: Three South Asian Women Writers". *The Massachusetts Review.* 29. No. 4 (Winter, 1988-1989), 655-665.

Said, Edward. *Culture and Imperialism.* New York: Knopf, 1993.

Sathupati, Prasanna Sree. "Psychotic Violence of Dimple in Bharati Mukherjee's *Wife*", *Indian Women Novelists.* Set III: Vol.3. Ed. R.K. Dhawan. New Delhi: Prestige Books, 1995, 110-116.

Sidhwa, Bapsi. *The Crow Eaters.* 1980. New Delhi: Penguine, 1990.

________. *The Pakistani Bride.* 1983. New Delhi: Penguin, 1989.

________. *Ice-Candy-Man.* 1988. New Delhi: Penguin, 1989.

________. *An American Brat.* 1994. New Delhi: Penguin, 1994.

________. "Why Do I Write?" *The Novels of Bapsi Sidhwa,* 27-34.

Singh, Randhir Pratap. "Buoyant Woman". *Bapsi Sidhwa.* New Delhi: Ivy Publishing House, 2005, 22-36.

Sujatha, S. "The Theme of Disintegration: A Comparative Study of Anita Desai's *Cry, the Peacock* and Bharati Mukherjee's *Wife*". *The Commonwealth Review.* Vol. 4. No. 2 (1992-93), 45-49.

Swain. S.P. "Dimple in Bharati Mukherjee's *Wife*: A Study of the Lacerated Self". *Indian Women Novelists.* Set III. Vol. 3, 117-126, also as "Dimple in *Wife*: A Study of the Lacerated Self " in *The Fiction of Bharati Mukherjee: A Critical Symposium:* 82-89.

________. "Problems of Identity: A Study of Bharati Mukherjee's *Desirable Daughters*". *Journal of Literature & Aesthetics* (Jan - Dec., 2003), 127-133.

Watling, Gabrielle. "Hybridity as Agency for the Post – Colonial Migrant: Bharati Mukherjee's *Jasmine* and Sara Suleri's *Meatless Days*". *Kunapipi.* vol. 21. No. 1 (1999), 60-70.

2

Expatriation to Immigration: An Individual's Passage of Exodus

> We immigrants have fascinating tales to relate. Many of us have lived in newly independent or emerging countries [...]. When we uproot ourselves from those countries and come here, either by choice or out of necessity, we suddenly must absorb two hundred years of American History and learn to adapt to American society [...] I attempt to illustrate this in my novels and short stories. My aim is to expose Americans to the energetic voices of new settlers in this country (Bharati Mukherjee "Interviewed", *The Times of India*, October 1, 1989).

Numerous women novelists focus attention on a journey, a move from one country or city to another, the experience of meeting other people, strange environments and all the paraphernalia that goes with actual, physical movement from one place to another. The undertaking involves two processes: the first representing upheaval and withdrawal of oneself from a familiar social set-up and, the second, braving a new and unfamiliar location which simultaneously lures and repulses. The second demands not only a mental and emotional acculturation of the new environment but also a physical reorientation in terms of surroundings, climate and terrain; in short, a substantial change of both landscapes—mental and physical. This is, precisely, the substance of immigration.

Expatriation may be identified as an emotional and psychological state of being between two worlds without belonging completely to either one or the other and operating in a space permeated by perpetually shifting alter-nativities.

A long sojourn away from home with a possibility of return ever present but perpetually deferred is expatriation. Besides, a constant shuffling of physical and emotional residence also signifies an expatriate consciousness. To emigrate is itself a political act because it implies a preference for a foreign country over one's own home, family, and familiar society as well as loss of faith in the systems one has grown up with—social, cultural, economic, or religious whatever the case may be.

Expatriation is a common phenomenon. George Steiner describes the expatriate writer as "the contemporary everyman" (10-11). Uma Parameswaran considers the phrase 'the expatriate sensibility' as a legitimate literary term in Commonwealth Literature (41). Christine Gomez in "The On-going Quest of Bharati Mukherjee from Expatriation to Immigration" defines the term expatriate as follows:

> Expatriation is actually a complex state of mind and emotion which includes a wistful longing for the past, often symbolized by the ancestral home, the pain of exile, and homelessness, the struggle to maintain the difference between oneself and the new, unfriendly surroundings, an assumption of moral and cultural superiority over the host country and a refusal to accept the identity forced on one by the environment. The expatriate builds a cocoon around herself/ himself as a refuge from cultural dilemmas and from the experienced hostility or unfriendliness in the new country.
>
> (72)

Faced with rejection, the new comer clings to his ethnic identity. Viney Kirpal in "The Third-World Novel of Expatriation: A Study of Émigré Fiction by Indian, West African and Caribbean Writer" observes: "Revival of ethnicity makes bearable to some extent the marginal shadowy existence of these migrants in the new land" (165). The main thrust of expatriation is on the native country and the traditions left behind. Immigration lays all emphasis on the cultural life of the host country. The expatriate dwells on his/her 'ex' status of the past, while the immigrant celebrates his present in the new country. As the very terms imply, expatriation focuses on the native country that has been left behind, while immigration emphasizes the country into which one has entered as a migrant.

The expatriate writers face a multi-cultural situation which may be combined with a personal anguish due to discrimination or a sense of rootless ness, if rejected by their host countries. They are able to project the cultural confusion and confrontation of a multi racial society. The clash of culture and the need for a deputation is a part of all expatriate experience.

The expatriate writers in India may be classified under the following heads:

(i) a very few who return to India and stay on as Nissim Ezekiel did.

(ii) those who came back to recover the lost patria but often returned disillusioned since they realized that home was no longer what it used to be, what far away in some foreign land they had loved and cherished—Sudhin Ghose and Meena Alexander.

(iii) Those who opt for a permanent exile abroad, yet continue to draw cultural and aesthetic substance and sustenance from their past—Mukherjee and Kamala Markandaya.

(iv) those who retain their contact with the original source of culture cherishing their land in their memory and dream by visiting and revisiting in search of roots—Raja Rao and A.K. Ramanujam.

(v) those who constantly moving between India and another home abroad—Amitav Ghose and Vikram Seth.

While expatriates share the experience of exile along with refugees, exiles and emigre's, there is one essential difference. Expatriate lives in an alien country out of an option deliberately exercised and the possibility of return not entirely ruled out. Thus expatriation is a voluntary and terminable form of exile. An expatriate may opt for migrant status or permanent residence in a foreign country and become an immigrant. Immigration is the movement of people into one place from another. While human migration has existed throughout human history, immigration implies long-term permanent or forced indefinite residence (and often eventual citizenship) by the immigrants. (http://en.wikipedia.org/wiki/ Immigration)

The twentieth century has witnessed massive migratory movements of various peoples across national and continental boundaries. The reasons for migration vary; the destinations differ. Yet all immigrant experiences share certain fundamental characteristics. The history of immigration is essentially a story of alienation and its often troubling consequences. The migratory experience invariably entails pain, for it involves an unhealable rift from home and tradition. Even when migration offers new forms of personal and political freedom, the pleasures are subverted by a sense of loss, discontinuity, and broken identity. Migration creates problems like adjustment, adaptation and assimilation in relation to religion, language, and culture. Among races and communities, it creates racial, cultural and linguistic confusion. On the other hand, cultural mixing makes a way for hybrid-culture.

Bill Ashcroft and others in *The Empire Writes Back* say: Post-colonial culture is inevitably a hybrid phenomenon involving a dialectical relationship between grafted European cultural system and an indigenous ontology, with its impulse to create or recreate an independent local identity" (195). However, the new capitalistic culture which has emerged in post-modern days is an outcome of American dominance. Frederic Jameson in "Post-Modernism or The Cultural Logic of Late Capitalism" affirms: "Post-modern culture is the internal and super structural expression of a whole as new wane of American military and economic domination throughout the world: in this sense, as throughout class history, the underside of culture is blood, torture, death and terror" (5). The process of migration to America started in the mid nineteenth century and finally it settled down in the end of the twentieth century to experience / confront qualitative cultural transformation / assimilation / negation.

The phenomenon of emigration and expatriation are by no means new but their scale in the present times is dramatic. The growing incidence of expatriation, particularly in the post-colonial societies in the second half of the twentieth century, and the psychic states attendant upon the awareness of connections and disconnections it effects, however, constitutes a contemporary phenomenon. This experience of inhabiting two geographical and culture spaces simultaneously is wrought with subtle and involuted tensions which get polarised into patterns such as dislocation vs relocation, domicile vs diasporic consciousness, dispossession vs integration, heritage vs hybridity and exile vs involvement. Such tension has proved to be an active source of creative energy and resulted in the emergence of a powerful and impressive body of creative writing. It is a Commonplace of modernism that the immigrant writer benefits from his or her uprooting, and that what is left behind is seen more clearly from a distance.

An increasing number of third world writers have emigrated to the west and have chosen to write in English language. The style and content of their writings have been greatly influenced by the extent to which they have been able to identify and adapt to their new surroundings. Manju Sampat in "Bharati Mukherjee: The Fiction of Alienation and Identification" says: "Those who still feel alienated in their new country tend to write about people and events which are 'typical' of their country of origin and are anxious to infuse Indian local colour in their writings. However, those who have been able to identify with their new host country are blessed with a bi-cultural perception which enables them to write from a wider and more exciting angle" (140).

The immigration is naturally followed by a process of adjustment and transformation of the personalities of the immigrants. The transformation of immigrants is effected in several ways. They can effect marital union between them irrespective of caste, culture or value systems. The immigrations and transformations have left behind them a sense of revolt against the traditional systems obtaining in the old-world cultures. The transformations undergone by them are accompanied by some kind of nostalgia too. Particularly, married life would become disgusting. The psyche of an immigrant is always tragic as a result of the tension created in the mind between the two socio-cultural environments, between the feeling of rootlessness and nostalgia. According to

Uma Parameswaran, a central tension in expatriate Indian writing stems from the writers' inability to either wholly repatriate or wholly impatriate themselves into their adopted country (46). In Mukherjee's writings, one can see that her writings chronicle the transition from an expatriate sensibility to an immigrant one. A novel of migrancy and belonging, *Jasmine* is the culmination of a literary trajectory initiated by *Daughter,* a semi autobiographical novel reflecting a postcolonial expatriate consciousness. Once these people left their original home-land, they were really alone. Even while standing in a crowd of a hundred thousand people such a person feels isolated, alienated and totally alone. So the first step that the immigrant takes in the New Land—the Promised Land, the land of golden opportunity where getting rich is easy—is the outcome of his deliberate independent choice to emigrate from his mother country. From now on, he will be an individual in stark contrast to his role in his previous existence. The new immigrant has to deal with people essentially different from himself. He has to learn and understand alien ways and language. He has to face unaccustomed problems. In short, he has to survive in a grossly foreign environment.

The problem of identity is connected to geopolitical space that the immigrants occupy. It is manifested as nostalgia for one's country of origin. It is also felt as a need to construct a narrative of home for themselves. Rather than searching for roots and authenticity, migrant writing constructs itself in the space of in-betweenness between different cultures, societies and homelands. Culture is an approach. It is a set of various principles of life. It is not a highly coherent and unified movement with a fixed agenda. It is a loosely coherent group of tendencies, issues and questions. Culture offers appears a lot to the distinct field of human existence. A cross-cultural condition erupts when the people of two cultural groups come in closer contacts. They bring near, along with some other nations, their willingness in parting with their much-sustained totality of heritage, habits, customs and facts. On the other hand, the same group would be reluctant in accepting the others' conventions and customs. Even this group predisposes; it cannot merge to divergent cultural identities. This occurs due to the individual's strong indigenous psycho-cultural background, which put him / her at the social cross roads.

Cross-cultural immigration has become an irrevocable precursor to the re-negotiation of identity, the re-mapping of boundaries, the re-naming of the self within and re-structuring of the life. It is due to the globalization of economy all over the world. It has reflections in other discourses like colonial discourse and so on. Celly in "Stuck in Dead Space: The Sense and Sensibility of the Indian American in Bharati Mukherjee's Short Stories" says: "Cross-cultural immigration in today's world has become an irrevocable precursor to the re-negotiation of identity, the remapping of boundaries, the re-naming of the self within and a re-structuring of the life without" (153). The cross-cultural confrontation brings a new concept, called multiculturalism. It is defined as: "Multicultural is best understood neither as a political doctrine with a pragmatic content nor a philosophical school with a distinct theory of man's place in the world but as a perspective on or a way of viewing human life" (Parekh, Bhiku. "Multiculturalism" 24 July 2005, http://google.com/). In 1954, the term 'culture shock' has been introduced by Kalvero Oberg.

> Culture shock is a term used to describe the anxiety and feeling (of surprise, disorientation, confusion, etc.) felt when people have to operate within an entirely different cultural or social environment, such as a foreign country. It grows out of the difficulties in assimilating the new culture, causing difficulty in knowing what is appropriate and what is not. Often this is combined with strong disgust (moral or aesthetical) about certain aspects of the new or different culture (en. Wikipedia.org/wiki/cultureshock).

The culture shock gives an opportunity for redefining one's life objectives. The culture shock grants for learning and obtaining new perspectives. It also develops a better understanding. The symptoms of culture shock can appear at different times:

1. Sadness, loneliness, melancholy
2. Preoccupation with health
3. Aches, pains and allergies

4. Insomnia, desire to sleep too much or too little. [...]
5. Longing for family
6. Feelings of being lost, overlooked, exploited or abused (www.pbs.org/wgbh/cultureshock)

The Parsees are ironically aware of how unwelcome their mass migration to Britain would be, despite their cordial relations with the colonial power. Unlike the Jews and the Chinese, the Parsi immigrant yearns for neither a spiritual, nor a familial homeland. Their allegiances are to the tribe, not the place of settlement.

A writer can effectively migrate without moving from the spot of his or her birth. To move into English if it is not the hearth tongue is an act of mental migration. Havely in "Pattern of Migration in the Works of Bapsi Sidhwa" observes: "Sidhwa creates a miniature of this in Faredoon Junglewalla's shift into English poetry and proverbs in his more expensive moments" (63). In Sidhwa's novels, migration is as much her theme as her lifestory. As a writer she sees a kind of constant mental migration as her trade. Sidhwa's immigration to the United States may have seemed like another repetition of a classic tale. Dazzled by success, the backwoods writer is lured to the metropolis and turns her back on the origins which were the raw material for her present fame. The writerly brain-drain seems to have been replaced by a celebration of immigration, though certain righteousness clings to those who have stayed on and roughed it out. Sidhwa's West migration is more subtly interwoven with the transformations of life. Parsees have long been westernized. Sidhwa has enjoyed many of the benefits of hybridization before leaving home.

In *Crow Eaters,* migration, though not sweeping and traumatic, involves certain of the features of dislocation, displacement, and even initial disorientation; however, after some initial confrontation they begin to assimilate the alien culture for either materialistic prosperity or for establishing amidenticy of their own. Freddy rises like a meteor. "Given his enterprising nature and possible hope Freddy can be regarded as an archetypal migrant. At the beginning of his quest, he is an 'outsider' struggling to achieve success and social recognition. He becomes a 'total insider' at the end of the novel' (Kumar V.L. 37). Considering Freddy as migrant Havely remarks: "In Sidhwa's works no migration or partition without loss. Even Freddie's jovial rise exerts its price. But the prevalent comedy of her also suggests that migration is one of life's essential rhythms and that the loses it incurs are made good with gains in self knowledge" (69).

In *Crow Eaters* Freddy's tale like that of Jasmine's in *Jasmine* is the immigrant's dream come true up the social ladder, beyond the laws which might frustrate a less aspiring spirit, to a marriage alliance with the fabulously wealthy, easy money family and the expansion of his commercial empire. Just as Freddy's dream Jasmine has a dream to fulfil as her husband failed to fulfil it. She wanted to go to America to fulfil her husband's desire and to perform 'Sati'. Immigrants recreate themselves into a new personality and form emotional ties with the place where they immigrate. The new self of the immigrant slowly makes them forget their native culture. When the immigrant returns to his native soil he / she may find that the taste and touch of their own soil have turned alien to him/her as it is with Feroza of *Brat* and Tara of *Daughter* and Jasmine of *Jasmine*. Similarly Freddy in *Crow Eaters* and Jasmine in *Jasmine* began to mimic the alien culture as they want to assimilate the alien culture with the determined will to do so on.

The immigrant is caught between the world left behind and the new one he or she faces. Like so many immigrants, Feroza of *Brat* is caught between communities, unable to go back fully, unable to go forward fully, until she discovers herself fully like Tara of *Daughter*. Even Feroza's mother makes this admission as she considers how much different her daughter's immigrant experience will be from her own, as Sidhwa admits: "Feroza would navigate her own course through life [...] along the dangerous and alluring trails Zareen had scented in the New world" (*AB* 308). In contrast, Zareen needs to return to her secure community in order to regain balance, thinking that all would be well as Sidhwa says, "once she was with her family and friends [...] she needed desperately to be with them, to be assured she had done the right thing." (*AB* 308) She is like Tara who returns to Calcutta after seven years in *Daughter* but not able to identify herself with Indian culture and ethos.

Crow Eaters celebrates the achievement of a tiny Parsi community which has survived migration. They have resettled peacefully without losing their cultural identity. Only after migration, Freddy has arrived a peaceful life, and he marries a girl from the fabulously wealthy Easy money family, and then he expands his commercial empire.

In Sidhwa's novels, there is no migration or partition without loss. Immigration is one of life's essential rhythms and that the losses it incurs are made good with gains in self-knowledge. In *Brat*, Sidhwa has returned to a lighter vein with the story of young Feroza's immigration and transformation into what her stay-at-home family sees as the brat, of the title. Feroza's immigration is risky like that of Dimple and Jasmine. Though Feroza will now never be entirely at home in the country she has left, she never has a wish to be totally absorbed into American culture like that of Jasmine.

Mukherjee's momentous decision to leave Canada and emigrate to the US is a movement away from aloofness of expatriation to the exuberance of immigration: India was Mukherjee's mid—point between her position as an expatriate in Canada and her decision to establish herself as an American immigrant. Mukherjee admits of being subjected to racial discrimination. Her works have not been identified in Canada while her husband's, Clark Blaise's, works have been accepted in Canada. She experienced herself as a psychological expatriate in Canada and clung to her ethnic identity. The process of change from expatriation to immigration got off during Mukherjee's stay in India in 1973-74. In *Days and Nights* she says: "The year in India had forced me to view myself more as an immigrant than an exile" (284). Later, the stories collected in *Darkness* mark a distinct departure in that Mukherjee is no longer an aloof expatriate writer. And as a result, in America, Mukherjee sees herself as an immigrant writer. From then on, she begins to explore the immigrant sensibility, recognizing its duality and flexible identity besides taking into cognizance alternate realities. In the "Introduction" to *Darkness* she admits: "The transformation as writer and as resident of the new world, occurred with the act of immigration to the U.S.A. [....] for me it is a movement away from the aloofness of expatriation, to the exuberance of immigration" (2-3). After discarding the posture of an expatriate writer she has chosen Bernard Malamud as her model.

The movement from expatriation to immigration is also reflected in the choice of the writers whom Mukherjee acknowledges as her models. When she experienced herself as an expatriate, Mukherjee saw Naipaul as a model but when she outgrew and discarded the pasture of expatriate writer she rejected Naipaul and took Bernard Malamud as a model. The shift from Naipaul to Malamud as literary models signified the transition from the exiled expatriate to the vibrant immigrant. Unlike the expatriate with his nostalgia for the past, the immigrant plunges into the present and gets enthusiastically involved in the environment. While the exile parades pain and grievance, the immigrant celebrates the fact of being alive in a new world, of being reborn. Immigrants are energetic resilient and able to accept things. They themselves change in their encounter with cultures. They bring about change in their environment. The immigrant never denies the past because it only means giving up a rigid holding on the past. In *Darkness,* Mukherjee says that she saw her Indianness not as "a fragile identity to be preserved against obliteration" but "as a set of fluid identities to be celebrated" (3). Usually, in Mukherjee's writings, the theme of expatriation is linked to fragmented, disintegrating, alienated characters, while the immigrants are well adjusted to the new country and its lifestyle. The movement from expatriation to immigration is a movement away from alienation to integration.

Sidhwa's immigrants are business men, Salesgirl and student. Mukherjee's immigrants are doctors, University Professors, Businessmen and women married to upwardly mobile professionals. They address themselves to the diasporic experience of cultural alienation. They speak and ape American. Their immigrants are confident, sophisticated, and poised as ones who will not melt into an American mainstream but expand the margins of what one may call 'the American experience'. These new Americans are neither nostalgic for their personal past nor afraid of the unfamiliar present. Their main strategy is adaptation without surrender as is evident in Carol of *Bride,* Feroza of *Brat,* Tara of *Daughter,* Dimple of *Wife,* Jasmine of *Jasmine,* Hannah of *Holder* and Tara of *Daughters* and *Tree Bride.*

In *Daughter* the expatriate sensibility takes the form of a questioning. Tara, on her return to India after a seven-year stay in the States, wants to understand India. But her efforts are destined to be futile for she begins the quest from outside, the India which lies outside the Catelli-Continental and under the layers of colonial Victorianism which is unapproachable and inaccessible. The hotel Catelli-Continental may be taken as a symbol of closed minds. It is inhabited by the rootless and the expatriates. It is also a symbol of India's colonial past. In *Daughter* when Tara accompanies her mother on visits to relatives, joins her school friends at gatherings at the continental, she wonders "how does the foreignness of the spirit begin?" (*TD* 37). She is not able to join in the excitement of her friends. She is not able to respond to the numerous queries about America and its affluence. She resents that no one asks about her husband. She finds herself misunderstood and thwarted as every one asks about her material affluence in America. In fact, she felt that she was not married "to a person but to a foreigner and this foreignness was a burden" (*TD* 62).

Whichever way she turns, Tara finds herself inadequate and incomplete, fragmented as if it were and unable to come together. Even when she joins her mother in the ritual of worshipping the household gods, she finds herself unable to recollect the prescribed actions. Mukherjee writes: "But she could not remember the next step of the ritual. It was not a simple loss, Tara feared, this forgetting of prescribed actions; it was a little death, a hardening of the heart, a cracking of axis and center" (*TD* 51). Jasmine, who luckily escaped death right at birth, and whose future was predicted dark and dangerous develops a sort of defence mechanism, drawing strength from her culture – she transcends personal tragedy, challenges the forces of death and destruction and seeks personal identity in a bewildering and inimical world. Amarjit Singh in "Symbolism in Bharati Mukherjee's *Jasmine*" says:

> Bharati Mukherjee in *Jasmine,* seems to use symbolism purposely to underscore the thematic concern of clash of cultures which results in confusion and chaos. The old stable societies crumble under the weight of new technologies engendering violence and discontent. An individual can neither attain personal integration nor maintain harmonious relationship with others and often gets crushed under the juggernaut of impersonal forces.
> (169)

O.P. Budholia also in "Dialectics of Culture / Accultaration in Bharati Mukherjee's *Jasmine* and Anita Desai's *Journey to Ithaca*" says: "Based on metaphor of collective memories (semantic and episodic) *Jasmine* becomes symbolic of the duality of cultures—the East and the West. Jyoti, the protagonist, experiments with life in terms of human feeling, institution, sensation and the dilemma of an expatriate who voluntarily leaves India and comes to America" (21). In *Jasmine,* the protagonist shares the poetic qualities of the novelist so far as the range of imagination and the objectivization of human emotions are concerned. It solves the question of otherness and assimilation through the logocentric dialectics of culture. It is through Du, their adopted Vietnamese son, that Jane wishes to sustain her identity as an immigrant. All the forces in Iowa would eventually freeze her to conformity or continual alienation. However, she realizes that she cannot remake herself through Du. In evaluating her past and present and envisaging her future, she confronts the complexity and multiplicity of her identity as an immigrant woman. Jane in an interior monologue says:

> I still think of myself as caregiver, recipe giver, preserver. I can honestly say all I wanted was to serve, be allowed to join, but I have created confusion and destruction wherever I go. As Karin says, I am a tornado. I hit the trailer parks first, the prefabs, the weakest links. How many more shapes are in me, how many more selves, how many more husbands?
> (215)

Jasmine's restless move from one place to another betrays her gripping alienation and bewilderment. She realizes that she is an 'outsider' and 'other' in America – an illegal immigrant without passport, living among aliens where ways she knows nothing about like Zaitoon who doesn't know anything about the tribal men among the hills in *Bride* to whom she is to be married and later to be brutally treated physically and psychologically. In both these cases the initial elation dries slowly.

There are other immigrants too in *Daughters.* Andys Karolyi, a Hungarian refugee-immigrant in the United States is very much in line with Du, the refugee immigrant in *Jasmine.* Andy's father organizes the escape of an entire village and keeps it a secret from the authorities. Twenty families comprising grandparents down to babes-in-arms like Andy, poured into refugee buses parked inside the Austrian border. Happenstance brings the Karolyis to the United States as it took others to Australia and Canada. Andy's family follows the Petocz family which has relatives in San Francisco. Before leaving Hungary, Petocz, the old man takes some vine clippings and cultivates them in Napa soil. This helps his son Jason Peters, Andy's life long friend to inherit a winery. On some week ends, Andy and Tara take the Peters—winery—turned—country—inn rides so that Andy can enjoy "the old language, the private wines, the comfort foods of home, the hot tub, the whole California good life" (*DD*: 74). She understands all that, though she is a different kind of an immigrant.

Danny Jagtiani is a survivalist – immigrant like Frankie Fong in *Leave.* Though both are high rollers in American society, the only difference between them is that Danny feeds the carvings of the ethnic side of an immigrant whereas Frankie feeds the American needs with Asian wants. Like Frankie, Danny has started from scratch, but now he has gone up the social ladder. Such wholesalers of the ethnicities in American life also demonstrate other ways of belonging.

While Tara and Dimple become isolated, rootless aliens because of their ambivalent attitude to their native tradition as well as the culture of the new world, Jasmine like Feroza, enjoys the assimilated status of immigration by a sheer will to bond herself to her adopted land. She journeys through different continents and through hunger, violence, rape and murder but she is not frightened at any moment. In order to fulfil her desire, she is willing to make all compromises and adjustments. She hops from place to place and person to person trying to find her real place in life. From Jyoti to Jasmine, to Jase and Jane may appeal to be real transformation of the personality from Hasnapur to Jullundhur to Florida, Manhattan, Iowa may appear to be moving from old world values to the brave new world.

Mukherjee's *Darkness* contains uneasy stories about expatriation. In the short story "Isolated Incidents", true to its ironic nature, Ann Vane has to file complaints from immigrants on problems concerning human rights but they are considered isolated incidents and not racial in nature. The title is ironic as cases of discrimination or hostility towards visible minority will not be related to racism but with always be ignored as isolated incidents. In another short story 'Hindus', Mukherjee juxtaposes an expatriate against an immigrant. In it, Leelaharini reveals an immigrant's fluid stability while Maharaja Patwant Singh of Gotlah is an obvious expatriate with a grievance against India for not having treated him well. The story implies a meaning that the expatriate stance is futile as Maharaja parades his pain and grievance and Leela celebrates her rebirth in a new land like Feroza of *Brat.* In "Angela" the protagonist is an immigrant with no nostalgic longing for her country Bangladesh and in "The Lady From Lucknow" Nafeesa and others are immigrants. "Tamurlane" focuses on the illegal immigrant and reverts to the violence that Indians are subjected to in Toronto. In "Visitors", Vinita is caught in the expatriate dilemma of being transfixed between two worlds. Like Dimple, she is not able to cope with the confusion arising from cultural collision.

Mukherjee's *Darkness* is a collection of angst-ridden stories about the lives of immigrants from the subcontinent in North America. Three of the stories, in particular "The World According to Hsu", "Nostalgia", and "Visitors", are powerful explorations of certain aspects of immigrant experience. "The World According to Hsu" is set in an island-nation off the coast of Africa, where an Indian woman and her Canadian husband, Graeme, are on a holiday from their home in Montreal. The story focuses on the wife's consciousness as her husband reveals his decision to accept an academic job in Toronto. Memories of her own personal encounters with racism on the streets of Toronto and images of newspaper headlines that impersonally report racially motivated physical assaults on 'visible minorities' flood her mind. The story ends on a poignantly ambivalent note: the protagonist savours her temporary Vacation / Vacatim away from Canada, even as she begins to confront her very real terrors of life in Toronto. "Nostalgia" examines another dimension of the immigrant dilemma. The protagonist, Dr. Manny Patel, is a successful New York psychiatrist with an American wife. He decides to have an affair with a young, thoroughly assimilated Indian immigrant salesgirl who reminds him of a Hindu goddess – only to find out that she is a semi-prostitute whose uncle uses her to blackmail him for immigration purposes. Sexuality and danger are at the core of "Visitors" as well. The focus is on Vinita, a young immigrant housewife with a caring, wealthy husband. Her life appears to be stable until Rajiv, a lonely young student, visits her while she is alone in the house. The conflicting emotions Rajiv's visit provokes in her –fear and anxiety, desire for sexual freedom and autonomy – force her to face the shallowness of her life in her husband's opulent condominium. Rajiv's visit releases in her a longing for liberation from her 'golden cage' so that she may embrace the danger, the magic and the adventure that America represents.

Mukherjee's *Middleman* deals with immigrants. In it, there is a definite movement away from expatriates who were marginal men and women to immigrants. In *Middleman* the characters in short stories "Middleman" and "Danny's Girls" are successful immigrants who are hustlers, while characters in "A Wife's Story" and "The Management of Grief" are independent and introspective women who have accepted their life as immigrants and observe the host country with sensitivity and objectivity. Her other stories "Loose Ends", "Orbiting", "Fighting for the Rebound" and "Fathering" present the impact of immigrants on the native America. These stories mainly present immigrants from the American point of view, though sometimes the viewpoint is suddenly reversed and Americans are seen through immigrant eyes.

Mukherjee's *Middleman* consists of 11 short stories and depicts the problems of emigrating to America and the dream of a new life which tempts them to go to America. The characters hail from the different countries of the world – India, China, Italy, Hungary, Iraq, Trinidad, Pakistan, Sri Lanka, Germany, Philippines, Vietnam, Afghanistan, and so on. These immigrants from the Third World undergo considerable suffering as the middleman claims a big chunk of money to arrange fake visas, passports, transports and jobs. The emigrants face these travails and tribulations because of their realization that America is their ultimate destination.

Mukherjee's *Holder* re-inforces expatriation as a journey of the human mind. Like Feroza and Jasmine who travel westward, Hannah's voyage to the orient is a pre-determined truth which effectively voices and manifests the latent tensions, aspirations and ambitions of the protagonist. Hannah, like Jasmine becomes an expatriate as a result of a quest for a ritual life of feeling and emotions. Her movement to the physically conscious, self-indulgent and fastidiously passionate world of the east is no accident nor is her role of an expatriate that of chance. Her early life points most emphatically to a new life of passion and feeling. It is a life denied to her in Puritan New England. She as an expatriate can only embrace the new world in its entirety; for it is this world that she has been in quest of ever since the fateful evening of her mother's abduction. Just as Jasmine is destined to go to America, Hannah is fated to go to India to be in the arms of an Indian lover. She has to participate in passions and emotions alien to the world to which she belongs.

On the other hand, Didi of *Daughters* represents the way of life of hundreds of immigrants in the United States. To feed the nostalgia of Indian settlers in the United States is her cultural mission and also her survival strategy. It is a good proposition for the new entrants to the host culture. In contrast, Tara's way to belong is a complex one. In the United States, she internalises the progressive views of the host country and its culture. But, at the same time, she understands that there is no support system to back her life-style. So, she falls back on her family, native culture, and homeland. From her ancestor Tara Lata, she learns the courage to face life in the midst of difficulties. From Parvati, she learns confidence and clarity in life. From her parents, she learns the care and concern that are the hallmarks of the family tradition in India. With a fine blend of tradition and modernity, she becomes a new woman of the twenty first century.

Daughters is a multilayered novel that attempts to bridge countries, cultures and generations. It works at multiple levels as it tries to bridge between the past and the present and the world of suspense and the underworld. It is also a telling commentary on the many—hued lives of the American Indian community today. In *Daughters*, Mukherjee has delineated the individual self quagmire in the kaleidoscopic spatio temporal reality of the American as well as the Indian society. The novel traces the life of the three Brahmin daughters, Tara, Padma and Parvati, all agog to forge an identity of their own in very trying and complex socio-cultural situations. They are born into a wealthy Brahmin Bengali family presided over by their fond father and a tradition-bound orthodox mother. The daughters are intelligent and artistic. They never feel bogged down or suffocated by a conventional society which has little regard for women. They rebel against this hackneyed and constraining socio-cultural set up and chart out their own course of action. Moving in different directions and different straining circumstances, each of them tries to carve out a unique identity of their one. But it is an identity in flux since all of them are ever on the go towards self-realisation and self-actualisation. Each of them tries to connect her past with the present, memory with desire. Each of them is on the move. Mukherjee portrays through these three moving and identity-shifting characters, who have partial affiliations, disinterested identities, tactical belongings, their sense of belongingness, which is constantly reinvented and relocated. Tara of *Daughters* has deep affiliations with her ancestry and her culture. She wants to connect her own with the mythic Tara Lata, the "Tree Bride". This myth provides the base for Tara Lata's curiosity to establish her identity through interrogations of cross-cultural re-approachment and conflictual cultural ties. The novel is not just an idyllic tale of the three desirable daughters and their diverse circumstances of upbringing but it is a complex transational narrative commenting on the intricate and enigmatic process of growing up and of the feminist struggle of these three sisters to stick to their own protean self, their cultural moorings in times of crisis. Their fascinating childhood reminiscences are dovetailed with dramatic scenes from Indian history:

> In a palanquin borne by four servants sit a rich man's three daughters, the youngest dressed in her bridal sari, her little hands painted with red lac dye, her hair oiled and set. Childish voices chant a song, hands clap, gold bracelets tinkle [...]. A Bengali girl's happiest night is about to become her lifetime imprisonment. It seems all the sorrow of history, all that is unjust, in society and cruel in religion has settled on her. Even constructing it from the merest scraps of family memory fills me with rage and bitterness.
>
> (*DD*: 04)

The novel is not only a nostalgic romanticisation of the past but also a reconstruction and revalidation of Tara's identity. It is her inverted story of mobility. The events and locales that form a part of her identity have been nostalgically delineated by the narrator. The spatio-temporal construction of her identity is based on fragments of place memories, of desires and experiences describing the cross-cultural impact on her identity partly Indian and partly Americanized. The novelist portrays her as a hybrid subject, mimicry of the American socio-cultural ethos. She travels through a hybridized space where the novelist reconstructs the notion of home/land in the context of a rapidly transitional society in the era of hectic globalization and consumerism.

The concept of home and migration is much embedded in the narratology that Mukherjee presents in *Daughters*. It is the sense of migration which brings about a change to the identity of Padma, who has finally made New York her home, her land of choice. But her inalienable attachment to her home makes her the sustainer and preserver of Bengali tradition in America. The alien culture thus fails to subvert her traditional identity. On the other hand, it only remaps and reconstructs her cultural identity. Hence, migration plays a crucial role in restructuring individual identities and cultural attitudes and perceptions. In order to assert her femininity and reconstruct and redefine her identity, Tara leaves her husband for a life of her own, chooses a school for her son which is "slanted to the arts" (153) and even takes the bold step of sharing her house with her lover Andy.

Mukherjee looks at India from the perspective of a Third World writer, an expatriate and an immigrant. India figures in the novel as a part of memory, as a Third World place, as a fragment of nostalgia. Experiences, psychic or fictional which are so commonplace like that of Tara Lata, the Tree Bride, to be of little or no importance to the readers become extraordinarily significant to the expatriate novelist. The 'Indian' self of the novelist is receding and then tries to restore or save it through her writings, a typically postcolonial situation. Writers like Mukherjee provides the west a picture of India such as Westerners themselves might not have dared to provide. India in this novel is not an identifiable presence. It is just a psychic reality. Though far away from India, Parvati is still conscious of her tradition. This is what she writes about in her letter to Tara:

> We Indians don't run to psychiatrists for every problem. Come to think of it, I don't know a single psychiatrist [...]. I hope you aren't doing bad things to yourself like taking prozac and having cosmetic surgery. Please, please, don't become that Americanised.
>
> (*DD* 104-105)

Tara says:

> The rhetoric of modern San Francisco makes me invisible. I am not 'Asian', which is reserved for what in outdated textbooks used to be called 'oriental'. I am all things. When

> the little kids climb on my lap to be read to, or just listened to, I don't think they see me as anything different from their teachers. I thrive on this invisibility. It frees me to make myself over, by the hour.
>
> (*DD* 78)

Tara's positioning is different from Padma in the sense Padma is a hyphenated immigrant. Mukherjee vociferously talks against the status of a hyphenated immigrant because the hyphen marginalizes the Asians as minorities. Parvati symbolises the traditional life of an Indian woman with a western orientation. Each one traverses her own path of immigrant life quite happily but often has a nostalgic past which continues to linger on the immigrants as talking about the society to which she belonged, Tara says:

> To be Calcutta bhadra Lok, as we Bhattacharjees were, was to share a tradition of leadership, of sensitivity, of achievement, refinement, and beauty that was the envy of the world. That is the legacy of the last generation of Calcutta high society, a world into which we three sisters were born, and from which we have made our separate exists.
>
> (*DD* 22)

Parvati's consciousness of the Indian tradition and an Indian's socio-cultural identity is further manifested in the following lines which describe her Daddy's renunciation and detachment from the mundane world: "Daddy is becoming more and more detached from the world, which I suppose is a good thing, at least it is something we are supposed to aspire to, but in his case I feel Daddy is feeling this world, rather than seeking the next [...] (*DD* 106). Parvati alludes to Aunt Bandana's love of the Bengali tradition and the laws of Manu. Aunt Bandana wants a suitable Bengali girl for her fourth son, a good Hindu Brahmin family settled in California. A good family is indeed but not an Indian citizen. Aunt Bandana's two main requirements are: "that the girl be an American citizen or green card holder who can legally sponsor her husband's immigration to the United States, and that she be a Brahmin" (107). Parvati's identity crisis is not so acute as in the case of Tara.

Parvati is a static type of identity with her emphasis on tradition and convention whereas for Tara, identity is dynamic; it is in flux, constantly changing. Her lifestyle is totally different from her other sisters. Dislocated as she is, she lives in San Franscisco, still cherishing the American Dream of possibilities and promises, but to her utter dismay, she finds that life fails to deliver these promises. Hence, she frustrates and feels lonely. The milieu dissatisfies and disappoints her. She feels in her a longing for the past:

> It has a happy landscape, I like to think, reaching from the shallow depression of Golden Gate Park and climbing to the communication towers atop Twin peaks. The area is given to summer fogs that make conventional gardening impossible, but that remain, me, not unhappily, of mountain resorts in India. I almost expect the chattering of monkeys, corn and peanuts smoking on open braziers, the tinkling of women's bangles and Buddhist prayer wheels.
>
> (*DD* 24)

Tara is but partially assimilated into the alien soil of America. Her attachment to the American culture is only skin-deep and superficial. Mukherjee has brought out Tara's marginality and also her estrangement in the following lines:

> The moment I step outside the bookstore on to the crowded Haight street, I lose the heady Kinship with the world that I feel through my reading. Nobody pays attention to me other than to ask for spare change or press a handbill into my closed fist. I am not the only blue-jeaned woman with a pashmina shawl around my shoulders and broken-down running shoes on my feet. I am not the only Indian on the block. All the same, I stand out, I'm convinced I don't belong here, despite my political leanings; worse, I don't want to belong.
>
> (*DD* 79)

Thus it is evident that Tara has a searing feeling of being cut off from her community and its style. She 'stands out', she is in the milieu but not with the milieu. As a racialized subject, She has to encounter the racist and nationalist ideology segregating her, pushing her away from the centre of American experience. Thus she 'stands out' from the rest.

Mukherjee's inability to return to India and the sense of her difference from other Indian women finds resolution in her art. She has to live and write on the cultural divide. Unlike a writer in exile who writes about a lost home, she feels that as an immigrant writer she needs to focus on her present surroundings and invent "Indians of the mind" (Rushdie 10) with the help of a constantly evolving imagination. Displacement in her novels leads characters to alienation and a search for self. Her protagonists face a multi-cultural society and exhibit a deep awareness of the social reality surrounding them. The multi-cultural ethos with which they are confronted leads to a struggle for a new life but not a complete break with the past.

Sidhwa's and Mukherjee's works emphasize the need for immigrants to choose their home by constantly adapting themselves to the new homeland. The immigrants' relationship with the old home and the new home is neither static nor monolithic. Hence, they emphasize the heterogeneity of the immigrant experience. They express their concerns related to contemporary themes such as quest for identity of their immigrants in America's frustrational and multicultural milieu for a materially better life. They make the immigrants face the tensions of adaptation and assimilation through the emotional and psychic syndromes. Their characters are the victims of double civilizations in their migrated souls. They struggle in distant bends in search of identity. They understand that the new home, the host society to immigrants is a melting pot of multiculturalism where the expatriates become immigrants truly breaking the umbilical cord with their home land.

Sidhwa and Mukherjee probe deep into the inner conflicts of well-educated, sensitive, adults whose traditional codes of economy of passion and material desire collapse amid their inadequate comprehension of the American paradigms of life, liberty and the pursuit of happiness. They show their protagonists living in between two cultures, constantly journeying into new meanings and fashioning new identities.

In Sidhwa's and Mukherjee's works there is no migration without loss. Migration is one of life's essential rhythms and the loses it incurs are made good with gains and self-knowledge. Feroza, Jasmine, Tara and others realize that they are poised between two cultures. Their journey is risky, and arrival both provisional and tentative. They will never be entirely at home in the country they have left neither do they wish to be totally absorbed into American culture.

Works Cited

Ashcroft B. ed. *The Empire Writes Back: Theory and Practice in Post-Colonial Literatures.* London and New York: Routledge, 1989.

Blaise, Clark and Bharati Mukherjee. *Days and Nights in Calcutta.* 1977. USA: First Hungry Mind Press Printing, 1995.

Budholia, O.P. "Dialectis of Culture / Acculturation in Bharati Mukherjee's *Jasmine* and Anita Desai's *Journey to Ithaca.*" *The Quest.* Vol.20. No. 1 (June, 2006): 20-29.

Celly, Anu. "Stuck in Dead Space: The Sense and Sensibility of the Indian American in Bharati Mukherjee's Short Stories". *The Indo-American Review.* Vol.12, 153-167.

en. Wikipedia.org/wiki/cultureshock.

Gomez, Christine. "The On-Going Quest of Bharati Mukherjee from Expatriation to Immigration". *Indian Women Novelists.* Set III, Vol.3, 71-87.

Havely, Cicely. "Patterns of Migration in the Work of Bapsi Sidhwa". *The Novels of Bapsi Sidhwa,* 61-70.

http://en.wikipedia.org/wiki/Immigration.

Jameson, Frederic. *Post-Modernism or The Cultural Logic of Late Capitalism.* London: Verson, 1991.

Kirpal, Viney *The Third World Novel of Expatriation: A Study of Émigré Fiction by Indian, West African and Caribbean Writers.* New Delhi: Sterling Publishers, 1989.

Kumar, Narendra V.L.V.N. "The Twain Shall Meet: Bapsi Sidhwa's Novels". *Parsee Novel*: 34-75.

Mukherjee, Bharati. *The Tiger's Daughter.* 1971. New Delhi: Penguin, 1971.

______. *Wife.* 1975. New Delhi; Sterling Publishers, 1976.

______. *Darkness.* Canada: Penguin, 1985.

______. "Interviewed. "*The Times of India*". October 1, 1989.

______. *The Middle Man and Other Stories.* 1988. New Delhi: Prestige, 1989.

_______. *Jasmine*. 1989. New Delhi: Viking, 1990.

_______. *The Holder of the World*. 1993. New York: Fawcott Books, 1993.

_______. *Leave It To Me*. 1997. New York: The Ballantine Publishing Group, 1999.

_______. *Desirable Daughters*. 2002. New Delhi: Rekha Printers Pvt. Ltd., 2004.

_______. *The Tree Bride*. 2004. New York: Hyberian Books, 2004.

Parameswaran, Uma. "What Price Expatriation?". *The Commonwealth Writer Overseas: Themes of Exile and Expatriation*. Ed. Alaistair Niven. Brussels: M. Didier, 1976: 41-52.

Parekh, Bhiku. "Multiculturalism". 24 July 2005, http://google.com/.

Rushdie, Salman. *Imaginary Homelands: Essays and Criticism 1981-1991*. London: Granta Books, 1991.

Sampat, Manju. "Bharati Mukherjee: The Fiction of Alienation and Identification". *Indian English Fiction 1980-90: An Assessment*. Eds. Nilufer E Bharucha and Vilas Sarang. Delhi: B.R. Publishing Corporation, 1994, 139-150.

Sidhwa, Bapsi. *The Crow Eaters*. 1980. New Delhi: Penguine, 1990.

_______. *The Pakistani Bride*. 1983. New Delhi: Penguin, 1989.

_______. *Ice-Candy-Man*. 1988. New Delhi: Penguin, 1989.

_______. *An American Brat*. 1994. New Delhi: Penguin, 1994.

Singh, Amarjit, "Symbolism in Bharati Mukherjee's *Jasmine*". *Symbolism in Indian Fiction in English*. Ed. K. Ramesh Srivastava. Jalandhar: ABS Publications, 1997: 163-169.

Steiner, George. *Extra-territorial: Papers on Language and Literature*. London: Faber and Faber, 1968.

www.pbs.org/wgbh/cultureshock.

3

Women's Journey through Sexual Violence to Routes of Escape and Assertion: A Case Study

> Th' expense of spirit in a waste of shame
> Is lust in action; and till action, lust
> Is perjured, murd'rous, bloody, full of blame,
> Savage, extreme, rude, cruel, not to trust:
> Enjoyed no sooner but despised straight
>
> (William Shakespeare, *Sonnet* 129)

Journey in a metaphorical sense may be taken as a process of translation or the process of undergoing changes. Cultural translation is for Bhabha, a part of the "spatial histories of displacement". He argues that culture is both "transnational" and "translational". It is transnational because contemporary postcolonial discourses are rooted in specific historical situations of displacement such as the Middle Passage or the migration of Third World peoples after World War Two. It is translational because it makes "the question of how culture signifies, or what is signified by culture, a rather complex issue" (172).

Sidhwa's and Mukherjee's novels translate culture by creating a virtual space in which the narrator can suspend time, effectively dehistoricizing the narrative. This critical move allows them to consider how location influences experience and allows the immigrant woman to construct a subject position. In other words, the novel allows them in the postcolonial world to question the translational and transnational aspects of culture along with a critical examination of the historical contingencies that produced them by playing with the concepts of history, time, and space.

Bride provides an incisive look in to the survival of women through a journey into wilderness of past and innocence. This novel pictures the cruel tradition of the tribal community into which Zaitoon, an innocent girl has been eventually married to a tribal man. Zaitoon in her journey discovers that reality is harsh and her romantic dreams become erroneous. She rebels against the cruel treatment of beatings and mistrust of the tribal man. She also realizes that her imagined ideal community is no longer "a region where men were heroic, proud and incorruptible, ruled by a code of honour that banned all injustice and evil [...] their women beautiful as houris and their bright rosy – cheeked children, lived besides crystal torrents of melted snow" (*PB* 16).

Makarand R.Paranjabe in "The Early Novels of Bapsi Sidhwa" says: "Zaitoon's story itself can be divided into three parts: her childhood (4; 5; 6); the fixing of her marriage and the Journey to the hills (10-17); and her fight for survival (18-30)" (95). Sidhwa shows Zaitoon's heroic struggle for survival against all odds. With barely enough food for a full meal and with a blanket, she ventures through the unfamiliar hills towards the bridge across the river. All the tribes men set out to hunt and kill her for there can be no mercy for any woman who tries to escape the tribe. Like an animal at bay, she proceeds in the harsh and cold terrain. Barefoot; ill-clothed, she crouches up the hills, terrified of being detected and killed. All along the tension is heightened by the author's shifting the focus from Zaitoon to her pursuers and from them to the army-men, those who might be able to save her.

Zaitoon begins to hallucinate. She sees visions of Sakhi now cruel. Vultures begin to trail her. Nearly a week passes since she has set out. She hasn't eaten anything for days. She is nearly killed by a leopard. The next morning, she reaches the rivers. Recklessly, she is rapped by two strangers. Finally, delirious, bruised, half-dead, ten days after her ordeal begins, she crawls to the base of the granite bridge that will lead to her freedom. The tribesmen too have reached the bridge. But luckily she is spotted by the army sentries first. Carrying her, and bundle her, with her old blanket Major makes his way across the bridge. Sakhi follows him. Major Mushtaq tells him that the girl is dead. He lies to his fellow tribesmen that he has buried her with his own hands. Thus Zaitoon survives at the end of the novel in her journey in order to assert her individuality and feminity like that of Jasmine who has been raped by Half-Face and thereby having a longing to exist in the materialistic world of hopes and dreams.

Zaitoon's odyssey from the plains to the Snow Mountains and back to the plains is symbolic of the inner journey of the young woman from the fantasy world of love, romance and heroes to the harsh and hostile realities of life, where man is the hunter and exploiter, cruel and inhuman treating woman and animal alike. It is a barbaric world of uncivilized people that Sidhwa brings to life and light.

In fact, Sidhwa, through Zaitoon's experiences within purdah society and Carol's experience from outside the purdah society, stresses the all-pervasiveness of purdah-a mark of segregation to women. Both men and women are affected. Men never look at women. It is stressed when Qasim is invited by Nikka to eat with them. Neither Qasim nor Nikka's wife looks at each other. Even their conversation is through the medium of Nikka. But an outsider is treated badly. Carol comes to realize this when she notices three tribals gazing at her. She feels uncomfortable at the way they stare. Carol asks Mushtaq, "Haven't they ever seen a woman before?" (*PB* 113). Mushtaq explains that it is the segregation of the sexes that causes the men to stare at her in that insolent manner. In fact, a meeting between Zaitoon and Carol suggests that though the Muslim girl lacks free and easy ways of the American, underneath the shyness and modesty is an awareness of the ways of men and women. Niaz Zaman in "Images of Purdah in Bapsi Sidhwa's Novels" stresses that

> the segregation of the sexes, the separation into men's spheres and women's, the world outside and the world within, creates a world highly charged with sexuality. It may be noted that in ordinary circumstances most children in third world countries sleep in the same room as their

> parents and therefore aware of what goes on in the marriage bed. Zaitoon, however, with no family, is not given a glimpse into these mysteries. Nevertheless, despite this innocence, Zaitoon lives in the highly charged atmosphere that emerges from enforced segregation.
> (163)

Zaitoon is not ready to be a martyr to the imaginary insults and infidelity that is attributed to her by her husband. Her husband, Sakhi's, a tribal man's thoughtless, cruel and inhuman behaviour drives her to despair and to the only alternative of running away. Sidhwa presents in a 16 year-old Zaitoon a powerful character who prefers death in the mountains to dying slowly and gradually, to being beaten into a spiritless woman like her mother-in-law Hamida. She knows that escaping is almost impossible. The mountains are treacherously pathless. She even does not know where she would be going at the end of her journey. She simply feels that if she could escape and cross the bridge, she may get help. To avoid being caught up by the members of her family, she chooses an indirect difficult and untrodden path and is lost in the mountains: "Zaitoon knew that somewhere in the serpentine vaults of the ravine and in the glacier-riven valleys she had lost her direction, and that the river gorge could be anywhere in the myriad furrows between the mountains [...] and mountains closed in on her like a pack of wolves" (*PB* 197). The mountain she had loved, whose magic and splendour she had admired, were now her enemy, a hostile inscrutable menace.

For nine days and nights Zaitoon wanders the mountains like a wounded animal hunted by the tribal men. At times she has glimpse of her life's end, her destiny of dying at the hands of her husband: "She feels him move and her destiny is compressed into seconds. She hurtles in a short-cut through all the wonders and wisdom of a life unlived. Instantly old, her tenure spent, she is ripe to die" (*PB* 235). She is aware of Sakhi and his relentless pride and sense of honour; "for him it is not an act of personal vengeance; he is dispensing justice—the conscience and weight of his race are behind him" (*PB* 235).

Experiencing the terrific claws of death, Zaitoon has an unexpected insight into the future that was to be her destiny. It is a common one to any woman of the mountain tribal world. The tribal woman has to suffer physically, mentally and sexually as it seems to be patriarchal in nature. Realising this Zaitoon tries to escape from her prison-like conditions. It is not escaping to freedom. She instinctively hides herself courageously to survive. She succeeds in her struggle to reach freedom by the timely lap of Major Mushtaq and his military camp.

Zaitoon's decision to run away is not due to militant feminism or deliberate defiance of male order. She is portrayed as a device, affectionate, obedient child. She has become a symbol of all oppressed and exploited women. Hers is a spiritual struggle to survive. Her escape to freedom is a great victory against the oppressive system. On her way to freedom, she is raped on the river bank by two strangers. When she walks up, she is a total wreck. Sidhwa narrates:

> The men had kept her hostage for two hours. When Zaitoon regained her consciousness, her body screamed with pain. She wept, putting her trembling legs through the salwar. Her brown skin gaped through new rents in the cloth. She had not seen her legs for days and gazed in revulsion at the twitching, fleshless shanks. A red spot spread on the cloth between her thighs. She folded her legs quickly and covered the skin with the front of her shirt. Printed with faded lavender flowers, it was torn down the front and the shoulders.
>
> (*PB* 230)

The oppression of a woman is shown in the molestation of a starved, raped and oppressed woman, Zaitoon. It is then Zaitoon remembers the mad woman she has encountered at Lawrence Gardens, Lahore: "She now knew the woman had been raped. Abandoned and helpless, she had been living on the charity of her rapists [...] and on theft" (*PB* 231). Though she survives, she could become mad like her. In the end, Mushtaq says:

> She would be all right, he mused. In a few hours he would quietly stow her away in the vehicle taking Farukh and Carol to Lahore. Let Carol take care of her! She could hide her in the States! Or perhaps Ashiq could propose marriage after a decent interval—she would be as securely hidden in his village.
>
> (*PB* 245)

The atmosphere of dislocation and partition is sustained throughout *Bride*. Carol is a character in dislocation with her environment in Pakistan and in a way 'Partition-ed' from her home and culture in America. She is totally an alien to the culture and her surroundings. She has left America but is unwilling to adapt to the way of life of the strange customs and traditions of Pakistan. They are inferior to her civilized way of life.

"What she had imagined to be exotic has failed to live up to the harsh image of reality, as it is apparent in her personal relationship with her husband, Farukh; yet, she chooses to stay in Pakistan because it is still better than the life she had in San Jose [...]. Carol chooses to stay in Pakistan because she is able to have an identity which would have been non-existent if she had continued to work as a shop-assistant in a departmental store in San Jose. Sidhwa conveys the tears and boredom of a single woman worker by making Carol stay in Pakistan, with its alien and sometimes claustrophobic culture, rather than return to the drudgery of American life that she would lead if she chose to go back. And so Carol chooses not to renew her contacts with the land and culture that is Hers." (Farukh Khan 144-145)

Sidhwa provides a parallel to Zaitoon's romantic fantasies and frustration by introducing the American shop girl and college drop-out Carol. Both Zaitoon and Carol are shocked by their husband's moral code and sense of honour. As an ordinary young American working in a store, Carol has not completed her studies. To her, Pakistan appears to be a land of romance and adventure, and Farukh seems an answer to all her drudgery in life. Though she fails to understand the world of veils and Zenana, after a year or so, she slowly realizes that "the repressed erotic climate was beginning to affect her. In the

States, what she had thought was a unique attraction for Farukh, had in fact been her fascination with the exotic, and later the attraction had disconcertingly extended itself to include his friends and relatives—and even acquaintances" (*PB* 176) like Hannah in *Holder* who has had an exotic feeling for the Raj and particularly on Raj Devsingh. At first, she hardly understands that her causal American ways, in a country where few women were seen unveiled, attracted the men. She is flattered by this attention and does not realize that for the men it is merely a passing affair. She is impressed by the bronze liquid-eyed men of Pakistan. Though she tries to conform to the norms of the country, Farukh's jealousy combined with the flattering attention she receives shatters her resistance when she comes across Farukh's friend Major Mushtaq.

The Major is an attractive handsome young man who seems to have stepped out of the romantic poetry. In Farukh's absence she flirts with him and thinks that she has really fallen in love with him. She decides to divorce Farukh and marry Mushtaq since "growing up in the 1950s, Carol was inexorably conditioned to marriage. She had only one recourse with which to reconcile her feelings and her actions. She had found her love. He must marry her" (*PB* 179). Little does she realize that in Pakistan men marry their cousins and as Mushtaq explains: "In spite of what you hear about our being able to have four wives, we take marriage and divorce very seriously. It involves more than just emotions. It's a social responsibility [...] For one thing, at the very least, my wife's life would become unbearably confined, drab and unhappy. And we're cousins, you know, our families would make my life—and yours—miserable. We'd be ostracized" (*PB* 181).

For Mushtaq, it is one thing to have an affair with the American woman who is liberal in her ways, since she could fulfill his need for a woman in the loneliness of his remote posting, and another thing to have a permanent relationship of marriage with the wife of his friend. Besides, he cannot even dream of forsaking his wife and children and distinctly points out the differences between the two ways of life: "you'd find her

[Zaitoon's] life in the Zenana with the other woman pitifully limited and claustrophobic—she'd probably find yours [...] terrifyingly insecure and needlessly competitive" (*PB* 180).

After being rejected by Mushtaq, Carol turns back to Farukh, thinks of having children, and making her marriage successful. She even dreams of going into the tribal world and imagines herself a goddess ministering and enlightening the handsome savages and cavemen. But this fantasy too, is shattered when she comes across a young tribal woman's head bobbing up and down in the dark waters of the river. In a crude and painful manner, all her romance and fantasy crush to disillusion: "Women get killed for one reason or other [...] imagined insults, family honour, infidelity [...] even imagined infidelity" (*PB* 223), all the time in Pakistan though Mushtaq asserts that jealously is universal.

Carol faces the realities of woman's life in the east and comprehends fully the fallacy of her fantasies: "That's really what's behind all the gallant and protective behaviour I've loved so much here, isn't it?. I felt very special, and all the time I didn't matter to you any more than that girl does as an individual to those tribals, not any more than a bitch in heat" (*PB* 224). The novelist poignantly describes her disillusion with life: "Her fantasy, set off by his startling handsomeness, his intense animalism, and her fascination with tribal lore and romantic savagery—took wing" (*PB* 221) only to be shattered into thousand pieces. She could not even salvage her marriage to Farukh as she has glimpses of the horror of generations of cloistered womanhood. The encounter with the floating face of a tribal girl triggers the avalanche of emotions bringing her firmly to the ground. She realizes the difference between the two cultures. In spite of her living in a "splendid modern structure surrounded by the antiquity of priceless possessions she has glimpses in the inner recesses of England and America-educated rich Pakistani women's minds and their insecure, uncivilized, cruel and brutal world dominated by men. She becomes fully conscious of her plight her independent attitudes would get her killed" (*PB* 227). Sidhwa brings into focus th issue of Pakistani women's plight through the eyes of an outsider, an American bride of the Pakistani man. This is apprehended through the plight of Zaitoon: "That girl has unlocked a mystery, affording a telepathic peephole through which Carol had a glimpse of her condition and the fateful condition of girls like her" (*PB* 228).

Carol's life so far has been a hopeless drift but Zaitoon with her dauntless courage and faith serves as a brake and deflects the direction of her life. Carol from the free world of fair and just social order can think in terms of her individuality but Zaitoon has no such notions; she simply does not wish to be a role-model of Hamida, always cowering, frightened to death and at the mercy of the cruel code of honour of man. She instinctively chooses to be herself. Sidhwa uses the image of the crippled but flying bird to emphasize the condition of Zaitoon. Such a bird cannot be easily caged or tamed even if it is maimed. Her fight is against both man and nature, which she can vanquish through her sheer will-power, "the strength of nature, a force, perhaps of God, within one", (*PB* 229). The novelist quotes the poet Iqbal here:

> Khudi ko kar buland itna,
> Heighter your 'Khudi' to such majesty,
> Ke har takdeer say pahalay,
> that before every turn of fate
> Khuda banday say khud poochay,
> God himself asks man -
> 'Bata teri raza kya hai?'
> 'Tell me, what do you wish?'
>
> (*PB* 229)

Crane in " 'A Passion for History and for Truth Telling' The Early Novels of Bapsi Sidhwa" shows the position of women as "Carol's experiences as the foreign wife of a Pakistani are juxtaposed with Zaitoon's ordeal as an 'outsider' married to a Kohistani tribesman, and together Carol's circumstances and Zantoon's awful plight are used by Sidhwa to highlight the position of women in Pakistani society" (52). Zaitoon, despite

Miriam's objections, is sent to school but taken off when she is eleven as soon as she begins to menstruate. From then on, she spends her time in segregation of the Zenanna. Life in the Zenanna does not offer much. In Zenanna she can experience "smells of urine, stale food and cooking hung in the unventilated air, churning slowly, room to room, permeating wood, brick and mortar" (*PB* 56). Women are segregated and curtailed. It is Carol through whom Sidhwa speaks when she cries out against the oppression of women:

> Women the world over, through the ages, asked to be murdered, raped, exploited, enslaved, to get importunately, imprcgnated, beaten-up, bullied, disinherited. It was an immutable law of nature. What had the tribal girl done to deserve such grotesque retribution? Had she fallen in love with the wrong man?.
>
> (*PB* 226)

In the novel *Bride* Zaitoon's and Carol's stories remind one of the position and treatment of women in a male dominated society. The picture of the oppression and degradation of women is strengthened by the images of violence, oppression and subjugation of woman. In fact, the tribal society treats women as valuable commodities. "Any girl—and he had made sure this one was able—bodied—was worth more than the loan due"(*PB* 7) thinks Qasim's father when a fellow clansman offers him his daughter in lieu of a loan that he owes. Afshan, the woman to be Qasim's wife is fifteen, five years older than Qasim, yet has no choice but to accept him. Qasim's father's decision to give the girl to his son is in fact generous because "To begin with he had thought of marrying the girl himself. He had only one wife; but in a twinge of parental conscience, he decided to bestow the girl on Qasim. It was his first duty" (*PB* 8).

A few years later, before the marriage is consummated, Afshan is really raped by a stranger when she sees her bathing, protected by Qasim alone, who is only a boy. The first chapter in *Bride* reveals the ill-treatment of women in the novel. Women are hartered and traded like commodities. It is as Makarand R. Paranjape remarks in "The Novels of Bapsi

Sidhwa": "Once married, they become part of the property of their husbands which the latter must protect; otherwise someone else may molest them. Finally, they have no choice but to accept whatever husband is chosen for them by their fathers; first they belong to their fathers, then to their husbands" (94).

Bride is a damning indictment of the Kohistani community in particular and the Pakistani society in general with regard to its brutal treatment of women. The women are marginalized. Qasim is offered as a bride at the tender age of 10. Afshan is sold into marriage to compensate for her father's failure to come up with money. It makes woman as a bargaining commodity. K.Nirupa Rani in "Gender and Imagination in Bapsi Sidhwa's Fiction" says: "The American and Pakistani brides become subjects of their husband's suspicion and both take pragmatic decisions to overcome their crises. Carol decides to make it up to Farukh and contemplates to have a child to bring anchorage to her loveless marriage. Zaitoon decides to take a visionary course of action and runs away, knowing fully well that the punishment for such an act is death" (121). There is a world of difference between these two women. Mushtaq explains to Carol: "It wouldn't be easy for you really to understand her. You'd find her life in the Zenana with the other women pitifully limited and claustrophobic-she'd probably find yours-if she could ever glimpse it—terrifying insecure and needlessly competitive" (*PB* 180).

Both Zaitoon and Carol are lured by their romantic imagination into an immense journey which deposits them on either side of the Indus in the high Karakoram. For both women, marriage is more than the literal sense a journey to a foreign land. For Carol, it is an escape from disappointment and for Zaitoon, the crossing of an imperative divide between daughter and wife. They uniformly share a romantic yearning for a larger life than the conventions of their respective cultures.

Zaitoon and Jasmine are survivors and fighters. Zaitoon fails to adapt to the life of the hills but Jasmine, even though assaulted physically and sexually like that of Zaitoon by strangers, adapts herself to the American way of living. Jasmine's journey through life leads Jasmine to many transformations—Jyoti, Jasmine, Jase and Jane via divergent geographical locales like Punjab, Florida, New York, Iowa and finally California. However, one can find that at every step both Zaitoon and Jasmine revolt against their fate and courageously trail on the path drawn for them.

The marriage and the interlude of joy that follows, are both short lived. Zaitoon's torture begins on the very next day after marriage. She is broken by her tyrannical husband who "beat her on the slightest pretext" (*PB* 147). Two months after her marriage, Zaitoon is severely beaten for going up to the river against the commands of her husband. The river is the boundary between the tribal territory and the army. Seeing her wave at the jawans across the river, Sakhi nearly kills her. After that, she decides to flee from her nightmarish world. In *Jasmine*, on the contrary, the marriages are happy: Jasmine's to Prakash, Nirmala's to Profersarji because "He was following an ancient prescription for marital accord: silence, order, authority. So was she: submission, beauty innocence" (*J* 141). The woman believes in the husband. Jasmine's mother tries to throw herself on her husband's pyre. Then, failing which, she shaves her head and sits in a corner. Jasmine is freely determined to go to America to fulfil her vision "of lying severely on a bed of fire under palm trees in a white sari" (*J* 120).

Jasmine as a girl is relegated to a marginal position even before she is born. Jasmine admits: "If I had been a boy, my birth in a bountiful year would have marked me as lucky, a child with a special destiny to fulfill. But daughters were curses. A daughter had to be married off before she could enter heaven, and dowries beggared families for generations. Gods with infinite memories visited girl children on women who needed to be punished for sins committed in their incarnations" (*J* 30). Jasmine's mother tries to strangle her moment she is born because "bad luck logged dowryless wives, rebellious wives, barren wives. They fell into wells, they got run over by trains, they burned to death heating milk on Kerosene stoves" (*J* 41).

Sidhwa firmly believes that inter-community marriage is a failure one. She depicts two inter-community marriages in *Bride*. The marriages between the white American woman Carol and the Pakistani Muslim Farukh and between the girl from the plains of Zaitoon and the tribal from the hills, Sakhi are failures. Both Carol and Zaitoon are victimized and the marriages cause them intense agony and unhappiness. Inter-community marriage between the Hindu Ayah and her Muslim admirer, Ice-Candy-Man in *Candy-Man* is also a failure.

The perennial Parsi problem of inter-faith marriage arises when Feroza wants to marry David Press, an American Jew. The family assembles at Lahore and treats the situation as dire emergency. Reprimanding a young cousin who defends Feroza's choice of marriage, Grandmother Khuthibai resorts to histrionics while relating tales of the horrors of excommunication. Khutlibai contrived to make her vigorous person look crumpled and close to death while she spoke, so that the spirit of rebellion in Bunny and other youngsters was nipped in the bud.

Feroza succeeds in getting her mother's reluctant permission to attend college in America. When she tells her mother that she wants to marry a Jewish boy Zareen make Machiavelli seems alive. The young Feroza would never have dreamed of making such a momentous decision on her own. In the end, Feroza sees herself as a member of a community that needs to accept a certain amount of change. Sidhwa writes:

> As for her religion, no one could take it away from her, she carried its fire in her heart. If the priest in Lahore and Karachi did not let her enter fire temple, she would go to one in Bombay where there was so many Parsees that no one would know if she was married to a Parsee or a non. (*B* 317)

Feroza in *Brat* is dependent on her friends and community for strength. She consciously attempts to recognize the conflicting truths of life. She is compelled to accept exploitative relationships because of parental / religious / cultural authority. She chronicles the glamour and efficiency of the USA but also delineates the seedy and violent aspects of life in a post-industrial, consumerist and technology dominated society. For Feroza, Bloomingdale's on Lexington Avenue in New York, "was like entering a surreal world of hushed opulence, festooned by all manner of hats propped up on stands and scarves and belts draped here and there like fabulous confetti" (*B* 73). The dazzling wares in the shops at New York have bewitched Feroza. However, Feroza's maverick uncle, Manek also shows her the other side of New York, "the lookouts, runners, drug dealers, elegant transvestites, male prostitutes and hubs of poverty" (*B* 80).

Feroza is also shown the Port Authority bus terminal, in which the homeless and discarded, "ragged and filthy men and women were spreading scores of flattened cardboard boxes to sleep on in the bus terminal" (*B* 80). She was used to the odour of filth, sweat, urine, open drains and reek of poverty in Pakistan. Those were smells and sights she was used to. However, she struggled to adjust to the poverty and stench of filth in the First World.

> "This was an alien filth, a compost reeking of vomit and alcoholic belches, of neglected old age and sickness, of drugged exhalations and the malodorous ferment of other substances she could not decipher. The smells disturbed her psyche; it seemed to her they personified the callous heart of the rich country that allowed such savage neglect to occur." (*B* 81)

Sidhwa thus aptly shows that "America is not all Saks and skyscrapers" (*B* 81). In Feroza's bewildered reaction to the filth and poverty of New York, the novelist raises a pertinent question about the distribution of wealth in the USA and the perpetual puzzle of why such poverty exists amidst so much opulence. At this stage, Sidhwa's novel is similar to Mukherjee's *Jasmine*, an Indian immigrant's encounter with the New York and her transformation as she gradually imbibes the new culture. Feroza's shock at the poverty of New York is similar to that of Jasmine's dismal view of the Florida swamps that she gets on her first entry into America. "Eden's waste; plastic bottles, floating oranges, boards, sodden boxes, white and green plastic sacks tied shut but picked open by birds and pulled apart by crabs"(*J* 107).

Jasmine is the story of an immigrant from the Third World to the United States who had been uprooted and re-rooted in an alien soil, America, where she has to confront uncertainties. Mukherjee writes:

> In America, nothing lasts, I can say that now and it doesn't shock me, but I think it was the hardest lesson of all for me to learn. We arrive so eager to learn, to adjust, to participate, only to find the monuments are plastic, agreements are annulled. Nothing is forever, nothing is so terrible, or so wonderful, that it won't disintegrate.
>
> (*J* 181)

Jasmine is an embodiment of old-world dutifulness. She is conscious of her sacred relationship with her husband who is always pushed from one disaster to another. In all her fights, Jasmine emerges not as a tragic character but as a one who is determined to change her destiny and explore the infinite possibilities among uncertainties in America as Mukherjee believed in the existence of alternate realities. *Jasmine* is in fact an account of adaptation and not defeat.

To all the men who enter Jasmine's life after her altered identities, it is her Indianness with its adaptability that endears her to them: "Taylor didn't want to change me. He didn't want to score and sanitise the foreignness" (*J* 185) and "Bud courts me because I am an alien, I am darkness, mystery, inscrutability. The cast plugs me into instant vitality and wisdom. I rejuvenate him simply by being who I am" (*J* 200). Her new role as Jane and Jase represents the possibilities of alternate realities, the ability to be reborn. She realizes that she has become a drifter moving in a world of uncertainties:

> I feel at times a stone hurtling through diaphanous mist, unable to grab hold, unable to slow myself, yet unwilling to abandon the ride I am on. Down and down I go, where I'll stop, God only knows.
>
> (*J* 138-39)

In *Wife* one can see that Mukherjee was going through her hostile stage in Canada. The novel shows her alienation, and marginality leading to a feeling of dispossession from her heritage in the character of Dimple. In Dimple's case, the dispossession culminates in a terrible brutalization of her psyche and a scanning of her character. Her to adjust to life in New York culminate in culture shock. She is driven to despair, madness, and violence. She ends up killing her husband.

In *Candy-Man,* Lenny's marginality and her separation from the colonizing forces is found in the second vignette of the novel. She and her Ayah are accosted by an Englishman who intends to straighten out Ayah's presumed laziness for letting Lenny ride in the pram. He begins to scold Ayah, who responds by telling the Englishman that Lenny cannot walk because she becomes tired. He continues to scold until Lenny lifts her pants and shows him the braces on her legs. He is startled at first, but he begins again to insist that Lenny be made to walk. By the time he recovers his voice, however, Ayah and Lenny are already strolling away (*ICM* 2). This section points out several borders in the novel. It shows not only the borders between the colonizing British and the indigenous people, but it also reveal the borders between the sick and the well, a border Lenny glories in. In addition, this section shows that though marginality may mean a lowering of status for the marginalized, it can also have its benefits, for one outside the structure is not always affected by its mores.

So Lenny is marginal in several ways, but marginality in *Candy-Man* cannot be confused with impotence. Ayah is also a marginal. She is a Hindu in a primarily Muslim community. Shanta, Lenny's Ayah, recreates Pakistan before Partition around her. Sikhs, Muslims, Hindus, a Chinaman, and various other men circle about her, and in her company, these suitors become equal. They create communities. Ayah's pacifying presence erases all borders between them. Lenny first begins to feel that Ayah's pacifying influence is waning when they join the Masseur, Ice-Candy-Man, and a variety of other suitors in a Lahore restaurant. An argument over the position of Lahore after the impending Partition swirls around Lenny and Ayah as they sit down, and though Masseur says, "There are no differences among friends [...] We will stand by each other", (*ICM* 131) but Lenny feels uncomfortable. Her discomfort comes not only in the realization that there are thirteen of them sitting around the table, but also from the synesthesia she experiences while Ayah's friends argue. She says:

> Blue envy; green avidity; the grey and black stirring of predators and the incipient distillation of fear tin their prey. A slimy gray-green balloon forms beneath my shut lids. There is something so dangerous about the tangible colors the passion around me have assumed that I blink open my eyes and sit up.
>
> (*ICM* 132)

So marginality does not mean impotence. Ayah provides a clear example of the dangers the marginal faces when the society in which he or she is marginalized and changes its borders. For Ayah, this shifting of the margins presents her scorned suitors with an opportunity to reclaim the control she has held over them.

In *Daughter* Tara returns home after seven years in America. In it, Mukherjee seems to be compelled to work out her from her psyche. In order to do so, she makes a metaphorical trip back to Calcutta of the sole sixties and early seventies with Naxal riots and protests. This novel exemplifies her hostility with implied alienation to both India and Canada. The novel shows her double alienation. In North America, Tara, in fact, Mukherjee felt, herself as an alien where she was racially an outsider. In India, she was not married to a person but to a foreigner and the foreignness was a burden. Thus, there her alienation is at two levels. In the end, the two worlds cannot be reconciled. As the alienation from the mother country seems stronger, Tara chooses to return to David and America.

Mukherjee's *Daughter* reflects the confrontation between illusion and reality. Tara being an immigrant, away from home, idealizes her own country and cherishes nostalgic memory of it. Tara was packed off by her father at the early age of 15 for America. In America, she experiences homesickness. Little things pained her and she sensed discrimination everywhere. She prays to Kali for her strength so that she would not break before the Americans. New York drives her to despair: "On days when she had thought she could not possibly survive, she had shaken out all her silk scarves, ironed them and hung them to make the apartment more Indian" (*T* 34).

Like Feroza and Tara, Hannah is a stunning creation, a bold mind striving for identity in strange surroundings, a timeless creature trying to survive in a rigid inexorably defined society. Her difference from others lies in her ability for establishing connectedness across cultural boundaries, Ostracism opens up unwalled worlds for her. She feels unfinished, unformed until she responds to the reality around her. She different because she is still connected to the emotional realities of human life at all levels and places. It is her openness to experience and connectedness to human beings that enable her to survive and identify her at any time or any place to be a Salem Bibi.

Ethnic women in America are clearly twice-marginalized: by virtues of their ethnicity and their gender. The central figures in Mukherjee's novels *Daughter, Wife*, and *Jasmine*—Tara, Dimple, Jasmine—fight two simultaneous battles against marginalization during their early expatriate experiences in America; coming as they are from (an) other world(s), their very identities are in question in America, calling out for a re-visioning and a re-defining at the start. The moments of change/ transformation / re-incarnation are crucial because, though the exercise is assertive / powerful / celebratory in its mainstream movement, the echoes at the margins valorize the anxieties of expatriation.

In *Bride* though Zaitoon is the heroine of the novel, it is through Carol that Sidhwa reveals the treatment of a Western, upper-class woman in the male-dominated society. Carol is a typically middle-class American of the sixties of twentieth century by birth and upbringing. After studying at Berkeley, while working as a sales girl in a cosmetic store, she falls in love with Farukh, a Pakistani Engineering student. Considering their relationship Makarand P. Paranjape in "The Novels of Bapsi Sidhwa" says: "Their relationship which began with what Carol had considered Farukh's charming and gallant possessiveness towards her, has degenerated into distrust and revulsion with Farukh's almost insane, jealousy and suspiciousness. Carol, too, has not been able to cope very well with the repressed sexuality of Pakistani society where she is constantly appraised and pressurized by men" (93).

Carol's Westernised habits are misinterpreted by Farukh and his friends. As he remains jealous in the hills, Carol finds herself being attracted by Major Mushtaq. She defiantly plunges herself into an affair with him when Farukh is away. But later in the company of Zaitoon, she realizes that she has become a plaything on the hands of men. This becomes more evident to her when Mushtaq refuses to marry her should she divorce Farukh. Finally, later, when she learns that Zaitoon has run away from the tribe and that she is being hunted by them, she wants to save her as she realizes that Mushtaq and Farukh would also treat her similarly in all probability. When she has an affair with Mushtaq, she begins to realize that he values her primarily as a sexual object. Even she realizes that her life is like that of Zaitoon's life. Sidhwa writes:

> In the instant their eyes met, the green and black of their irises fused in an age-old communion an understanding they shared of their vulnerabilities as women. For an intuitive instant Carol felt herself submerged in the helpless drift of Zaitoon's life. Free will she thought contemptuously, recalling heated discussions with her friends on campus. This girl had no more control over her destiny than a caged animal [...] perhaps, neither had she [...].
>
> (136)

Even her conversation with the Major makes her realize of the pitiable rule of women in a society as he observes casually: "oh, women get killed for one reason or other [...] imagined insults, family honour, infidelity [...]" (*PB* 223). Even when questioned, "Do you think Farukh would kill me?" by Carol, the Major casually answers: "Who knows? I might, if you were my wife" (*PB* 224). It makes Carol realize her position, a marginalized one as Sidhwa writes:

> Suddenly a great deal became clear to her. 'So that's all I mean to you' she said. 'That's really what's behind all the gallant and protective behaviour I've loved so much here, isn't it? I felt very special and all the time I didn't matter to you any more than that girl does as an individual to those tribals, not any more than a bitch in heat. You make me sick. All of you'.
>
> (*PB* 224)

Carol too, like Zaitoon, is exploited.

Carol and Hannah are not able to assimilate/syncretize their experiences of relocation and sexuality with dislocation. They are rescued not abducted by men, Mushtaq and Raja Jadav Singh respectively. Thereby, they gain sanctuary in an alien land. As the Pakistani boy never pays concerns to Carol, Hannah's husband Gabriel is neither faithful nor concerned about Hannah's welfare. Carol's and Hannah's rescue by Mushtaq and Jadav Singh is also the point at which they consciously cross racial boundaries / borders. Hannah like her mother, Rebecca, takes lovers from another culture. Sidhwa in *Brat* expresses the joys and terrors of the newcomer's, Feroza's, discovery of herself and her own body and representations of the micro politics of middle-class south Asian homes. In fact, she captures the human face of the homogenization of a polyglossic and multicultural population. It concerns itself with East-West relations. Being a member of a marginal community, Sidhwa deals with the questions of ethnicity and tribal affiliations to Pakistan.

Sidhwa's novels include a scene at Hira Mandir. The courtesans of Hira Mandi begin their evening with a classic Kathakali which would turn to be erotic in a classical striptease. Sidhwa explains that Pakistan is a segregated society and therefore its people are sexually obsessed. So Hira Mandi peddles romance and not sex. In *Bride* Qasim and Nikka visit Hira Mandi and are entertained by a dancer named Shahnaz. Shahnaz's song stresses the pretence that both courtesan and her clients maintain. The eroticism and coyness, the repression and the mystery, the double perspective of purdah society—all these are contained in Shahnaz's song.

In Sidhwa's *Candy-Man* the narrator's relationship with her cousin upholds the principle of equality as she does not allow him to manipulate her sexually. He remains a drooling figure, adoring her for her vivaciousness. Lenny's lameness never becomes a source of self-pity or a constricting force on her psyche. She remains assertive, at times even aggressive. Ayah infuses in Lenny the ideas of independence and choice. In fact, she epitomizes the strength of the feminity of a female. She is extremely protective of Lenny. She suffers during the partition riots. She is abducted by the cronies of the Ice-Candy-Man, ravished and raped by the hoodlums, kept as the Ice-Candy-Man's mistress and then forced to become the Ice-Candy-Man's bride. Her name is changed from Shanta to Mumtaz and she is kept at a kotha even after her marriage. During the interregnum between her abduction and marriage, she is used like a sewer by drunks, Pedlers, sahibs, and cut-throats with the connivance of the Ice-Candy-Man. In the end she seizes her freedom.

Equally, Mukherjee's characters are raised in conservative, often sexually repressive communities. Mukherjee's characters desire the sexual freedom. The traditional concept of marriage which immigrants bring with them is challenged by the values of a permissive foreign culture. The structures that keep marriages intact in India are absent in the west, thus leaving the immigrants' marriages fragile and vulnerable. Having an affair is not merely a sexual temptation, but it offers a way of reasserting one's autonomy, one's control over one's life. The danger is alluring. But as in the case of Dr. Patel, the desire for intimacy outside the boundaries of marriage might also be symptomatic of larger discontents of immigrant life—the loneliness, the uncertainty and the emptiness. Vinita in "Visitors" has a devoted husband, a fabulous condominium, and an apparently satisfying life. Yet the romantic overtures of the lonely Indian student, Rajiv, create in her a longing to leave her husband.

In Mukherjee's world, Jasmine empowers her in an alien culture after having been raped by Half-Face. Bhagmati in *Holder* is disempowered after her rape in a culture that values virginity and chastity; and Hannah by her liaison with Jadav Singh chooses to break social norms concerning interracial relationships and the power of women to choose their sexual partners like Zaitoon who has been raped and there by determined to cross the bridge in *Bride* and Tara who had a liaison with Andy even though her husband Bish is in her life. The rape / physical assault / molestation / deflowering empowers Zaitoon and Tara to face life with determination.

Though Jasmine has come to America with the crazy notion of erecting a funeral pyre for her dead husband's clothes on his University campus and burning herself on it, by grasping at the dream of a new life, she has to sacrifice herself and her original self. She needs to discard her ethnicity. It results in alternate identities as women have to change sexual behaviour. Dimple's and Jasmine's sexual behaviour with an American man and Half-Face respectively makes them detach from traditional sexual mores and assimilate the new world through their rapid Westernization / Americanization. Jasmine is released from her traditional identity as a de-sexual widow soon after she arrives in America, for in being raped by Half-Face. This helps her grow in confidence to live by. She like Zaitoon who in the words of Jasbir Jain in "The Male Presence in the "Purdah" Novel" "is escaping herself to every kind of risk when she decides to escape; it is a decision deeply rooted in her helplessness, in the sense of having been totally abandoned to the brutality of her life with Sakhi. Sexual desire, which very often, helps women to accept their lives, or timidity which compels them to do so-are, in Zaitoon's case, not adequate enough to stop her from this desparate act" (221). On the part of Carol, Farukh's excessive jealousy drives her to Mushtaq. His jealousy destroys her freedom. She hates what Farukh's jealousy has done to her:

> It had corroded her innocence, stripped her, layer by layer, of civilized American niceties. She was frightened to see a part of herself change into a hideously vulgar person.
>
> [...] And the atmosphere of repressed sexuality in Pakistan had not helped. Slowly Carol had begun to realize that even among her friends, where the wives did not wear

> burkhas or live in special quarters, the general separation of the sexes bred an atmosphere of sensuality.
>
> (*PB* 111)

Equally, Zaitoon's proposed entry into an alien culture is a reflection in of the Carol- Farukh relationship. Both the women have moved from relatively open cultures into closed cultures. In fact, Zaitoon, Carol, Jasmine, Dimple, Tara, Hannah and so on often surrender to sexual fantasies of male conquest and social fantasies of conquering the new territory of their husband's world. And it is the failure of these fantasies which pushes them to decide to escape in various ways—Jasmine kills Half-Face and goes with American men like Taylor and Bud, Dimple murders Amit, Tara returns to India and realizes the love for David and Hannah abandons Legge and surrenders to Jadav Singh only to return to Salem as Bibi-Salem Bibi. The worst fate is assigned to Zaitoon. First of all she is used as a sacrifice by Qasim to re-establish his link with his homeland and then she is left in a totally alien and hostile environment without knowing what identity to assume. She is almost raped by Sakhi on their first night of marriage. On top of that Sakhi, in accordance with the expectations of a man's role in Kohistani traditions, starts the frequent and brutal beatings in order to tame Zaitoon whenever she dares to go against his wishes. She is a virtual prisoner with Sakhi being the omniscient being, who knows every move she makes. She is abused and battered routinely. When Sakhi is taunted by his brother Yunus Khan for not being a man enough to control his wife, it leads to increased savagery on his part towards his possessions. In blind rage, he first batters his Ox, then his mother with a stick. In a rage he says: "'I'll teach you', he hissed, 'I'll teach you meddling women. You think you can make a fool of me? Do you?' " (*PB* 172). Even when Zaitoon tries to stop him from beating his mother, he begins to thrash her: "'You are my woman! I'll teach you to obey me!'" (*PB* 172-73). In this world of male chauvinism, being a woman almost implies being owned and being like a beast of burden. The violence against the women in the tribal society is more shocking. Sakhi beats Zaitoon not only with sticks but also with stones. He even kicks her. The violence is also sexual and verbal, not only physical. When Sakhi spies Zaitoon waving at an army track across the river, his anger is expressed in crude and vile invective:

> 'you whore', he hissed. His fury was so intense she thought he would kill her. He cleared his throat and spat full in her face. 'You dirty, black little bitch, waving at those pigs [...] Gripping her with one hand he waved the other in a lewd caricature of the girl's brief gesture. 'Waving at that shit – eating swine. You wanted him to stop and fuck you, didn't you.'
>
> (*PB* 185)

When Sakhi beats her, in an instinctive gesture Zaitoon butts her head into his groin undoing his salwar. Sidhwa writes:

> He slapped her hard, and swinging her politely by the arm, as a child swings a doll, he flung her from him. A sharp flint cut into her breast, and in a wild lunge she blindly butted her head between the man's legs. In the brief scuffle, the cord of Sakhi's trousers came undone and the baggy gathers at the waist of his salwar flopped to his ankles. Sakhi froze. Transfixed on the edge, he blanched. What if some one had witnessed his ultimate humiliation?.
>
> (*PB* 186)

Sakhi retaliates by kicking her between her legs until she faints with pain. Then only Zaitoon decides to run away. She nearly dies for it.

Sidhwa makes it quite clear and creates significant events to sharply focus the situation of life into which Zaitoon finds herself. She is revulsed by the faces around her, the rubbery bread offered to her and the cave like huts instead of the rosy picture of her dreams. She is haunted by the unpleasantness around her and dreams about her "standing by the river, admiring its vivid colours, when a hand had come out of the ice-blue depths and dragged her in, pulling her down, down" (*PB* 156). Her fear crystallizes; she senses the savagery of the people, their poverty and what the harshness of their fight for survival had made them. "Her mind revolts at the certainty that to share their lives she would have to become like them"

(*PB* 156). In her desperation she urges her father to take her back with him for she feels that "I will die rather than live here" (*PB* 157). The novelist places Zaitoon in the unfamiliar and savage surroundings and describes fully the mountain people and their life with her Dickensian insight. The conflict at this stage is presented deftly. To Qasim the mountain man, his honour is dearer to him than his own life or his daughter's life even though he has a nagging fear for the girl's life. "Qasim had an unreasoning impulse to take her back with him on some pretext or other [....] He should have listened to the child's violent plea the night they arrived. His departure imminent, he felt he had acted in undue haste. Too late, he tried to fight this wave of sentimentality and fear" (*PB* 166). But he seeks consolation in the fact that his own old fervent longing to be with his blood would be realized through Zaitoon's marriage to Sakhi. The novelist has added a dimension to Qasim's character by revealing this detail. Man's wish to realize his own dreams even by sacrificing his own child's life to insecurity and hardships of the cruel traditions of the tribal men is fully explored by Sidhwa. Gita Viswanath in "Modes of Resistance in the South-Asian Novel: A Study of the Fiction by Bapsi Sidhwa, Rohinton Mistry and Yasmine Goonerdne" says: "Zaitoon, a young girl is victimized by the debilitating patriarchal prescriptions of an insular tribal society. The woman is held as repository of moral values in a patriarchal society. Within this ideological framework, Zaitoon signifies the 'woman-as-victim paradigm in much feminist writing" (39). Sakhi stands between her and freedom. The rigorous code of honour of the tribal society in Kohistan rests on notions of sexual superiority and possessiveness. Yunus khan, brother of Sakhi, taunts him for not being manly enough to control his wife. He says: "How is your wife from the plains? You know, she requires a man to control her" (*PB* 170). In the perverse value system of the tribal society, the honour of a man is judged by how well he can oppress his women. Sakhi exercises his right of proprietorship on the wedding night itself. He says to his bride: "'It's my cunt!" he breathed, holding her crotch in a warm squeeze" (102). In this context, the violence is not only physical, but also verbal and sexual.

The episode of Sakhi beating the animal almost to death and his mother's attempt to save the animal, his beating his own mother and even Zaitoon brings into sharp focus the tribal manhood and the barbarious views of honour. The woman, be she a mother or a wife, is savagely ill-treated; it is man against woman; there is no code of respecting the mother or an elderly woman. Man is the master even if he is a child, as Sidhwa points out at the beginning, of the novel, describing Qasim the child husband of his grown-up young wife. No laws of civilized life affect the tribal men. They may kill their women for dishonour caused to them but do not hesitate to rape women if they get such an opportunity as is revealed by the author—an attempted rape on Qasim's wife earlier and Zaitoon being raped by the two tribal men of some other group.

Woman is a mere chattel and she is exploited both sexually and also for household work which includes collecting fuel and fetching water from the stream. She is not treated as an individual in her own right, nor given any status even as a mother. She is simply a slave to the men of the family and they whip her and beat her at their fancy any time even without reason. Sidhwa portrays with Zolasque details the life of the mountain tribals who remain cut off from the mainstream of life in Pakistan. Though here too, she shows that the Pakistani Muslim husband considers infidelity in his wife a sin which must be punished either by maiming her or by killing her. The Major makes this clear to Carol who is a privileged bride since she is an American white woman, but she too is doomed if she is unfaithful and her husband comes to know about it.

The molestation of Zaitoon, a starved and raped girl, becomes an eloquent appeal against the oppression of women. Even Carol considers Zaitoon as emblem against male dominance:

> Carol had a sudden sinking realization of the girl's plight. She remembered the curious communication between them; and her large sensitive eyes. She now felt they had revealed more than just the hopeless drift of her life; they had communicated faith and a dauntless courage. Through an awesome act of will the girl had chosen to deflect the

> direction of her life. Carol felt a compulsion to help her even risk to herself.
>
> (*PB* 245)

She even resolves to assist Zaitoon in case the fugitive survives: "Christ! If she comes through, I'll do something for her, I really will" (*PB* 229).

The *Bride* displays a rare awareness of women's oppression and exploitation in the society. Zaitoon is a child of Partition whose epic struggle for survival becomes central to the narrative. Sidhwa questions the androcentric ideology that pervades the tribal world to which Qasim, father of Zaitoon belongs. In the novel, there is not mere recognition of sexism; it is accompanied with a conscious effort by a challenge to patriarchy. Patriarchy and Imperialism served as complementalities and rebellion, if there is any against Imperialism should also be concurrent with the contemporary subversion of the patriarchal order. Zaitoon's struggle highlights one of the pivotal issues in feminist discourse, viz., the position of, and the treatment meted out to, women.

Like Carol, in Mukherjee's *Daughter* Tara makes her a misfit in the company of her friends and relatives. Her alienation is deepened as she is welcomed by her relatives as 'Americawali' and her husband as in 'meccha'. Such labels of distinction intensify the alienation in the mind of Tara and they deepen the angst of her mind. Tara returning to India after seven years in the USA experiences the alienation of an expatriate who senses a gulf between herself and her native people and traditions. She realizes that her alienation extends further back into her Indian past, to her education under Belgian nuns: "How does the foreignness of the spirit begin? [...] Does it begin right in the centre of Calcutta, with forty ruddy headdresses, long black habits intensifying the hostility of the Indian Sun?" (*T* 37).

Dimple also experiences an intense loneliness of the expatriate. There is a progressive and total estrangement from the environment, from herself and from existence itself. "She [illegible] so much worse than ever, more lonely, more cut off from [illegible] from the Indi[illegible] left alone with borrowed disguises, she felt like a shadow without feeling" (*W* 200). Her loneliness and foreignness is similar to that of Sindi Oberoi in *The Foreigner* where Oberoi comments upon his mode of life: "I was foreigners in America. But then, what difference would it have made if I had lived in Kenya or India or any other place for that matter? [...] my foreignness stayed within me and I couldn't leave myself behind wherever I went" (65). America represents a freedom which is often excessive. It is increasingly a corrective to the growing fundamentalism in Pakistan. Feroza is caught up in the religious politics of the country. "The growing fundamentalism of Pakistan is initially portrayed as a series of inconveniences which do not seem to warrant the drastic action of a close of American culture. The horrors of the growing criminalization of women's bodies to make themselves present but in a rather diluted form; Feroza discovers the victimization through American media" (*AB* 108).

In *Candy-Man,* when the riots erupt, the Ice-Candy-Man seizes his chance to debase the Ayah and leads a Muslim mob to Lenny's house. The Parsi family and its Muslim servants hide the Ayah, but Lenny unwittingly betrays her. Ayah is dragged away by the mob and raped. After her degradation, the Ice-Candy-Man sets up her in a house in the prostitutes' Quarters in Lahore. Having proved his mastery over her, he now professes to be crazily in love with her and wants to marry her. She, having been betrayed by him and physically abused by the mob, refuses to accept him. Ayah suffers in silence. The novel as a whole discusses the issue of sexual transgression. Matti Katherine Pennebaker in "The Will of Men: Victimization of Women During India's Partition" says: "The fact that Ayah is forced to prostitute her body and coerced into having sex with Ice-Candy-Man indicates that women's bodies have been historically become territory in which men act out their aggression" (http://www.tamu.edu/chr/agora/summeroo/ Pennebaker. pdf). Feroza and Dimple discover the victimization through American media. Mukherjee's *Wife* presents an intense inner world of neurotic and solipsistic individual. Rootlessness and unreal existence make a deliberate distortion of Indian womanhood.

Dimple is an instance of the forlorn and all ill-accomodated self of an Indian wife. S.P. Swain in "Dimple in *Wife:* A Study of the Lacerated Self", says: To understand the reality of Dimple's psyche one has to delve deep into the inner recesses of her mind, the intricate stirrings of her feelings" (83). Dimple in *Wife* dreams of an independent flat. But actually in America "she was much worse than ever, more lonely more cut off from Amit, from the Indians, left alone with borrowed disguises, she felt like a shadow without feeling" (*W* 200). Later, she begins to resent her own passivity. She feels she is falling apart. She kills her husband with the Kitchen Knife, the very knife with which she chopped chicken and mutton in the same kitchen on the same counter.

Dimple's journey in *Wife,* unlike Tara's in *Daughters,* is undertaken in search of fulfilment and self-expression. Dimple has been educated in India and is married to an Indian husband; yet she is ill at ease in her world. She appears to be constantly bored with herself. She moves from one unreal objective to another; from the dream of marriage as an escape from this boredom to the hope of emigration. "Marriage, she was sure, would free her, till her with passion" (*W* 13) like that of Mohini who aspires to wed in order to get rid of her old-mother in Bhattacharya's *Music for Mohini.* But when her marriage to Amit remains unfulfilled, she turns to thoughts of America. In order to be able to begin life afresh, she decides to induce an abortion. "She had skipped rope until her legs grow numb and her stomach burned; then she had poured water from the heavy bucket over her head, shoulders, over the tight little curve of her stomach. She had poured until the last of the blood washed off her legs, then she had collapsed" (*W* 42).

Shyam M. Asnani in "Identity Crisis in *The Nowhere Man* and *Wife*" says: "In contrast, Dimple is unwilling to brave the new world outside, feels bored, dejected and dismally ignorant of actual patterns of social interaction in America and is ultimately driven into an entropic state of inertia, nervous debility, and mental decrepitude. Her sudden forays into the world outside the apartment prove abortive. Her displacement ends on a tragic note" (46). In Dimple's case the loss of identity is not only due to being an exile in America but also due to her constitutional temperament and her alienation from her husband. More so, due to her self-alienation, she loses the contact with reality. Her coming to America might have aggravated her feel of alienation. She is perilously estranged from her own self. She is alien to it. It is her self-alienation that breeds a terrible anguish in her and prompts her to murder Amit as "Her own body seemed curiously alien to her, filled with hate, malice, an insane desire to hurt, yet weightless, almost air borne" (*W* 117). She is an alien to the world of Amit, an outsider to her husband.

In the case of Dimple, though she is at times shocked at her own intensity of feeling and her capacity to hate eventually, she exercises her ungratified passion through violence alone. S. Indira in "Exploration of Inner Space: Anita Desai's *Cry, the Peacock* and Bharati Mukherjee's *Wife*" says: "Neither the cultural conflict nor a feminine need for freedom can account for Dimple's bizarre, blasphemous imagination and behaviour" (64). In *Wife* Dimple has to cope up with her traumatic mental condition all alone as Amit fails Dimple on all planes—physical, mental and emotional. She turns towards Ina, Leni and Milt Glasser in her moments of crisis. Ina and Leni fail her as friends. Milt proves to be a temporary transgression. She is an alienated being undergoing the supposed after-effects of alienation—psychosis, psychosomatic disorder, delinquency and contemplation of suicide.

S.P. Swine in "Dimple in *Wife:* A Study of the Lacerated Self" says: "It is the gloomy corridors of her psyche, that Mukherjee probes with a keen and penetrating psychological subtlety. Dimple moves from a state of mute resentment to an escalating disgust and intolerance which finally culminates in disaster" (84). Initially, she decides to marry a neuro-surgeon but finally agrees to marry an engineer for affluence. As a being, she is a partial woman and her psychic obsessions are about the inadequacies of her figure and complexion. Lake of communication stifles and chokes her voice and disintegrates her sensibility. It takes away the sanity of her mind. She has nightmares of violence, of suicide and of death. She even has the sensation of being raped and killed in her flat. Thoughts of illusion and reality alternate in her psyche—the illusion of committing suicide and the reality of butchering her husband. It is to admit as S.P. Swain further states in "Dimple in *Wife:* A Study of Lacerated Self": "Dimple suffers from a terrible angst. The anxiety of living haunts her. She loses her balance of mind. Mentally deranged, she begins to develop nausea for things around her. Tedium vitae and apprehension phobea split her self, breeching a morbid fear of the milieu" (88).

In *Wife*, Dimple appears to indulge in masochistic suffering in order to ease the pain of disappointment with life, especially with married life. As the masochist neurotic seems to convert every chance occurrences into painful experiences, she converts even the chance occurrences into painful dreaming, hallucinations and nightmarish experiences. It is primarily used by her to narcotize the pain. As female masochism is largely a culturally-determined phenomenon, Dimple's masochism forms apart of what Karen Horney calls "the general principle of finding satisfaction by losing the self" (270) in even greater misery and it is practised by dissolving the individuality with all the doubts, conflicts, pains, limitations and isolation attendant on it. M. Rajeshwar in "Sado-Masochism as a Literary Device in *Wife*" says: "Dimple's life is a long tryst with death. Her masochism makes her moribund consciousness look almost transparent. As her need to die increases in intensity, she becomes more and more neurotic and vice versa. However, death should also be viewed here as the logical and final goal of the conservative instincts in order to do justice for its employment as a literary device. It can therefore be understood that her awareness of death is partly a thematic necessity and partly an aesthetic necessity" (94).

Dimple is an escapist, lost in her private world of fantasy. In the beginning, at home in Calcutta, she dreams of marrying a neuro surgeon. She has lived so long in the fantasy world of advertising and advice columns. She is emotionally incapable of understanding others. She aspires for freedom and love in marriage. This brings her indignation, grief, resentment, peevishness, spite and sterile anger. She is trapped between two cultures. Despair sets in her life. She thinks "marriage had betrays her, had not provided all the glittering things she had imagined" (*W* 101-102).

There are two important encounters with death in Dimple's life – one symbolic, another actual. The first is her sadistic killing of a mouse. It has a surrealistic touch to it. It occurs after Dimple's marriage to Amit and particularly after having undergone series of frustrating—experiences which propel her to think of death. She chases the rodent and kills it shouting hysterically.

> 'I'll get you!' she screamed. 'There is no way of this, my friend'. She seemed confident now, a woman transformed. And in an outburst of hatred, her body shuddering, her wrist taut with fury, she smashed the top of small grey head.
>
> (*W* 35)

Equally, when she inflicts an abortion on herself, causing death to the Foetus, she outwardly passes from sadism to masochism.

Dimple being frustrated devises at least ten different ways of terminating her life under the central metaphor of her life as 'a dying bonfire': getting her head caught in the oven, slicing open her jugular vein, consuming pesticide, getting suffocated in a garbage bag, starving, falling on bread-knife, getting her head with shovels and finally getting mugged and killed in the laundry room in the basement after mid night. She also begins to view herself as already dead, first in dream:

> An after dream persisted when she woke up: someone had murdered her the night before and concealed her corpse among the Bedouin brasses and baskets of indoor plants. She wrapped her blue bathrope tighter around her breasts and hips and did all the things she normally did between seven and eight on weekday mornings, but she knew that she was dead and that Amit would recoil from her as soon as he sat down at the table for his wheaties and two fried eggs.
>
> (*W* 185-86)

Her sado-masochist drives further compel her to inflict the same kind of punishment upon Amit. She wishes to die but by forming a reaction she kills. Maya Manju Sharma in "The Inner world of Bharati Mukherjee From Expatriate to Immigrant" says: "Dimple's moral and cultural suicide is symbolized and effectuated by an act of abortion, the destruction of an actual or potential human life merely because it has begun, like Dimple herself in India" (15). In an interview with Geoff Hancock, who asks, "Is infidelity and murder the only solution?", Mukherjee replies:

> Dimple's decision to murder her husband is her misguided act of self-assertion. If she had remained a housewife living with her extended family in India, she probably would not have asked herself questions such as, am I happy, do I deserve to be unhappy. And if by chance she had asked herself these questions, she might have settled her problems by committing suicide. So turning to violence outward rather than inward is a part of her slow and misguided Americanization.
>
> (44)

Meera Manvi points out: "The dialectic of 'appearance' and 'reality' is [...] projected through Mukherjee's narrative technique; the interplay of the 'real', the 'unreal', and the 'televised' in the extreme. Denied self-hood, Dimple's only act of self-assertion is murder. The instrument which symbolized her bondage – as a 'Wife [...] becomes the instrument of murder" (149). Jasmine is also put through the most grueling confrontations with death (of her husband Prakash), murder (the killing of Half-Face who raped her), assault and crippling (of Bud) and suicide (of her neighbour Darvell).

Violence in Sidhwa and Mukherjee "stems from an instinctual recognition that if everyplace, including the so-called Third World is assimilated to the status of simulacrum of spectacle, then it is also true that for the diasporic every place is no place that all places are homeless, uncanny [....]" (Samir Dayal 82). On the question of violence put forth by Sharmani Patricia Gabriel in conversation with, Mukherjee answers:

> Risk-taking and the consequences of that risk-taking can be very, very violent. The uprooting from what you know

> to land somewhere where you have no clue as to what is expected of you, let alone what you expect of yourself, is a traumatizing experience. And, so, as a writer, I have to find metaphors for talking about the psychic violence of up-rooting and re-rooting. That is why there is so much physical violence in my fiction. The physical violence can take either the form of sexual violence or of actual homes burning down [....] .
>
> (132-133)

Mukherjee introduces violence, a kind of psychic violence in Tara, Dimple and Jasmine. Brinda Bose in "A Question of Identity: Where Gender, Race, and America Meet in Bharati Mukherjee" affirms:

> The level of violence escalates as one moves from Tara's horror as she is, in two climatic scenes, seduced by a middle-aged politician and stranded in the midst of a bloody political riot, to Dimple's frenzied killing of her husband, and finally to Jasmine's reincarnation as an avenging Kali in her desperate bid to find a foothold in the American way of life. Tara is convinced by these experiences that she needs to discard her past and embrace her home away from home, and to her this is a physical wrench; both Dimple and Jasmine are eased into the notion that if circumstances require that they do more than merely escape, they must do so to save themselves. For them, murder evolves into an acceptable signifier for discarding nostalgia and starting over; it is neither the end nor even merely the means to an end; it is a beginning.
>
> (53-54)

Matti Katherine Pennebaker in "The Will of Men: Victimization of Women During Partition" also admits:

> In Sidhwa's novel, acts of violence against women are not limited to acts of religious hatred and demophobia. Lenny's mother, a Zoroastrian; is a victim of the will of men as Well. Lenny states, 'Although father has never raised his hands to us, one day I surprise mother at her bath and see the bruises on her body' (224).

Thus Sidhwa reminds the reader that victimization and abuse of women not always occur in the context of warfare and religious hatred but in the daily course of domestic life. The forgoing depictions of violence against women are shockingly savage. These acts of brutality indicate what women's bodies symbolize for these religiously diversified groups. The appalling physical injuries inflicted on these women suggest that in this time and place the female body became a territory to be fought over, conquered, and subsequently "branded" by the assailant through rape or disfigurement. (http://www.tamu.edu/chr/agora/summeroo/pennebaker.pdf)

A loss of self-esteem is one of the commonest experiences of women in all cultures. Women in general become trapped in a self-destructive gender based situation not because they form a destructive relationship but because the relationship is thrust on them as is the case with Zaitoon, Carol, Jasmine, Dimple, Tara, Hannah and so on who are compelled to accept exploitative relationships because of parental/ religious/cultural authority. The pressure of the male power as experienced by Zaitoon from Sakhi, Carol by her sexual need which is not fulfilled by her Pakistani husband, Farukh and her lover Major. Mushtaq, Jasmine by the brutal rape by Half-Face, and Dimple by her materialistic husband who fails to read her mind, Hannah by Gabriel Legge and Tara by Andy so on, often frustrates the redemptive exercises initiated by women. These are fictional accounts of women's struggle in their culture or in an alien culture. They celebrate victory/survival/escape of the female protagonist or through culture/ religion/society prohibit the articulation of female voice.

One major obstacle in Zaitoon's and Dimple's quest for identity is their husbands. Basically Sakhi is tradition bound and takes Zaitoon as a commodity or an animal to be tamed and Amit is basically too absorbed in his search for economic security. They have no time to either understand or sensitize the complicated changes that is going on in Zaitoon and Dimple. Sakhi never wants Zaitoon to be what she is but Amit seems to be happy when Dimple becomes American but not too American. Assessing the reasons for Dimple's insanity and madness, Kalpana Wandrekar in *The Ailing Aliens: A Study of the Immigrant Psyche in Six Indian English Novels* says:

> Displacement distances Dimple from Amit. She is lonely and alienated. When the outlets to relate to people around her get blocked Dimple's personality indicates fragmentation. She suffers from insomnia which is a direct result of the feeling of insecurity and fear. This development in her character indicates a lag between social and psychological evolution in which the psychic needs could no longer be satisfied by the usual role in the stratification of the society.
>
> (68)

Dimple's mental aberrations cannot bridge the hiatus between the dream-world of imagination and the drab-world of reality. Her mental make up at this stage throws light on the connection between repressions and pseudo-acts. The realisation of her shattered dream-world is an emotional threat to her which creates anxiety and then dormant destructive tendencies emerge. The burden of the feeling of being trapped weighs more on her. The sick mind begins to contemplate death and suicide.

Psychoanalysts have identified the journey as a voyage of self-discovery which provides the missing parts of the traveller's experience and helps identify her individual needs and desires. In it, the goal is the psychic liberation that provides a sense of identity and self-worth and allows her to interact with her social environment as an individual. Zaitoon's adoptive father, Qasim, on the other hand has the opposite purpose in mind as he undertakes another journey from Lahore to Kohistan, in a bid to re-establish his lost connection with his past and his people. Though he might be going back to his people, he is not alone, he is taking a gift as an atonement for his long absence and to show his commitment in desiring a renewal of his ties. It is another example of Partition and the necessary migration/ dislocation which comes with it for Zaitoon, who had known nothing about her life in India and had thought of Lahore as her home. When Qasim arranges Zaitoon's marriage, it is Miriam who brings out the contrast and points out how Qasim himself has changed: "they are savages, brutish, uncouth and ignorant [...] most of them are bandits, they don't know how to treat women" (*PB* 93).

Zaitoon is brought up in liberal ways of life in Lahore, is educated and really belongs to the plain. Miriam is even prepared to adopt her as daughter since she has doubts about the ways of the tribals. She tries to explain this to even Zaitoon but Zaitoon does not listen to her. Young as she is, she is guided by the vision of the glorious home of her father's forefathers and of the lover her fancies envisaged" (*PB* 98). Thus begins the journey of Zaitoon to the unknown yet romantic mountains into the civilization entirely different from the one to which she is born and brought up. Zaitoon is aware of this: "I cross this spot and my life changes she thought with sudden reluctance. But the step into her new life had been taken a month back and she was moving fatefully on its momentum" (*PB* 153). Even though she is just 16 years of age she is aware of her predicament. She steps into the closed world of mountains, almost pathless wilderness. Sidhwa writes: "Before them stretched centuries of an intractable wilderness, [....]" (*PB* 154).

Through Zaitoon's fight and escape from the inhospitable environment and Kohistani men, Sidhwa seems to make a statement with regard to women's plight in a country like Pakistan. The path to 'freedom,' in this case of a personal nature, can come about only after a 'partition.' And as with the Partition of India, those in power would use whatever means they have in their disposal to prevent the person or a nation of attaining statehood/self-hood. Sidhwa articulates that women, though jealously coveted by their men from outsiders are more at risk from the very people who are supposed to 'guard' and 'value' them. Zaitoon's story runs parallel in a number of ways to the nation's turbulent history. Just as the Muslims of this country felt stifled and suppressed in India, Zaitoon knows that it is almost impossible for her to survive in the Kohistani community. Just as there was vehement opposition of the majority of population of India to Pakistan's freedom, the whole of Sakhi's tribe hunting for Zaitoon is an apt parallel between two stories. The desperate and trying struggle of both displays the resolve, will-power and the courage involved in the initial desire and the eventual achievement of freedom.

The Pakistani nation's internal weaknesses, which can ultimately pit the society against itself, are laid bare by the way the patriarchy treats its women. And so the imagined 'homeland' where a woman can be safe still retains the elusiveness of an often dreamt fantasy, as the 'dislocated' and 'partitioned' relationships of Nikka and Mariam, Sakhi and Zaitoon and Carol and Farukh dominate the domestic scene in the novel.

Even though the tribals come across a very cruel and repressive community, one questions the desire of the so-called 'plain's civilization' to 'civilize' them. For it is quite obvious that one side is not on a higher moral ground in terms of their treatment of the women in their community. After all, it was Qasim (who had become a semi 'plains person') who brought an 'outsider' to the mountains. Her escape and final return to the plains seems to suggest that it would be better to leave these two distinctly cultures as far apart as possible.

In Zaitoon, Carol and Mukherjee's Jasmine one can find the melodramatic intensity as women infringe their husbands' moral code and sense of honour. In their cases, one can find a cessation of romanticism and the flight of the frustrated wives. In Zaitoon and Jasmine, the flight is a permanent one as they desire to escape from their culture into alien culture but in Carol's case it is a temporary one. Carol returns to her husband but it is not so in the case of Zaitoon and Jasmine to whom future is ambiguous. As Jasmine gives herself to so many men, Zaitoon gives herself to Ashiq, the orderly of Major Mushtaq. For both Zaitoon and Carol, marriage is a journey to a foreign land. For Carol, it is an escape from disappointment. For Zaitoon, the crossing of the imperative divides between daughter and wife. But neither is content in the place of arrival. Carol's dreams are satisfied neither by her wealthy Pakistani husband, nor by her dashing lover. Zaitoon's daydreams are more brutally destroyed. The destruction of Zaitoon's life does not share Carol's imperialist tinge. But, both ironically share a romantic yearning for a larger life than the conventions of their respective cultures have previously permitted.

Sidhwa's inclusion of the Mushtaq-Carol sub-plot is to provide another perspective on purdah. As an American married to a Pakistani, Carol comes face to face with a society very different from the one she has known. Zaitoon is a part of purdah society. Carol is outside it. Her boredom and infidelity become less important than her realization that women, both Pakistani and American, belonging to a purdah or non-purdah society are equally vulnerable. But while Zaitoon is saved by Mushtaq, Carol leaves Pakistan empty handed. Pakistan hurts her because it is a civilization "too ancient, too different" (*PB* 229).

Carol's and Hannah's journey to the East is fraught with images of adventure, action, and passion. It projects a sort of escape from the rigid world. They are highly imaginative and quickly embrace the new exotic world – Pakistan and Mughal India. After the neglect of her Pakistani husband, Carol comes to Mushtaq. Hannah also comes to Raja Jadav Sing after the death of Gabriel. Realising their potential as individuals, they exemplify an enduring strength and pugnacity for achieving personal recognition and an intrinsic contender for life's vicissitudes. They emerge as women who are inquisitive, vital and intensely aware of self and purpose. They are so magically entranced by Pakistan and India. They easily forget their old world as Pakistan and India seem to them as a place of endless possibilities and sensuous pleasures which they could not dream of in their lands. Just as Jasmine adopts herself to the western life style, Carol and Hannah find great contentment and joy in their adapted lands. They transport from place to place, and from person to person. Their whole personality undergoes a change as they move in and out of places physically as well as mentally. In it, they succeed in burying their past. Sidhwa's *Bride* is not a mere study in victimology but a study in escape from a tribal husband and his family, propelled by her own free will after being a victim of inductable fate. Carol being equally oppressed in her relationship with Farukh decides to break free.

Struggle is again the underlying motif of *Brat*. Feroza's frustrated question, "Why am I a Paki Third Worlder?" (27) sets the theme. Throughout her journeys to and in America, Feroza struggles to know who she is, why she is and how she relates both to the body politic of her own Parsi community and that of the larger community of America. In that regard *Brat* is certainly a bildungsroman. Jussawalla posits in "Navjote Ceremonies: The Location of Bapsi Sidhwa's Culture", that the bildungsroman is the "primary form and characteristic of the postcolonial novel" (Dhawan, 80). As she states:

> The bildungsroman journey seems to be the basis of every so-called postcolonial [...] novel. It is the initiation process that leads not just to a general self-awakening process, but to an awakening into one's nationalism and to an understanding of one's self as located in a particular place and in a particular cultural-political framework.
>
> (80)

Feroza's journey to self-awareness begins with her flight to America. A group of friends from her school are there, along with Feroza's many family members to see her off. As Feroza leaves to board the plane, "the girl's hand reached out reluctant to let go as Feroza pulled away, giving the impression if stretched, elasticized bodies being torn apart" (49). Thus Feroza's body proper is violently detached from the body of her family and community. She now stands alone. Once settled in America, she tries to reconnect to another body in the person of her roommate, clinging to "the umbilical cord by which she had attached herself to Jo" (214). Sadly for her, this connection doesn't adequately satisfy her need for belonging, and she remains isolated and still searching for identity. Then sometime later when she first arrives in America, Manek takes her sightseeing in New York City. They visit Bloomingdale's an entrancing new world for Feroza: "It was like entering a surreal world of hushed opulence festooned by all manner of hats propped up on stands and scarves and belts draped here and there like fabulous confetti [...] Feroza felt she had never seen such luxuriant textures or known the vibrant gloss of true colors" (*B* 73). While in Bloomingdale's, Manek insists he can smell a desi (a native of the subcontinent), and he "sleuth(es) off to prowl the twilight periphery of the elegantly embellished space" (*B* 74). His nose, however, leads him directly back to Feroza, the "smelly desi" (*B* 74). And he chastises her for not practising the American custom of wearing deodorant. When

Feroza emerges from the store some time later, she has bought, along with her new clothes, the all-important stick of deodorant.

Several parallels between the body proper and the body politic are apparent in this incident. Bloomingdale's, of course, represents America. As a newcomer in America, Feroza is awed by its opulence; she in fact becomes "witless" as she is overcome by its "suctionlike force" (*B* 73). Her foreignness is highlighted by her objectional body odour; the very essence of her body proper is alien in America. Further, when Manek looks for the desi he knows is in the store, he looks not in the heart of the elegance, but in the darkened periphery. Feroza, the self-avowed "Paki Third Worlder" belongs only in the margins of the American body politic. She attempts to centralize herself by adapting to American mores, represented by her purchase of the deodorant. This is the first step she takes in her quest to locate herself within the framework of the body politic.

Another incident happens to Feroza while vacationing in New York City that is equally telling of her relationship to the body politic. She and Manek are staying at the YMCA for the duration of their stay. After mistakenly getting off the elevator on the wrong floor, she is led into the fire escape by an apparently, though not necessarily, well-meaning woman. Once inside the stairwell, she is locked out of the building. A terrified Feroza spends half an hour in malodorous darkness trying to discover an unlocked door. Though her prayers don't help, eventually her screams are heard, and she is rescued. While Bloomingdale's represented the affluence of America, the YMCA stairwell represents another, more malevolent, aspect of the country. It seemed to Feroza that once the door shut on her, she was "shut [...] out of New York" (88). Indeed:

> America assumed a ruthless, hollow, cylindrical shape without beginning or and without sunlight, an unfathomable concrete tube inhabited by her fear. She was sure something monstrous was crouched in the imprevious shadows that patrolled this alien domain[...].
>
> (90)

Sidhwa's descriptions of Feroza's futile efforts to rescue herself include many visual images of the ineffectiveness of her body.

She tries doorknocks, knocks tentatively, and finally resorts to pummeling the door with her hands. All of her puny efforts are useless against the monolithic structure that represents America. This metaphor foreshadows that Feroza's journey to inscribe herself, not in the margins of America, but in its heart, will be traumatic like that of Dimple who has been ostracised in the opulent world of America and let herself to be all alone. It is as Mallikarjun Patil in "Bharati Mukherjee's *Wife:* A Post Modernist Novel" says: "The novel, *Wife,* depicts an Indian Woman's exile to America and her spoiling of her own self-conscience" (122). It is to say as the motto of the novel, *Jasmine* reads: "There are no harmless, Compassionate ways to make oneself. We murder who we were so we can rebirth ourselves in the images of dreams" (*J* 25). Dimple kills her husband, Jasmine cuts her tongue, burns her past, sheds her cultural baggage, changes her clothes, alters her walk and her name, and instead of becoming in this violent process of nullification a nonentity, a husk void of self, she acquires the desired and desirable identity of Jase or Jane, the identity of a while banker's or professor's wife. In Jasmine, Mukherjee endorses what Adrienne Rich called the two powerful pressures in present day American culture: "one is the imperative to assimilate; the other, the idea that one can be socially twice-born" (141).

The simple village girl, Jyoti, renamed Jasmine in Bharati Mukherjee's *Jasmine,* reveals socio-psychological traumas relating to the life of an exile or expatriate. Based on mnemonic metaphor (gross from of memories as semantic and episodic), Jasmine works out the transoceanic, transmutationist, transnational and transcultural issues as alien native in America. In India, her marriage to Prakash Vijh absorbs her light and changes her into a modern girl, Jasmine. It is Prakash who effects her transformation for Jyoti to Jasmine. Usha Anand in "Jasmine: A Study" says that "America on the other hand comes across as the land of freedom and promise and self-fulfillment where there is a premium on individual effort and where man-woman relationships are based on mutual and equal partnership". Further she elaborates: "America, in the novel, is also synonymous with a liberated sexual morality [...].

The new woman in the novel Jasmine rejects the moribund Indian values and avidly accepts America and American values" (214).

Relocation within a First World community substantially alters the post-colonial subject's experience of cultural hybridity. By definition, the postcolonial migrant is a subject who interpellates and is interpellated by a broad range of discourses, not all of which co-exist unproblematically, but Western humanist expectations require that the subject consolidate his or her identity into the autonomous, unambiguous 'I' of the humanist tradition. Hybridity thus becomes shorthand for 'assimilation', a fixation of the self which requires that the migrants weed out the ambiguities born of her engagement with multiple discourses and recreates herself as 'one of us'. To put that another way, the post-colonial migrant is expected to take on western individuality and so becomes a 'readable' member of the First World community. Most migrants oscillate between their cultural base and the dominant First World culture, but Sidhwa's and Mukherjee's characters increasingly regard the movement back and from between their Indian friends, family and culture and their adopted America as a sign of failure.

Jasmine's early efforts to negotiate America are typical of the difficulties faced by the Third World migrants in the First World, but, in adopting American values on behalf of Third World migrants, Sidhwa's and Mukherjee's works systematically overlook the very forces which help to relegate the Asian migrant to second-class status. In short, Sidhwa's and Mukherjee's women go beyond the adaptation which would allow them to renegotiate America on their terms and become Western humanists - self-asserting individuals for whom the voluntary negotiation of multiple discourses is anathema.

The journey of Junglewalla, Zaitoon, Carol, Feroza, Tara, Jasmine, Hannah and so others comes to a spiritual change after material dialectics. Since their journey is meant for socio-psycho-historical dialectics of human thought, it reveals an analysis of dissociation and association of human sensibilities. They leave a message of human exploitation, post colonial reactions and post-structural viewpoints. The linguistic epithets used in the text *Jasmine* such as 'tornado', 'rubble maker' create the situational and contextual referents which make them a helpless being in society.

Further, Mukherjee's use of time travel to help Beigh unrave the mystery of the Emperor's Tear is a clever ruse. And also, in the final analysis, Beigh's searches around museums, East India company documents and colonial literature, her travels to India and auctions all over the world, are commendable efforts to reconstruct a daring woman's odyssey. She makes it seem plausible that seventeenth-century puritan women could have ventured into a different culture and met a Mughal ruler, 'contemporary of the Sun King, of Peter the Great and of Oliver Cromwell'. Beigh's painstaking piecing together of Hannah's life is like building a picture-puzzle across time. Solving the last clue through computer magic turns it into the stuff of high-tech occult. While it satisfies emotionally, one remains unconvinced.

Hannah's journey to India is fraught with images of adventure, action and passion. She returns to her native land, not as a reformed American, but as a rebel on the fringes of a society. Like Feroza and Jasmine, she finds final contentment and joy in the adapted land. It is the morality of the land that she carries along with her. Her voyage is mental and interior rather than physical. For Faredoon, Zaitoon, Carol, Lenny, Feroza, Tara, Dimple, Jasmine, Tara and Hannah there seems to be no way out. The distance they covered cannot be retraced. They are immigrants both in place and mind. Theirs is the foreignness of the spirit. They belong nowhere. Zaitoon's, Carol's, Feroza's, Tara's, Dimples Jasmine's and Hannah's journey out – i.e. away from the heroines natural country – is generally undertaken in the hope of progress towards a goal but there is no return to Feroza, Tara, Dimple, and Jasmine. Meera Manvi in "Reading Indian Womanhood: A Note on the Narrative Structure of *Wife*" says:

> [...] Mukherjee further underscores [...] her as a prototype of female psychosis – a victim of patriarchal oppression seeking ineffectually to integrate a last and divided self.

> Dimple's quest is to prevail as an authentic self against role prescriptions, her inability to survive psychologically, her failure to assert individuality, and the belated efforts to do so which result in the act of murder, are an indication that Mukherjee sees madness a political event'.
>
> (140)

Sidhwa's and Mukherjee's women who take journey into the wilderness of others may be classified as follows:

1. An un-nurtured, lonely woman who perceives strangers as enemies and employs primitive strategies to retain her power—Zaitoon and Dimple.
2. A woman of status and privilege is divested of her position and privileges when she enters a new world, experiencing profound devaluation and devastation as a result of making the journey which is, by its physical and psychic nature a descent into darkness—Ayah, the initial experiences of Feroza, Tara and even Carol in Pakistan.
3. the realization that in order for the heroine to regain her lost status and powers there must be a 'pay off'. The experience of her humiliation and vulnerability can never be denied or removed. It must be acknowledged and given an appropriate place in her experience in order for 'wholing' to take place. This acknowledgement allows her to overcome subsequent obstacles without losing completely that which she loves and values – her identity, the restoration of her self-worth and a more liberated personality which allows her to make difficult choices as appropriate for her.—Feroza, Jasmine, Tara and Hannah.

Likewise, Sidhwa and Mukherjee suggest the way for the exodus in their women's arduous journey; but it is realized that some prefer to return to their native culture to establish and realize their roots and identity being hallucinated by the alien opulence (Zaitoon, Tara), some prefer to stay on in an alien culture (Feroza, Jasmine), some perform the act of murder (Jasmine, Dimple), some cherish the memories of an alien culture (Carol, Hannah) some desire to return but cannot stay on (Tara), and some return and wish to belong to (Tara of *Tree*

Bride). Theirs is a case study-a socio-cultural and psychological maladjustment.

Works Cited

Anand, Usha. "*Jasmine*: A Study". *Women in Indo-Anglian Fiction: Tradition and Modernity*. Ed. Naresh Jain. New Delhi: Manohar Publishers and Distributors, 1988, 214-218.

Asnani, Shyam M. "Identity Crisis in *The Nowhere Man* and *Wife*". *Quest for Identity in Indian English Writing*. Ed. R.S.Pathak. New Delhi: Bahri Publications, 1992: 38-47.

Bhabha, Homi. *The Location of Culture*. London: Routledge, 1994.

Bhattacharya, Bhabani. *Music for Mohini*. Delhi: Orient Paper backs, 1984.

Bose, Brinda. "A Question of Identity: Where Gender, Race and America Meet in Bharati Mukherjee". *Bharati Mukherjee: Critical Perspectives*: 47-63.

Crane, Ralph. J. "'A Passion for History and for Truth Telling': The Early Novels of Bapsi Sidhwa" *The Novels of Bapsi Sidhwa:* 48-60.

Dayal Samir. "Creating, Preserving, Destroying: Violence in Bharati Mukherjee's *Jasmine*". *Bharati Mukherjee: Critical Perspectives:* 65-88.

Hancock, Geoff. "An Interview with Bharati Mukherjee". *Canadian Fiction Magazine.* 59 (1987), 30-44.

Horney, Karen. *The Neurotic Personality of Our Time*. New York: W.W.Norton, 1937.

Indira, S. "Exploration of Inner space: Anita Desai's *Cry, the Peacock* and Bharati Mukherjee's *Wife*." *The Fiction of Bharati Mukherjee: A Critical Symposium:* 59-65.

Jain, Jasbir. "The Male Presence in the "Purdah" Novel". *Margins of Erasure: Purdah in the Subcontinental Novel in English*. Eds. Jasbir Jain and Amina Amin. New Delhi: Sterling Publishers, 1995, 216-230.

Joshi, Arun. *The Foreigner*. Delhi: Hind Pocket Books, 1968.

Jussawalla, Feroza. "Navjote Ceremonies: The Location Bapsi Sidhwa's Culture." *The Novels of Bapsi Sidhwa*: 80-87.

Khan, Farukh. "Women. Identity and Dis-location in *The Bride*". *The Novels of Bapsi Sidhwa:* 140-151.

Manju Sharma, Maya. "The Inner World of Bharati Mukherjee: From Expatriate to Immigrant". *Bharati Mukherjee: Critical Perspectives:* 3-22.

Manvi, Meera, "Rereading Indian Womanhood: A Note on the Narrative Structure of *Wife*". *Osmania Journal of English Studies*. Vol.25 (1989): 140-150.

Mukherjee, Bharati. *The Tiger's Daughter*. 1971. New Delhi: Penguin, 1971.

_______. *Wife*. 1975. New Delhi; Sterling Publishers, 1976.

_______. *Jasmine*. 1989. New Delhi: Viking, 1990.

_______. *The Holder of the World*. 1993. New York: Fawcott Books, 1993.

_______. *Desirable Daughters*. 2002. New Delhi: Rekha Printers Pvt. Ltd., 2004.

_______. *The Tree Bride*. 2004. New York: Hyberian Books, 2004.

Paranjape, R. Makarand. "The Novels of Bapsi Sidhwa". *Commonwealth Fiction*: 80-103, also as "The Early Novels of Bapsi Sidhwa" in *The Novels of Bapsi Sidhwa:* 88-106.

Patil, Mallikarjun "Bharati Mukherjee's *Wife*: A Post Modernist Novel". *Indian English Fiction: Readings and Reflections*. Eds. Gajendra Kumar and Uday Shankar O'sha. New Delhi: Sarup & Sons, 2003, 116-123.

Patricia Gabriel, Sharmani. "'Routes of Identity': In Conversation with Bharati Mukherjee". *Ariel*. Vol. 34. No.4 (October, 2003), 125-138.

Pennebakar, Mattie Katherine. "The Will of Men: Victimization of Women During India's Partition". *Agora*. No.1. Issue 1 (Summer, 2003) <http://www.tamu. edu/chr/agora/summeroo/pennebaker.pdf>

Rajeshwar, M. "Sado-Masochism as a Literary Device in Bharati Mukherjee's *Wife*". *Indian Women Novelists.* Set III: Vol.3: 127-139 also in *The Fiction of Bharati Mukherjee: A Critical Symposium:* 90-99 and also in *Indian Women Novelists and Psychoanalysis: A Study of the Neurotic Characters:* 34-44.

Rani, Nirupa. K. "Gender and Imagination in Bapsi Sidhwa's Fiction". *The Novels of Bapsi Sidhwa:* 118-124.

Shakespeare, William. *Sonnets*. New Delhi: Mac million, 1983.

Sidhwa, Bapsi.. *The Pakistani Bride*. 1983. New Delhi: Penguin, 1989.

_______. *Ice-Candy-Man*. 1988. New Delhi: Penguin, 1989.

_______. *An American Brat*. 1994. New Delhi: Penguin, 1994.

Swain. S.P. "Dimple in Bharati Mukherjee's *Wife*: A Study of the Lacerated Self". *Indian Women Novelists.* Set III. Vol. 3, 117-126, also as "Dimple in *Wife*: A Study of the Lacerated Self " in *The Fiction of Bharati Mukherjee: A Critical Symposium:* 82-89.

Viswanath, Gita. "Modes of Resistance in the South – Asian Novel: A Study of the Fiction by Bapsi Sidhwa, Rohinton Mistry and Yasmine Gooneratne". *The Fiction of Rohinton Mistry: Critical Studies*. Ed. Jaydipsingh Dodiya, New Delhi: Prestige Books, 1988, 38-43.

Wandrekar, Kalpana. *The Ailing Aliens:* (A Study of 'the Immigrant Psyche' in Six Indian English Novels) Gulbarga: JIWE Publications, 1996, 63-77.

4

Cultural Dislocation and Quest for Identity

> The dialectic between change and continuity is a painful but deeply instructive one in personal life as in the life of a people. To 'see the light' too often has meant rejecting the 'treasure found in darkness'.
>
> (Adrienne Rich)

Literature is a subsystem of a given culture. It offers an illustration or exemplification of some general pattern or syndrome. Minority discourse is characterized by an urge to adapt and assimilate. It is also characterized by a culture of protest and resistance. Culture is not merely an organizational principle holding together the members of a community. It is also a means of establishing its separateness from and resistance to other communities.

In the twentieth and twenty-first centuries, cross-cultural confrontation has received a pronounced impetus due to migration, expatriation and immigration. The word 'culture' is very difficult to define as several sociologists, anthropologists, historians and men of letters have tried to define the term from time to time. Eliot in *Notes Towards the Definition of Culture* says: "culture may even be described simply as that which makes life worth living" (27). Further, he categorizes culture into two:

> Now there are of course higher cultures and lower cultures, and the higher cultures in general are distinguished by differentiation of function, so that you can speak of the less cultured and the more cultured srata of society, and finally

> you can speak of individuals as being exceptionally cultured.
>
> (*Notes* 120)

Eliot uses the term 'culture' in three senses. He says: "The term culture has different associations according to whether we have in mind the development of an individual, of a group or class, or of a whole society" (*Notes* 21). Thus, he maintains that there are three ways of regarding culture: as the culture of the individual, as the culture of a group or class, or as the culture of a whole society. Further, he asserts:

> The culture of the individual is dependent upon the culture of a group or class, and that the culture of a group or class is dependent upon the culture of the whole society to which that group or class belongs. Therefore, it is the culture of the society that is fundamental.
>
> (*Notes* 21)

Language is more important in the development of culture. The cultural standard depends upon the use of language. Environment is also important for the development of culture. It provides the base for cultural formation and its growth.

Misunderstanding, confusion and incomprehension are inevitable in any cross-cultural endeavour. In fact, Sidhwa and Mukherjee through their novels suggest the difficulties of passage in and out of Pakistan and India and point at bridges that cannot be built between cultures. Passage to and out of Pakistan and India will cause pain and bewilderment. Sidhwa as a Pakistani focuses her critical lens on the many cultural conflicts and divisions that she sees as part of life in Pakistan. Especially, the cultural conflicts must be continually faced by women in Pakistan. Sidhwa and Mukherjee juxtaposes different cultures, be it of American culture and Pakistani culture in Sidhwa's case and American culture and Indian culture in Mukherjee's case, but they fix their characters in a flux, not able to cope up either with their native culture or an alien culture. It results in cross-cultural confrontation due to culture shock.

Sidhwa and Mukherjee uniformly portray that their women and men characters are caught in the massive web of cultural-clash/shock. In *Bride,* Sidhwa introduces the young American woman, Carol, who is married to a modern, Western-educated Pakistani husband. Her presence in the novel emphasizes the cross-cultural differences between West and East and also shows the cross-gender differences that exist within Pakistani society. Sidhwa also makes a contrastive picture of the brutal ways of cultural behaviour of Qasim's people with the gentle life in Lahore where Zaitoon lives. Sidhwa sees the exploration of the culture divisions within independent Pakistan. In Mukherjee's *Daughter* when the 23-year-old Tara visits India, the alien Western culture which has almost become a second self to her is constantly in clash with the culture of her native soil. The clash is deeply felt in the psyche of Tara while she is in India. Even in India She finds it difficult to adjust with her friends and relatives in India. She feels loneliness in her own native land. She expected that her return to India would remove her displeasure of staying abroad. But to her dismay India too becomes too remote and alien

> For years she had dreamed of this return to India. She had believed that all hesitations, all shadowy fears of the time abroad would be erased quite magically if she could just return home to Calcutta. But so far the return had brought only wounds. First the corrosive hours on Marine Drive, then the deformed beggars in the railway station, and now the inexorable train ride steadily undid what strength she had held in reserve. She was an embittered woman, she now though, old and cynical at twenty-two and quick to take offense.
>
> (*TD* 25)

On her visit to Bombay, Tara feels that Bombay has become dirty but it is not Bombay but her outlook that has been changed by her stay in America. Her sickness at the present situation makes her think about her husband, David. Ananda Prabha Barat in "Bharati Mukherjee and the Immigrant Psyche: *The Tiger's Daughter*" says: "The thought of her husband symbolically suggests the second self developed in her. It seems that the alien land has become more of a home to her"

(55). Equally in *Wife,* for Dimple the loss of old culture is neither an exciting nor an exhilarating experience. She is disillusioned on all planes—physical, mental, and emotional. Freedom from caste, gender and family leaves her utterly lonely and desolate. Jaiwanti Dimri in "From Marriage to Murder: A Comparative Study of *Wife* and *Jasmine*" suggests: "Her killing of her husband is partly an act of desperation and partly an outcome of her guilty conscience. Judging herself by the Indian standards of marriage and womanhood, she is uneasy about her extra-marital relationship with Milt Glasser. Unable to cope with the crisis, she kills her husband" (75). Amit's inattentiveness blocks the outlay. Torn by her psychic and emotional tensions, she takes the drastic step of murdering her husband.

Shyam M. Asnani in "Identity Crisis in *Nowhere Man* and *Wife*" ascribes Dimple's mental state to the dilemma of cultures: "Dimple is entrapped in a dilemma of tensions between American culture and society and the traditional constraints surrounding an Indian wife, between a feminist desire to be assertive and independent and the Indian need to be submissive and self effacing" (42). At times, when loneliness becomes unbearable, Dimple contemplates ways of committing suicide. Linda Sandler in "Violence as a Device for Problem Solving" says: "She is uprooted from her family and her familiar world and projected into a social vacuum where the media becomes her surrogate community, her global village. New York intensifies her frustrations and unhooks her further from reality" (75).

Dimple slides into madness precipitated precisely at the point when she has the opportunity to be all by herself and particularly when she is free of the constraints imposed on an Indian wife by the constant presence of other members of her community. Linda Sandler in her interview with Mukherjee suggests that Dimple goes crazy in part because of her own instability but mostly because she has moved into a social vacuum. In the Greenwich village flat, where she has to spend almost all her time watching television because she is too terrified of the violent world outside, her frustrations intensify, and she gets further unhinged from reality. As Sandler observes, *Wife* suggests that Dimple has moved into "a vacuum where once was society and that violence becomes increasingly ordinary where there is no anchoring community" (76).

Gita Rajan notes that *Wife* centres "in the debilitating, corrosive influence of an alien culture on a fragile self " and that Dimple's self is ultimately "shattered, detonated by a raw and alien reality" (236-237).

In *Wife* towards the end of the novel Dimple almost freezes herself to death and Amit realizes for a moment that his wife is desperately unhappy and he can only diagnose her condition as the culture shock that all Indian wives in America go through. It is a condition to be distinguished from "one of those famous breakdowns that American wives were fond of having" (*W* 180).

Another obstacle in Dimple's path to self-realization is the expatriate Indian community in which she has to spend her time. *Wife* may be taken as a devastating critique of immigrant culture. Inevitably, Dimple and her expatriate friends suffer from alienation in a culture whose codes they are not able to decipher. Even before her coming to America, she had heard friends talk of America as a place where you could have fun but where you would have to be a foreigner all your life. At a farewell party given for her in Calcutta by Pixie, she had been told by a woman who seemed to know all about expatriation and aloofness in America: "You may think of it as immigration [...] but what you are a resident alien" (*W* 46).

Even in New York, Dimple hears Meena confess how inadequate she feels outside her community because she has such hard time understanding American humor or the English language. Dimple discovers in her first shopping expedition, like that of Feroza's in *Brat,* that it is difficult to do even the smallest chores in an alien land and culture where she cannot be understood. She finds herself "caught in the crossfire of an American communalism she couldn't understand" (*W* 60). It leads to frustration and a feeling of void. It makes her wonder how she could keep on living in a country "where every other woman was a stranger, where she felt different, ignorant, exposed to ridicule in the elevator" (*W* 112). However, Dimple keeps trying in her own confused and uncertain manner to put out feelers to see if she could immerse herself in this strange but exciting world. She displays desires that indicate that she would like to break free from some of the habits of thought she had imbibed as a Bengali wife. She dreams of working and of going to night school, of throwing her own parties for friends, and of having her own flat where she could be herself.

In fact, Dimple and Jasmine are faced with the problem of the loss of culture and both of them endeavour to assume a new identity. In their struggle to assume a new identity, they are driven to violence. Jasmine starts her life in America with a murder and Dimple rounds up her stay there with a murder of her husband, Amit Basu. Like Dimple's killing of Amit, Jane's killing of Half-Face is a kind of self-assertion. "Her decision to kill herself first, is a decision of a woman who loves for her deceased husband but the woman who kills Half-Face is prompted by her will to live to continue her life" (Nagendra Kumar 110). However, "In killing Half-Face" writes Samir Dayal "she experiences an epidemic violence that is also a life-affirming transformation" (11).

Sidhwa in *Bride* by presenting Carol in Pakistan and Mukherjee in *Holder* by presenting Hannah explore the complexities of cultural confrontation and the politics of otherness. They present the difference between the old world and the new world represented by America, Pakistan and India. By presenting a clash of value systems, a confrontation between an austere, stark society and culture in which nothing is in important than the celebration of beauty they present the fluid identity of their women.

Carol's and Hannah's arrival in Pakistan and India is set against a period of tumultuous political and economic activity. Hannah's primary concern in this new world is "to peel the superficiality and social grace and dwell beneath it in a quest for a meaningful life. In fact, as soon as she steps on the shores of the Coromandel Coast, she feels an instinctive sense of belonging and decides that she did not 'aspire to return to England upon the completion of Gabriel's tour" (104). She is aware of the fact that she belongs to India, on entering the new world, the world of Hindus. She discovers in herself an urge to be able to name and memorize the new" (*H* 225). She wants to embrace this new world only to sacrifice herself at the altar of true love: "She wanted the Raja and nothing else she would sacrifice anything for his touch and the love they made. What she felt for the Raja was of a different order [....] (*H* 229). Later, Jadav Singh's, the Raja's, the Raja of Devgad's, death and Hannah's encounter with Aurangzeb mature her experience in terms of her journey to the world of the mysterious East.

In *Bride* and *Jasmine* Zaitoon and Jane are expected to be silent women in their alliance / marriage to Sakhi and Bud Ripplemeyer respectively. They are, however, a complex blend of 'silent women', the speaking persons and teller of tales of past glory. Both of them, like silent women in their beginning of marital life accept the almost preplanned and tailor made itinerary of a certain way of life with their men – Zaitoon with Sakhi and Jane with Bud Ripplemeyer. But their suffocating world is heightened by their inability to share with them their memories or reflections of the past, which are as much as part of their identity as the present. Sakhi does not want to share anything with Zaitoon similar to that of Bud who prefers not to discuss Jasmine's painful past. Jane says "Taylor didn't want to change me. He didn't want to scour and sanitize the foreignness. My being different from Wylie or Kate didn't scare me" (*J* 165).

Sidhwa's *Bride* and Mukherjee's *Holder* are to be interpreted as quest narratives written to point how lives have been intertwined and can be intertwined across space and time. The theme of the subtle relatedness of lives is a development of the theme of immigration. It reminds one of the interconnections among cultures. Sidhwa and Mukherjee explore other ramifications of cultural confrontation in these novels. There is a tale about dislocation and transformation arising when two cultures come into contact with each other. Arshia Sattar in a review of the *Holder* says that this novel "has a wide canvas that sweeps across continents and centuries, cultures and religions. Immigration, exile, alienation, and foreign lands [....] (6). In *Holder*, there is an unlikely and intriguing meeting of two worlds, the Puritan Seventeenth and early Eighteenth century American world and the Mughal world of Indian life, which is responsible for the quest for identity and transformation and translation of protagonist's personality under the stress of the circumstances like that of meeting of two different worlds – America and Pakistan – in the characters of Carol and Farukh in *Bride*.

Cultural alienation is a world phenomenon today. The tremendous difference between two ways of life leads a person to a feeling of depression and frustration. This could be called culture shock. When an individual leaves his / her own culture and enters another, his / her values come into conflict with the new ones he / she finds.

Mukherjee's *Daughter* is a manifestation of cultural conflict in which a Bengali Brahmin girl goes to America for higher studies, marries an American and returns to India only to find herself confused, lost, totally strange and an alien in a native land, India. The young girl is Tara, the great granddaughter of Harilal Banerjee and the daughter of Bengal Tiger, the owner of famous Banerjee & Thomas (Tobacco) Co. Ltd. Tara is packed off by her father at an early age of 15, whereas Feroza of Sidhwa's *Brat* is packed off at the age of 14, to America for higher studies. Her initial reactions to American life are one of fear and anger:

> For Tara Vassar had almost been an almost unsalvageable mistake. If she had not been a Banerjee, a Bengali Brahmin, the great grand daughter of Hari Lal Banerjee, or perhaps, if she had not been trained by the good nuns at St. Blaise's to remain composed and ladylike in all emergencies, she would have rushed home to India at the end of her first track.
>
> (*TD* 10)

In America, she becomes homesick. She senses discrimination. Her roommate refuses to share her bottle of mango chutney.

In *Daughter* Tara's efforts to adapt to American society are measured by her rejection and revulsion of Indian modes of life. F.A. Inamdar in "Immigrant Lives: Protagonists in *The Tiger's Daughter* and *Wife*" makes a comment that "For Tara, Calcutta appears to be Conrad's *Heart of Darkness* with riots in the city, buses burning and workers surrounding the warehouses" (40). Seven years ago, Tara admired "the houses on Marine Drive"

(*T* 18) but her stay at Vassar has changed her outlook on Indian life. The very houses she admired then, "now their shabbiness appalled her" (*T* 18). It is again America's influence on her that makes Bombay's railway station "more like a hospital" (*T* 19). Tara's rootless self makes the scenery outside "merely alien and hostile" (*T* 25).

There is a strange fusion of the Americanness and Indianness in the psyche of Tara. They are confrontation with each other. Sometimes, she makes futile effort to establish her American self. But it clashes with her early life in Calcutta on her return from America. She can neither take refuge in India nor in her newly discovered life in America. The outcome of this confrontation is her split psyche. She becomes depressed and disgusted with the deteriorating situation of India. In fact, in the end of the novel, her new personality finds herself difficult to adjust with the situation. Finally, she wishes to go back to the USA and to her husband.

The cultural shock to Tara in *Daughter* is too big for her to bear. She has returned from America with high hopes of a fond reunion with parents, relations and friends. But at the end of the novel, she leaves for America in a hurry, suddenly informing her helpless parents about her decision to return to David and the United States. Her resolve is preceded by a gradual disillusionment with the Calcutta of her early youth. There are four important episodes that lead to the climax of her departure. The first of these is her visit to the burning ghats with an eccentric old man, Oyonto Roy Chowdhury, a tea estate owner, whom she meets at the Catelli. He decides to save her from the chaos surrounding the traditional way of life of his class in Calcutta, but in the process unwittingly administers the first serious shock to her sensibility.

The second episode is of the picnic organized by Tiger Banerjee friends at his factory premises for the entertainment of his daughter and her friends. A small snake is discovered in the swimming pool, where they frolic for some time before lunch is served. Tara is so horrified that she reacts by screaming loudly, which surprises even her parents. The third of her shocking experience is at the summer resort of Darjeeling, where a group of middle-class Indian tourists behave rudely towards her when she goes out riding with her friend Pronob and English girl they meet at their hotel. The last straw is her seduction by Tuntunwala at the Nayapur Guest House, where she goes, at the suggestion of her father, to calm her nerves after the Darjeeling experience. That is when Tara finally decides to return to America. Her disillusionment with an India in upheaval is complete, and she concludes that it would not be possible for her—though born, bred and educated in Calcutta—to adjust to the changed conditions after her exposure to life in the West. Like her author, she too is a middle-woman caught in a cross-cultural turmoil.

Tara realizes that America has transformed her completely. "Tara's westernization has opened her eyes to the gulf between two worlds that still makes India the despair of those who govern it" ("Oh Calcutta!..." 736). In India, she sees disease, despair, riot, poverty, the children eating yoghurt off the side walk. Now, she has started looking at the ugly aspects of India. Always in her mind, there is an ongoing conflict between her old sense of perception and outlook on Calcutta and her changed outlook. Jasbir Jain in "Foreignness of Spirit: The World of Bharati Mukherjee's Novels" says:

> Tara's consciousness of the present is rooted in her life in the States and when she looks at India anew it is not through her childhood associations or her past memories but through the eyes of her foreign husband David. Her reactions are those of a tourist, a foreigner.
>
> (13)

In fact, Tara starts a life of duality and conflict since her childhood. After marriage, she undergoes a traumatic dilemma enjoined upon her to belong to an entirely new set up. This in itself is a migration—a migration from one's own former self to an imposed one. And this conflict gets multiplied with migration to another country. Tara's situation is to be looked at from this angle. Brinda Bose in "A Question of Identity: Where Gender, Race and America Meet in Bharati Mukherjee" says:

> Duality and conflict are not merely a feature of immigrant life in America; Mukherjee's women are brought up in a culture that presents them with such ambiguities from childhood. The breaking of identities and the discarding of languages actually begin early, their lives being shaped by the confluence of rich cultural and religious traditions, on the one hand, and the new learning is imposed by British colonialism in India, on the other.
>
> These different influences involve them in tortured processes of self-recognition and self-assimilation right from the start; the confusion is doubled upon coming to America.
>
> (50)

Roshni Rustomji-Kerns describes her failure to her constant nervousness regarding her role as the Bengali wife of an American: "Tara's petulance and constant nervousness regarding her role as the Bengali wife of an American, visiting her family in Calcutta; overshadows her well-intentioned efforts to understand her world of diverse cultures" (657). In fact, Tara's confusion results from her own 'unstable self'. In *Wife* the cultural and social gulf dividing the two worlds – India and America – makes her feel frustrated and lonely due to dull existence in the apartment. She used to contemplate on the methods of suicide. She becomes depressed and neurotic. She feels neglected by her husband like that of Carol by Farukh in *Bride*. Dimple seduces Milt Glasser as Carol does in *Bride*. Carol seduces Major Mushtaq knowing that he will not marry her. It becomes a traumatic experience for Carol and Dimple, who feel transformed after their act of betrayal to Farukh and Amit. It gives them strength to reject Pakistan and India. Jasbir Jain in "Foreignness of Spirit: The World of Bharati Mukherjee's Novels" states that it is very difficult to treat the novel *Wife* related to a theme called culture-shock or cultural confrontation. He says:

> It is difficult to treat the novel as a study of cultural shock for even while in Calcutta. Dimple is an escapist and lost in her private world of fantasy; it is difficult to approach it as a statement about the feminine need for freedom [....]. Dimple's dreams are very vaguely related to independence or self-realisation but more directly related to a sexual

> awareness, to the sexual power a woman can exercise and how she can successfully step out of the limits put down by the Sita legend. *Wife* is also not merely a study of the East-West encounter and its aftermath. Dimple's silent criticism of her situation or her circumstances is primarily concerned with appearances and with affluence: at no juncture does she posit a world which is more integrated or more free than the one in which she is placed. The reasons or causes for Dimple's neurotic behaviour are not sufficiently elaborated [...] Even the cultural conflict does not adequately account for Dimple's behaviour.
>
> (17)

It is quite true that her isolation is not rooted in loneliness or in cultural differences but in her estrangement from her own past and her own inner being. But when a person visits an unknown land, he / she is an outsider in a no-man's land. There he/she has to struggle a lot for his / her survival. He / she recreates himself/herself into a new personality and forms emotional ties with the place he / she lives in. The discovery of a new self makes him / her forget his/her own native culture. On his return to his/her native lands he / she finds himself/ herself alien in his/her native land by having lost his / her native roots. His / Her mind is again torn apart between the cultural clashes of two environments. He / She is forced to fight with his / her split personality. Hence, it may be taken that Dimple's case is related to this alienness in a new culture with her split personality which is the result of cultural void/divide.

An important concern of the post colonial literature is related to place and displacement. The concern with identifying a relationship between self and place leads to a crisis of identity. The self may be eroded either because of dislocation or because of cultural denigration. Ashcroft in *The Empire Writes Back* says: "Beyond their historical and cultural differences, place, displacement and a pervasive concern with the myths of identity and authenticity are a feature common to all Post-Colonial literatures in English" (9).

The theme of exile is frequently concerned with place and displacement and establishing of new relationships. Ashcroft maintains: "the theme of exile [...] is one manifestation of the ubiquitous concern with place and displacement [...] as well as with the complex material circumstances implicit in the transportation of language from its place of origin and its imposed and imposing relationship on and with the new environment" (29).

Sidhwa and Mukherjee suffered a literal geographical displacement and are confronted with social and cultural alienation. Mukherjee's work makes metaphorical reference to 'uprooting' and 'unhousement' of the immigrants in their attempts to construct a future by dealing with the notion of place and displacement in her writings.

In Sidhwa's and Mukherjee's novels not only is expatriation a major theme but it becomes a metaphor for deeper levels of alienation like existential alienation and self-estrangement which results in exile. Fakrul Alam in *Bharati Mukherjee* says: "*The Tiger's Daughter* is designed to capture the predicament of someone returning to her homeland after a period of self-imposed exile: to such a person, home will never be home again, and life in exile, bitter draught though it often is, will be preferable to what home has become" (22).

Jasmine is an exile in flight from the old-world of India and old cultural values. Her sense and sensibilities are actively engaged with the world outside her. Faced with rejection as a new comer Jasmine, clings to her ethnic identity as Viney Kirpal in *The Third World Novel of Expatriation: A Study of Émigré Fiction by Indian, West African and Caribbean Writers* says: "Revival of ethnicity makes bearable to some extent the marginal shadowy existence of these migrants in the new land" (165).

The dictionary meaning of the word 'to identify' is to 'become identical', which means becoming the same as or essentially alike. The word 'identity' also implies certain homogeneity and coalescence; in other words assimilation. Identification can be on many levels; psychological, sociological, linguistic, cultural and emotional. The extent to which identification has been achieved on all these fronts will qualify how complete one's identification has been to the new surroundings. The quest for identity by marginal groups in developing multi-racial societies emerges as one of the major concerns in literature.

In Sidhwa and Mukherjee, one can find a common, shared focus on ethnic groups struggling for identity. Both writers show how the ethnic groups, the Bengali Brahmin and the Parsees, strive to retain their identity by upholding traditional values and customs as well as seeking assimilation in a multi-racial, modern, and changing society. Sidhwa and Mukherjee perceptively reveal the process of change and the contradictions that stem in the period of flux.

Diasporic experience is a double identification that constitutes hybrid forms of identity. Such forms of identity differ from the essentialised notion of national and ethnic identity. It also explores multiple belongings that enable people to inhabit more than one space at the same time. Tara is a fictional rendering of such cultural hybridity. Tara says, "I am both" (*DD*: 6). Being simultaneously an Indian and an American she has gained the third space of enunciation.

Sidhwa's identity-crisis and evocation of Parsiness is further complicated by yet another diaspora, the one engendered by the Partition. So in *Crow Eaters* and *Candy-Man*, her Parsi protagonists have not only to contend with the imminent departure of the colonial rulers but also with the question of which one of the two new nations was to receive their allegiance. Being neither Hindu nor Muslim, their choice of either India or Pakistan was not an automatic one, they could in theory actually make a choice. In reality, the actual geographic location at the time of the Partition usually dictated the option exercised by the Parsees. However, this was not an easy choice and the Parsees had to exercise extreme tact and diplomacy in order to convince their new rulers of their neutralityvis a vis the Hindu-Muslim conflict and their loyalty to the selected nation. This was a difficult task but the Parsees had to also contend with the fact that either choice would lead to divided families, loss of Hindu/Muslim/Sikh friends colleagues and business partners, which in turn would result in psychological trauma and yet another diaspora. *Crow Eaters* presents a community which has survived migration, re-settled peacefully and prospered without losing their cultural identity

The escapist behaviour of Yazdi, the second son of Faredoon Junglewalla, exemplifies another aspect of identity crisis on the verge of paranoia among the Parsees. Yazdi, as a sensible boy, is aggrieved at the conspicuous commercialism and sycophancy of the Parsees like that of Noah Adler in Richler's *Son of a Smaller Hero*. Like Adlers refused to marry outside their Jewish ghetto, Yazdi is not allowed to marry a childhood sweet heart, the Anglo-Indian Rosy Watson. It makes Yazdi revolts against the existing system in his family. Yazdi, as a note of protest, takes charity to the extreme. He has given his shoes to an orphan in his class. Later, when he is transferred to a boarding school, he becomes a drop-out, and a modern-day hippy. Finally, Yazdi makes a total break from his family by using his money to feed dying children and by becoming a follower of Mazdak, the first communist.

In Canada, Mukherjee claims to have experienced an anti-Indian attitude. Canada's hostility to Indians and the non-recognition of her writings in Canada are the twin recurring themes in her novels. She experienced herself as a psychological expatriate in Canada and clung to her ethnic identity. In fact, Mukherjee had to come to terms with her own identity in an alien land, caught as she was between two conflicting cultures. She had to contend with racial discrimination during the years she spent in Canada, precisely between 1972 and 1980. She managed to overcome both the crises and this brought in her a sense of elation and confidence. So, Mukherjee's novels deal with the theme of identity and the dichotomy in her attitude to her homeland and also with the paradoxes and contradictions in the immigrant psyche. Mukherjee's *Daughter* and *Wife* reflect a world that refuses to hold together both at the individual and cultural levels. They are novels of and about isolation. The protagonists Tara and Dimple are preoccupied in exploring the nature of their own identities. They remain voiceless. Their voiceless emotions arise out of a questioning of cultural issues.

While trying to establish an identity of her own in America, Dimple miserably fails to do. As she has been caught between two different cultures and not able to establish her identity, Amit appears to Dimple a projection of her neurotic self which she wants to annihilate and hence her committing the act of murder. She murders Amit in a fit of neurotic frenzy. She feels herself possessed by demonic power. The murdering of Amit is an assertion of her American identity. P.S. Swain in "Dimple in *Wife:* A Study of Lacerated Self" says:

> The novel traces the psychic break-down of an Indian wife in America and the concomitant deep culture-shock leading to neurosis. Free and rebelling throughout, Dimple has the inhibitions. Her predicament transcends the plight of the alienated self enmeshed in the vortex of the limbo of culture – shock. A lacerated and anguished spirit Dimple, like Tara, is the nowhere woman. She is neither of India nor of America but a stunned wanderer between these two worlds, yet to attain a distinct identity. Neither does she belong to the T.V. world nor to the world of reality but keeps on shuttling between the two. She is yet to get out of her schizophrenic self. A waylaid traveler she is yet to reach her destination and carve out a niche for herself. Her quest is a quest for a voice, a quest for identity.
>
> (88-89)

Like Dimple's, the American experience shocked Jane and disgusted her many a time. In the process of her transformation Jane was seized by a longing to belong. She closely identifies herself with Bud's adopted son 'Du' a Vietnamese, because he was an immigrant like herself. Pushpa N. Parekh in "Telling Her Tale: Narrative Voice and Gender Roles in Bharati Mukherjee's *Jasmine*" says:

> As the Jasmine—Jane protagonist learns to cast herself in different roles, she finds her initial identity in America immuned in the volitional silence and invisibility of a law breaker in two senses. She is an illegal alien who has defied the immigration laws and a murderer who defies the ruthless violence of a male-powered capitalist society. An adept at defiance as a model of survival from her childhood days, Jasmine—Jane characterizes her voice with the tone of defiance. This defiance born of inner monologues and reflections, and of the sanity and capacity of the human will to survive, is distinct. It is at times a brash, willful defiance, at others quietly enduring.
>
> (117-118)

Jasmine discovers her identity as difference, as a multiply split subjectivity: Jyoti/Jasmine/Kali/Jase/Jane. She does not remain Jyoti (light) but recognizes her multiplicity only after the violence – the rape. After the violence, she forsakes her identity and recognizes within her Jasmine, the caregiver and also Jase, the fireless adventurer. She becomes a nomad and a hybrid and shuttles between different identities including the veritable Kali, the Killer of Half-Face. It is through her internalized mode of India that Jasmine works out the theory of karma and kal (Time). For the theory of Karma, she brings forth the unconscious mode of her thinking. She says, "My grandmother may have named me Jyoti, light, but in surviving I was already Jane, a fighter and adapter" (*J* 40). As a mystery, the fighter Jane becomes submissive before the powerful yet unseen hands of Time. She swings without any certainty between real and human time which makes her disillusioned between the reality and maya (illusion) of time. As a fighter and adapter, and even after so many transformation of herself into different names, she still enquires, "who I am" (*J* 197). She quotes the words of Karim who says about her: "I am tornado [...] How many more shapes are in me, how many more selves, how many more husbands" (*J* 215). Here she expresses the inner pangs of an exile and an expatriate who lives in America.

Tara in *Daughters,* belongs to both tradition and modernity. Her identity is highly assimilative. She can adapt and accommodate herself both to her traditional Indian way of life and to her newly adopted American ethos. But she does not stick to the value systems of either of these ways of life. She moves on both the planes-the Indian and the American. She vacillates between two lives: "may be I really was between two lives [...]" (*TD* 251). Yet to strike roots, yet to belong to any of these lives, she exemplifies the existential dilemma, of diaspora and the problem of an immigrant who has a fluid identity associated with mobility and plurality rather than stasis and singularity. She wants to redefine herself and to reconstruct her feminine self in time with her novel experience in an alien soil. She wants to have a new identity but she fails. Inspite of her liberated and emergent attitudes, her desire to construct hybridity, her acceptance of her son's gay sexuality and live in-relationship, she fails to transcend the tradition-bound life of an Indian woman. Hence, Mukherjee is quite right in calling Tara a cosmopolitan character without a focus. Rashmi Gaur aptly observes:

> Tara represents the dilemma of an average migrant. The demands of tradition and their hold on one's psyche are never ultimately rejected [...] She tries to create a personal space for herself through compromise. Rejection of her husband and associated security is a bold step for an Indian girl of Tara's background. Despite an obvious diffidence, she questions, at least for sometime, traditional notions and shuns the cliche'd answers provided by conventions. She wants to redefine herself and create fresh gender relations.
>
> (*Indian Journal of English Studies*: 209)

Mukherjee is fascinated by people with a fluid identity, people who are adventurous, who are constantly on the go, people who live a life in transit, who have to forgo their former identities in order to accommodate and assimilate themselves in another country in order to acquire the identity of the other. Though Tara is all-embracing, she is essentially Bengali upper class Brahmin elite. She says, "even as proud members of the majority community, we were a blessed, elite minority and we knew it" (*DD*: 29). Sometimes the readers suspect whether Tara is a status-conscious, caste-conscious snob. There are many instances in the novel in which she deliberately flaunts her Brahmin heritage. "We are Bengali Brahmins from Calcutta and nothing can touch us" (*DD*: 44) are Tara's resonating words in praise of her Brahmin lineage. But these facets of her personality do not hinder her strategies of survival in the adopted land. For six long years, she flouts the Indian tradition of arranged marriage and lives with a Hungarian refugee. The reconciliation of the broken family also symbolises the reconciliation of cultures. The bombing of her house symbolises the end of a 'single' existence. Cultures need not conflict with one another or be mutually exclusive. Materialism of the West can be complemented with the spiritualism of the East, subjugation of the East can be offset by the liberation of the west. In the end, Bish learns that running after money can never lead to fulfillment. Tara learns the meaninglessness of her attempts at sexual liberation. Rabi, the second-generation immigrant learns that his parents' cultural legacy is a treasure-trove of spiritualism and wisdom.

Sidhwa's and Mukherjee's women find their ethnic and American identities. They have to find their identities with self, with tradition, and with the wonders and horrors of a new culture with growing aspirations, hopes and desires. However, her growing concern is that these new born identities should not suffer from the horror and terror of marginalization. Mukherjee's women evolve from the homesick: Junglewallas long to return to India, Zaitoon decides to escape to Lahore, Carol decides to go back to America, Tara returns home to find herself alienated and Dimple's and Jasmine's confusion turns violence to kill Amit, and Half-Face. It is due to a fluid identity which torments them to alternate between the desire for remembering and the need for forgetting with its accompanying pain. Tara's memory has played tricks on her during her prolonged expatriate experience in America. Even on returning to India she feels herself an outsider and an alien to the native soil. Mukherjee's works *Darkness, Jasmine,* and *Holder* show her preoccupation with her sense of place and location both geographically and ideologically. Nalini Iyer in "American / Indian: Metaphors of the Self in Bharati Mukherjee's *The Holder of the World*" admits:

> As geographic space, location becomes a metaphor for self; self-fashioning for the immigrant character in her work. As ideological space, location in Mukherjee's narrative is the authors' interrogation of such self-fashioning by questioning gender, race, and ethnicity as they render, identity as a fluid rather than a fixed entity. In addition, Mukherjee also questions the location of a writer within a specific literary canon and ideology of such canon formations.
>
> (30)

Both Sidhwa and Mukherjee talk about the changing social milieu and identity crisis in Parsee and Bengali community in British India. Their characters like Junglewalla and Banerjee's

(Tara, Padma, and Parvati) do not consider westernization or Americanization as a conscious abandonment of their own group identity – to Sidhwa Parsee and to Mukherjee Bengali Brahmin identity. Sidhwa in *Crow Eaters* writes:

> They entertained continuously at small, intimate, 'mixed' parties where married couples lashed and danced decorously with other married couples. 'Mixed' parties were as revolutionary a departure from Freddy's all-male get-togethers at the Hira Mandi, and Putli's rigid female sessions, as in a discotheque from a Victoriam family dinner. The parties were fashionably cosmopolitan, including the various religious sects of India: Hindus, Muslims, Sikhs and Christians, the Europeans, and the Anglo-Indians.
>
> (*CE* 245)

S.P. Swain in "Problems of Identity: A Study of Bharati Mukherjee's *Desirable Daughters*" admits: "In *Desirable Daughters,* Bharati Mukherjee has delineated the individual self quagmired in the Kaleidoscopic spatio-temporal reality of the American as well as the Indian society" (127).

The self is the distinct and characteristic individuality of a person. The human self is a self-organizing, interactive system of thoughts, feelings and motives that characterizes an individual. The self or self-concept is defined as organized, consistent, conceptual gestalt composed of perceptions of the characteristics of the 'I' and 'me' to others and to various aspects of the life, together with the values attached to these perceptions. Self, the result of man's awareness of himself as a separate entity in the social environment, enables him to regard himself and emotionally experience his own integrity and identity in relation to his past, present and future. Self and society are interconnected and this link is a kind of web, the construction of which is partly under guidance from self and partly the prevailing social pattern. The subtle by-play between society and the individual by which the individual develops a sense of self through participation in social interaction, and yet possessing a feeling of separation from others is a fundamental social process which perpetuates culture and society.

In this modern era, the self finds it difficult to come to terms with the social environment because the inner values nurtured by the self and the outer social demands are incompatible. This inability to connect the self with the society results in the alienation of self. In the words of O.P. Saxena:

> [...] self alienation, however, means the loss of contact of the individual self with any inclination or desires that are not in agreement with the prevailing social patterns, as a result of which an individual is forced to manipulate in accordance with the social demands or feels incapable of controlling his actions.
>
> (71)

The process of social change that have taken place in the twentieth-century England have played havoc with the personal accommodation of selves into society. In the twentieth century, the Victorian idea of 'Permanence of Institution' was displaced by the sense of universal mutability, marked by a bewildering flux of ideas and of tentative experiment. The twentieth century witnessed crises of unparalleled magnitude and scope: two world wars, a severe economic depression, revolutionary movements of tremendous magnitude and fury and threat of nuclear holocaust, Cybernation, technological development, globalization and mechanical pace of living have had significant effect on the social fabric of the society. New attitudes towards morality, marriage, female sexuality and divorce have emerged. The institution of marriage retains its sanctity for those who desire permanent relationships and the stability of family life, while it does not lose its popularity among the flippant who keep divorce in view as a back door of escape when the sentimentalities and social trivialities pall.

These drastic changes that have taken place through the late twentieth century into the twenty first century have given rise to a relatively new set of complexities regarding self, identity and alienation. Today, people are hungry for meaning, identity, for some roots in existence, for some purpose in human experience, for some protection against anxieties and frustrations. But as the forces of cultural and societal expectations are a Herculean obstacle to overcome, the individual self finds itself in a state of conflict. The disparity between what an individual wants to desire for and the societal expectation is wide. This lack of compatibility between the self and society is the essence of Sidhwa's and Mukharjee's novels as is strongly evident in *Daughter*. S.P. Swain in "Problems of Identity: A Study of Bharati Mukherjee's *Desirable Daughters*" comments: "This novel is not just an idyllic tale of the three desirable daughter (sic) and their diverse circumstances of upbringing but it is a complex transational narrative commenting on the intricate and enigmatic process of growing up and of the feminist struggle of these three sisters to stick to their own protean self, their cultural moorings in times of crisis" (128).

Likewise, in Sidhwa's and Mukherjee's world, the issues of diaspora globalization, consumerism, transnationalism, cultural hybridity, alienation and identity crisis have become the leit-motif due to cultural dislocation. In the quest for identity, the self is dislocated in space and time from its roots and has a homing instinct-the desire to discover its 'in betweenness' in a transnational and trans – cultural space.

Works Cited

Alam, Fakrul. *Bharati Mukherjee*. New York: Twayne Publishers, 1996.

Ashcroft B. ed. *The Empire Writes Back: Theory and Practice in Post-Colonial Literatures*. London and New York: Routledge, 1989.

Asnani, Shyam M. and Rajpal, Deepika. "Identity Crisis in *The Nowhere Man* and *Wife*". *Language Forum*. 1-2 (January–December, 1992), 38-47.

Bose, Brinda. "A Question of Identity: Where Gender, Race and America Meet in Bharati Mukherjee". *Bharati Mukherjee: Critical Perspectives:* 47-63.

Dayal Samir. "Creating, Preserving, Destroying: Violence in Bharati Mukherjee's *Jasmine*". *Bharati Mukherjee: Critical Perspectives*, 65-88.

Dimri, Jaiwanti. "From Marriage to Murder: A Comparative Study of Bharati Mukherjee's *Wife* and *Jasmine*". *American Literature Today*. Ed. Suman Bala. New Delhi: Intellectual Publishing House, 1994: 170-175.

Eliot. T.S. *Notes Towards the Definition of Culture*. London: Faber and Faber, 1948.

Gaur, Rashmi. "Gender Relations and Cross-Cultural Transactions in Bharati Mukherjee's *Desirable Daughters*". *Indian Journal of English Studies*.Vol. XLI. 2003-2004.

Inamdar. F.A. "Immigrant Lives: Protagonists in Bharati Mukherjee's *The Tiger's Daughter* and *Wife*". *Indian Women Novelists.* Set I. Vol. V: 187-196, also in *The Fiction of Bharati Mukherjee: A Critical Symposium:* 39-52.

Iyer, Nalini. "American/Indian". Metaphors of the Self in Bharati Mukherjee's *The Holder of the World. ARIEL.* Vol.27. No.4 (October, 1996), 29-44.

Jain, Jasbir. "Foreignness of Spirit: The World of Bharati Mukherjee's Novels". *Journal of Indian Writing in English.* Vol. 13. No. 2 (July, 1985). 12-19.

Kirpal, Viney *The Third World Novel of Expatriation: A Study of Émigré Fiction by Indian, West African and Caribbean Writers.* New Delhi: Sterling Publishers, 1989.

Kumar, Nagendra. *The Fiction of Bharati Mukherjee: A Cultural Perspective.* New Delhi: Atlantic Publishers, 2001.

Mukherjee, Bharati. *The Tiger's Daughter.* 1971. New Delhi: Penguin, 1971.

________. *Wife.* 1975. New Delhi; Sterling Publishers, 1976.

________. *Jasmine.* 1989. New Delhi: Viking, 1990.

________. *The Holder of the World.* 1993. New York: Fawcott Books, 1993.

________. *Desirable Daughters.* 2002. New Delhi: Rekha Printers Pvt. Ltd., 2004.

"Oh Calcutta! Bharati Mukherjee's *The Tiger's Daughter*". *Times Literary Supplement.* 29 (June, 1973), 736

Parekh, Pushpa N. "Telling her Tale Narrative Voice and Gender Roles in Bharati Mukherjee's *Jasmine*". *Bharati Mukherjee: Critical Perspectives:* 109-126.

Prabha Barat, Ananda. "Bharati Mukherjee and the Immigrant Psyche: *The Tiger's Daughter*". *The Fiction of Bharati Mukherjee: A Critical Symposium:* 53-58.

Rajan, Gita. "Bharati Mukherjee (1940 -)". *Writers of the Indian Diaspora: A Bio-Bibilographical Critical Source:* 235-242.

Rich, Adrienne. "Resisting Amnesia: History and Personal life". *Blood, Bread and Poetry.* New York: W.W. Norton, 1986, 136-155.

Richler, Mordecai. *Son of a Smaller Hero.* Toronto: McClelland & Stewart, 1965.

Rustomji-Kerns, Roshni. "Expatriates, Immigrants, and Literature: Three South Asian Women Writers". *The Massachusetts Review.* 29. No. 4 (Winter, 1988-1989), 655-665.

Sandler, Linda. "Violence as a Device of Problem Solving". *Saturday Night.* 90.5 (October, 1975), 75-76.

Sattar, Arshina. "Review of Bharati Mukherjee's *The Holder of the World.*" *The Sunday Times* (Sunday Review) (20 March, 1994), 6.

Saxena. O.P. *Glimpses of Indo-English Fiction.* Vol. 1. New Delhi: Jainsons Publications, 1995.

Sidhwa, Bapsi. *The Crow Eaters.* 1980. New Delhi: Penguine, 1990.

________. *The Pakistani Bride.* 1983. New Delhi: Penguin, 1989.

________. *Ice-Candy-Man.* 1988. New Delhi: Penguin, 1989.

________. *An American Brat.* 1994. New Delhi: Penguin, 1994.

Swain. S.P. "Problems of Identity: A Study of Bharati Mukherjee's *Desirable Daughters*". *Journal of Literature & Aesthetics* (Jan - Dec., 2003), 127-133.

5

Crafts(wo)manship

> Not to destroy the wonder of literature but to enhance it.
>
> (John Spencer)

Modern criticism, through its exacting scrutiny of literary texts, has demonstrated with finality that in art beauty and truth are inevitable and indivisible. For beauty one can substitute form and for truth content. So in literature one can speak of technique and subject-matter. Modern criticism shows that to speak of content is not to speak of art but of experience, but when one speaks of achieved content, it is form, the work of art as a work of art. "The difference between content, or experience, and achieved content, or art, is technique" (Schorer, 106). Further, he asserts:

> When we speak of technique, then, we speak of nearly everything. For technique is the means by which the writer's experience, which is his subject matter, compels him to attend to it, technique is the only means he has of discovering, exploring, developing his subject, of conveying its meaning, and finally of evaluating it.
>
> (106)

The style of a writer can be said to reside in "the manipulation of variables in the structure of a language or in the selection of optional or latent features" (Fowler 15). If language is always contextual, every writer has to choose a language to suit the particular situation of his / her writing.

Sidhwa and Mukherjee have experienced dauntlessly with language and technique which secures their position as leading

Post-Modern novelists of ideas. Their narratology exploits substantially several popular techniques adopted by different writers. They have blended faction, metafiction, magic realism and black humour in their powerful narratology.

The novels of Sidhwa are boisterous, slightly ribald, and ingenuously irreverent. *Crow Eaters* is satirical and exuberant. *Candy-Man* is an almost surrealistic story of Lenny, a young girl coming of age, told against the backdrop of the bloody struggles that were a part of partition. It is skilfully told through the unsophisticated eyes of a child. The sequel to these books, *Brat,* shifts the setting to America as it follows Feroza, another young Parsi, in her quest for identity and self-awareness. In *Brat*, Sidhwa explores the complex conflict between Parsiness, the Pakistani identity and the lure of the Western world. The Parsi girl, Feroza is packed off to a university in the USA to prevent her further contamination by what her family sees as regressive Islamic fundamentalism. Thus at the beginning of this text, Parsiness is perceived to be closer to Western values than to those prevalent in Pakistan. However, once in America, Feroza turns more western and liberated than her family would like her to be. So wheels are then set in motion to rescue her from the libidinous West. The general hilarity and comic situations thinly disguise the underlying dilemma of the diasporic Parsis, at home neither in the East nor in the West. Their understanding and acceptance of both are vitiated by the missing fragments of their own past.

When Mukherjee began writing, she chose the Omniscient point of view, and habitually used irony in order to distance herself from her protagonists. Later, she began to celebrate the immigrant voices instead of treating the life of exiles and expatriates with condescension. By the time she wrote *Darkness,* she had adopted American English as her language. She moved away from using irony and was no longer comfortable using an authoritative point of view. Manju Sampat in "Bharati Mukherjee: Some Essential Conclusions" points out that Mukherjee was influenced by British writers in her early novels but as she grew to "identify more and more with America, her writing style became more Americanised and she became increasingly influenced by other American immigrant writers like Roth and Malamud" (73).

Mukherjee uses language which is a mark of good style with inventiveness and originality. In *Leave* she abundantly uses hyphenated ajectives: 'diamond-hard light stars' (*LM* 9), 'Sand-yellow sun' (*LM* 9), 'eight-armed, flame-bright, lion-riding dispenser' (*LM* 5), 'spaced-out smile'(*LM* 60) 'Preaky-costumed freedom' (*LM* 65), night-vision implants' (*LM* 135); bile-poisoned self ' (*LM* 209), 'Junior – year growth spurt' (*LM* 16), 'Jazz-worthy Californian' (*LM* 96) and so on. She even describes the Goddess of Devigaon as: "a lasso, a trident, a fire-tipped spear, a demon-spitting disc, a bow and arrows, a death-dealing staff, a thunder-sparking axe, a pitcher of water and necklace of blessed beads [....]" (*LM* 5).

Leave develops the postmodern American paradigm in a more contemporary mode. In Deleuzian fashion, it subverts the inescapable Freudian model of the Oedipian subconscious, since the orphan narrator embarks on a quest of self-exploration on the heels of her mysterious parents with whom she has had very little contact. It is composed of a prologue, three parts and an epilogue. The prologue presents the story of Devi, the Earth Mother and Warrior Goddess cutting off the usurper's buffalo-head, as told by old Hari in the Indian village of Devigaon. Part I made up of five chapters, begins with the latest moment in the time-scale of the novel and doubles back to the early days and adolescence in upstate New York of 23-year-old Debby. Part Two which contains 19 chapter divisions is more or less linear in construction and presents Debbey alias Devi Dee's move from New York State to San Francisco, followed by her establishing useful contacts in her exploration of available indices about her biological parents. The main flow of narration is augmented by fax reports, letters and court transcripts from India (*LM* 105, 119, 144) concerning the sexguru serial killer of the 1970s who sired the narrator and sudden revelations of the past in Devi Dee's memory (*LM* 103,162,223-224). Part III with its chapters zeroes in on the showdown between Devi Dee's Bio-Mum and Bio-Dad and the Epilogue closes with an apocalyptic evocation of the house boat called "Last chance' being served from its moorings at the very moment that the

Big Quake hits the Bay area. Besides, the accumulation of gory scenes of violence and murder with far-fetched coincidences reveals the novel's melodramatic, black-buster orientation.

In *Leave* violence is presented as being more macabre, more planned and more deliberate. As Debbie set the Fong House on fire, she watches, "rivers of flame lick at vintage velvet drapes. Then split off and multiply, and crawl like amoebas across massive Oak doors and curved-glasswindows. A spectacular extravaganza of light, sound, and heat" (*L* 53).

Holder introduces a set of new elements in Mukherjee's cross-cultural vision. She communicates through it a new kind of global consciousness that provides a sense of connectedness beyond the barriers of time and geography. In this novel, a computer is used to resurrect history and interact freely with a virtual reality recreated from loads of information as is used by Amitav Ghose in *The Calcutta Chromosome.* The world in *Holder* is one in which the metaphoric freely merges with the literal and India becomes an example for such merging of realities. In fact, the novel is a bridge between the past and the present. It is a computerized history. It juxtaposes the conflicting world of luxuriant past and the mechanized present. The opening sentence of the novel, "I live in three time zones simultaneously, and I don't mean Eastern, central and Pacific. I mean the past, the present and the future" (*HW* 5) illustrates Mukherjee's attempt to look at the past in the present to preserve it for the future through the super computer. Nair in "A Puritan in a Mughal Court" admits:

> Mukherjee spins an absorbing story, full of the drama and spectacle of the seventeenth century being lustily colonized and raided, amidst racial and religious tensions that seem eerily contemporary. As an American writer of Indian origin, Mukherjee has written an interesting account of the colonial experience from a western perspective.
>
> (106-107)

Similarly, Sidhwa uses verbal jugglery in her novels with the use of style nearer to modernist or postmodernist. The influence of Salman Rushdie and the technique of Indianization of written English is obvious in her novels. It helps in the racy flow of her narrative. Her language resembles the rhythms, styles and nuances of everyday speech in the sub-continent. Sidhwa does not follow the non-linear, non-realist narrative forms. The influence of Dickens and the nineteenth century novelists is obvious. She firmly believes in the importance of a sound plot and gripping story in her novels. *Crow Eaters* and *Bride* display the novelist's purposeful control of language. Sidhwa's is a plain and supple style without ornate diction or unnecessary complications. Yet it can rise to poetic intensity when the narrative demands it. Her writings are consistent and moderate. Though, *Crow Eaters* and *Bride* are very lonely plotted, both lack a single uniting idea. Both the novels are very absorbing and dramatic. Sidhwa controls the tension throughout. Thus her overall prowess over the genre is impressive. Her range of settings, plots, themes and characters makes her one of the most exciting of the recent Commonwealth novelists.

In Mukherjee's novels the "emergence of the new type of immigrant woman is voiced in a language which integrates the old cultural vocabulary with the new one" (St. Andrews 56). Comparing Joy Kogawa, St. Andrews says:

> Language therefore becomes a metaphor both of belonging and not belonging. Kogana and Mukherjee create characters who wrestle with the idea of how language enfranchises and dis-enfranchises them.
>
> Focussing on immigrant characters [...] Mukherjee too warns society about this tactic of imposing silence or of using language to misrepresent experience [....]
>
> (56-57)

In *Wife* one can find Dimple's disgust with American English like that of Feroza in *Brat.* She is afraid to operate the self-service elevators. Linda Sandler in "Violence as a Device for Problem Solving" explains it in terms of her traditional upbringing:

> Dimple emigrates the electronic age with her traditional values almost intact, only partly modified by the pop-culture of modern Calcutta, she is unable to make the

> transition from Before to After and chooses violence as a 'problem-solving' device [....]
>
> (75)

In *Middleman,* while the pattern of each story is nearly fixed, the writer's use of language is unconventional. The spoken language of the characters corresponds to their actual thinking process. She also uses abbreviations like NJIT, BMW, Rencen, Sci-fi-novel, MCI, MTV, JFK and so on 'with slangs like' indies or 'gringes' and so on. In *Jasmine* Mukherjee's language is simple and straight forward. The storyline takes a linear progression with occasional flashbacks. In describing rural Punjab, she takes no metaphors or metaphorical images but uses realistic portrayal of the village that was Jasmine's entire world.

In *Jasmine* Mukherjee fashions her language into the casual shorthand beloved of Americans. This is primarily the voice of a village girl. The process of transformation figuratively centered in the death of one's old self and the birth of a new self, is a motif that vitalises the narrative language and structure. Sensory images reiterate at various levels the symbolism of cyclical patterns of birth, death, and new birth, in the content of the immigrants' life and expectations. *Daughter* adopted the technique of documentation to bring out the contrast between two worlds and two attitudes.

Sidhwa in *Bride* shifts the point of view from episode to episode, from Qasim to Sikander and Zohra to Nikka, to Carol and Mushtaq to Zaitoon. The section concerning Qasim's early days is a mini-saga of the life in the hills. Qasim is married at 10 to a girl of 15; he is also handed his first gun at that age. Before the consummation of his marriage, his wife is nearly raped and he nearly kills her molester. In a few more years his whole family, except himself, is wiped out by smallpox. The cycle of harsh, brutish, violence that life in the hills are established in this brief section.

Sikander and Zohra's story contains in it the germ of all Partition stories—communal frenzy, carnage, migration, and the break-up of families. Both Sikander and Zohra are killed, leaving the orphaned child Munni, later called Zaitoon by

Qasim in memory of his own dead daughter. Qasim and Zaitoon thus become the reconstituted family, the unlikely coming together of two cultures, the Kohistani and the Punjabi, the tribal and the urban, the hill and the plain, the fair and the brown.

Nikka's story shows the sophisticated evil of Lahore politics in comparison with the stark violence of the tribal society. Nikka is a professional assassin working for powerful political bosses. His story, which includes visits to brothels in Hira Mandi, familiarizes the reader with the ways of urban life. Finally, Zaitoon's marriage and flight constitute the main story proper. Even Carol's affair with Mushtaq, provides a commentary on the main events: here is depicted how a Western woman is treated by the male Pakistani society as compared to Zaitoon, who is a native. Such a reading will discover that the novel is more unified, especially thematically, than it appears.

However, in sharp contrast to such an episodic narrative, Mukherjee's *Daughter* has rather a British feel to it. Mukherjee adopts the Omniscient point of view and a great use of irony. This is because her concept of language and the notions of how a novel was constructed were based on British models. *Daughters* is not only a nostalgic, romanticisiation of the past in which reminiscences are dovetailed with dramatic scenes from Indian writing. Mukherjee writes:

> In a Palanquin borne by servants there sit a rich man's three daughters, the youngest dressed in her bridal sari, her little hands painted with red lac dye, her hair oiled and set. Childish voices chant a song, hands clap gold bracelets tinkle. A Bengali happiest night is about to become her lifetime imprisonment. It seems all the sorrow of history, all that is unjust, in society and cruel in religion has settled on her. Even constructing it from the merest scraps of family memory fills me with rage and bitterness. (04)

As Mukherjee's *Daughters* is reminiscence, Sidhwa's *Eaters* is a loosely constructed narrative which begins with an extended flashback. Junglewalla tells the story of his early years to a captive audience consisting of his seven children and some neighbouring kids. He tells how at the end of the nineteenth century, at the age of 24, he embarked on a journey to Punjab with his wife and mother-in-law, how he struggled many years with his mother-in-law for control over his household; how, through a fraudulent insurance scheme in which he set fire to his own shop and frightened his mother-in-law, how he became both the master of his house and rich; and how he rose to power and eminence in the community with hard work and craft. Life's movement, hence, is seen as cyclical, going from comedy through tragedy back to comedy. It is this movement that engrosses and engages the author, not so much individual characters. That is why the focus shifts from character to character in the novel.

The first section belongs to Freddy; in the middle, the attention shifts from Freddy to his children; finally, in the third section, it is Billy not Freddy to his children; finally, in the third section, it is Billy not Freddy, who is the chief actor. Money, love, sex, procreation, the passage of time, and the progression of society—all these comic concerns are seen merely as components of the larger rhythm of life: Yazdi's renunciation is one aspect of life, while Billy's acquisition another.

Though the novel always stays closer to Billy's side of things, by also depicting Yazdi's otherworldliness, it acknowledges or attempts to recognize life's totality. Soli, by the astrologer's prediction, is reborn as Billy's son after his (Soli's) death (274). Faredoon, towards the end of life, becomes philosophical and detached. Sidhwa fuses the key elements of low comedy with a vision that is largely and typically Indian as is the case with the typical Indian way of storytelling that is followed by Mukherjee in *Daughters*. This vision springs from a philosophic attitude which regards the world as Leela or play.

All characters perform their assigned roles within this pattern, none more or less valid than the other. The individual, no matter how enterprising and determined, merely plays his part in a larger purpose, which is ultimately inscrutable and mysterious. Faredoon himself realizes this when he cannot prevent his son's death and his other son's renunciation of the world he loves so much. *Crow Eaters* thus explores both the superficial and the more profound dimensions of the comic mode. Not only it is an entertaining satire and farce on the foibles of its main characters, but it also embodies a larger vision of the world, a vision which is best described as broad, tolerant, and sympathetic. This vision is comic.

Sidhwa's *Candy-Man* is narrated from the perspective of Lenny, a young parsi girl coming of age at the time of Partition and independence of India. As the narrative unfolds, it becomes apparent that her subjectivity is mediated by a community identity undergoing a double-edged crisis. The shift in power from a British to the Hindu and Muslim-Centric states of India and Pakistan respectively signals the end of Parsees privileged relation. The novel dramatizes the confusions and contradictions that face a young girl initiated into the norms of her community. In it, the locale of the Parsi community, Lahore, becomes a conjunctural site of belonging in determination "where the discursive meaning of 'belonging' is under revision" (Didur 46-47). Sidhwa's narrative in *Candy-Man* is what Arjun Appadurai calls in *Modernity at Large: Cultural Dimensions of Globalization* 'a local reading' of a macro event. It is to quote:

> [...] local readings [...] are often silent or literally unobservable, except in the smallest of passing comment [....] They are part of the incessant murmur of urban political discourse and its constant undramatic cadences. But people and groups at this most local level generate those structures of feeling that over time provide the discursive field within which the explosive rumours, dramas, and speeches of the riot can take hold.
>
> (Appadurai 153)

In *Candy-Man* a macro event, Partition of India, is given a local colour by placing the novel in the centre of Parsi Community in Lahore. The subject of the novel is the Partition of India but the focus is on a small group of individuals in Lahore. It focuses on the trauma of the 1947 Partition of India. Through a child-narrator's consciousness it visualizes the grim realities of the historical catastrophe. Manju Jaidka in "Hyphenated Perspectives on the Cracking of India: Bapsi Sidhwa's *Ice-*

Candy-Man" says:

> The novel traces a gradual but inevitable movement from outer spaces to the inner: from the Queen's Garden (18,88), where characters from different communities congregate under the statue of Queen Victoria [...], to the Wrestler's restaurant (127) which becomes the next venue for their meetings, then to the Lawn's of Lenny's house (147), and finally to the inner confines of the house (179-183) where the Ayah in vain seeks refuge from the blood thirsty mob. There is, thus, this centripetal movement, a zooming in of energies which only leads to a final explosion in the catastrophe, an irreversible tide of events that cannot be contained or explained or justified.
>
> (47)

Candy-Man is even more centrally concerned with the partitioning of India. This is a rather sophisticated narrative which utilizes several postmodernist features – fantasy, fragmentation of time and allegory. At the level of allegory, it details the political betrayal and symbolic rape of a hapless colony by a departing colonial power. Interwoven into this dark and sordid tale is the story of little Lenny and her troubled childhood. Lenny is the narrator of this novel and it is through this girl-child's eyes that the readers see the ghastly dismemberment of India. Lenny is a subaltern figure, hers is a triple-marginalisation. She is female, belongs to a minority community and is physically handicapped. Lenny is also an autobiographical character. The maimed girl-child could also be symbolic of the damaged Parsi identity which was once again under threat during the division of India. With the creation of the new Muslim state of Pakistan, Lenny's world shrinks, it loses its Hindus and Sikhs. Thus the Parsi identity in Pakistan becomes a reductive entity, a victim of yet another diaspora.

In the *Candy-Man* and to a certain extent in *Brat*, Sidhwa attempts the modernist / post-modernist vein of narrative – experimentation. She adheres to the Dickensian method of a gripping story but unlike Dickens with limited authorial intervention and the linear realist narrative. Similarly, in Mukherjee's *Daughter* the narration is almost passive: the characters fail to react. Events take place in time and a consciousness of the present is almost always there. Tara's consciousness of the present is rooted in her life in the States. When she looks at India anew it is not through her childhood associations or her past memories but through the eyes of her foreign husband David. Her reactions are those of a tourist and of a foreigner. Her *Wife* is also a scary story told with malice and charm. According to Meena Manvi, "the narrative structure of *Wife* is conceptualized through Mukherjee's evocation of the Sita myth at a strategic moment in the narrative; the examination of this myth is further strengthened by the opposition that is successfully manipulated between passive resistance / violence, female desire / male authority, enclosure / freedom, marriage a bond / female eroticism, reality / after 'dream', love/marriage" (141). In order to reverse and sometimes subvert readers' expectations, the novelist functions as a narrator and moreover it is essential for her purpose to initiate a dichotomy between narrator and reflector/focalizer.

Like the narrative in Sidhwa's *Candy-Man* in *Jasmine*, the narrative shifts between the past and present between India of her earlier life and America of the present. The past is Jyoti's childhood in the small village of Hasnapur like that of Lenny of *Ice-Candy* in Punjab and her marriage to Prakash, the present was her life at Iowa as Jane. In *Jasmine*, the narrative voice of the protagonist, speaking in the first person point of view, reflects her choice of rhetorical tools in telling her tale. Pushpa N. Parekh in "Telling Her Tale: Narrative Voice and Gender Roles in Bharati Mukherjee's *Jasmine*" says:

> The memory of Jasmine's personal history and environment shapes and directs the reception of her present experiences and content and is often countered by the acruing of memories of newer experiences. This double perspective of the shifts in time and space and their impact on the psyche of the immigrant woman can be explored through the tonal-shifts with which the Jasmine-Jane protagonist concretizes her emotional and intellectual reality-fear, anger, pain, bitterness, confusion, silence, irony, humour, as well as pathos underline her observations as she discovers for herself the undefined

> median between the preservation of the old world and assimilation into the new one.
>
> (117)

Like that of Sidhwa's *Candy-Man* in *Jasmine* the narrative shuttles between past and present between India of the narrator's early life and America of her present one. The past is Jyoti's childhood in the small village of Hasnapur, Punjab, her marriage to Prakash Vijh and the consequences leading to her departure to America. The present is her life as Jane in Baden, Iowa, where she is a live in companion to Bud Ripplemeyer, a small town Banker. Gurleen Grewal in "Born Again American: The Immigrant Consciousness in *Jasmine*" says: "The starkness of the rapid linear development from village to metropolis, of Jyoti reborn as Jane, is disguised by the non-linear narrative techniques of montage and jump-cuts, shuffling us back and forth in time. However from the opening page, the narrative constructs the native woman, Jyoti, as a beaming figure marked for exile and deliverance from the dark and static Being of India" (186). The narrating consciousness proceeds to dissociate itself not only from India but from Jyoti as well Jane. The narrator declares that she was named Jyoti but she has transformed herself into Jane.

In *Leave* Debby's encounter with existential verities reveals Mukherjee's narrative skill in which descriptions as well as conversational language resort to deft metaphors and colloquial expressions. Through bold images, pithy dialogues and engaging divulgement, Mukherjee presents a firm conviction that a woman is no more a subaltern, cannot be exploited as the weaker sex. Her *Holder* is a virtual reality novel in which the narrative is strung uneasily together by Mukherjee's ideas on diverse subjects ranging from Hindu fatalism to multiculturalism to intertextuality. It recaptures historical and imaginative reality through a virtual database to make infinite reality withdrawals from both time and place. In *Holder* the movement of the narrative is circular since the story ends in the same vein as it opens but the person (Hannah) does not remain the same. The narrative makes the readers move from Salem to Stephney, Coromandel to Devgad and then back to Salem.

The structure of *Holder* is complex; it spans two historical periods, the seventeenth and the twentieth centuries. The primary narrator, a twentieth-century American assets hunter, Beigh Masters, from Massachussetts, uses the help of her Indo-American lover (a computer scientist) to recover the narrative of a seventeenth century woman, Hannah Easton Fitch Legge. Beigh's initial motivation for piecing together Hannah's story is to find the Emperor's Tear, a jewel given to Hannah Easton by the Mughal Emperor, Aurangzebe. Beigh's narrative traces the story of Hannah from her New England origins through a brief stay in England as the wife of an English sailor to her subsequent travels to India with her husband, who becomes an East India Company factor and later a pirate. Hannah's existence as a Company spouse is transformed radically by her husband's wanderlust that leaves her in India at the mercy of a Hindu king and eventually as the mistress of the Raja. Beigh juxtaposes the narrative of Hannah with a narrative of her own life where one can see her growing understanding of her role as writer, narrator, historian, and assets hunter. As Beigh delves deeper into Hannah's life, she begins to lose interest in the Emperor's Tear and becomes very involved in the intricacies of Hannah's extraordinary life. The jewel ceases to be a material object and becomes symbolic of the essence of Hannah's existence. Very early in the narrative, Beigh recognizes her changed objective and comments, "I couldn't care less about the Emperor's Tear, by now. I care only about the Salem Bibi" (*HW* 19).

Beigh constructs the narrative of Salem Bibi (the name given to Hannah by Mughal India) through meticulous research into artifacts such as paintings, embroidery, diaries, and folk narratives, and begins to put a book together. Her more traditional academic research and narrative methods are contrasted in terms of objectivity by the virtual reality program created by her lover that enables him to feed vast amounts of seemingly random data to produce in virtual space the actual event. Her narrative and Venn's recreation of experience uneasily coexist in the novel, and Mukherjee uses them to question subtly the relationship between experience and its narrativization.

In this novel, the tension between Beigh's narrativization of experience and Venn's virtual recreation of the experiences suggests that the Salem Bibi / Hannah Legge's identity and the cultural space she occupied are constructs, and in imposing a narrative structure on her life both Venn and Beigh are structuring their own individual and cultural identities. For Beigh this self-formation is through identification with Hannah as an American woman (she even sees a remote family connection between herself and Hannah), and for Venn the identity construction is in opposition to Hannah as a white woman complicit with early mercantile imperialism in India. As they read Hannah's diaries and interpret stories about her, she eludes both their attempts to categorize her. At the end of the novel, Beigh's research data is fed into Venn's computer program. This brings both their narrative methods together in an attempt to allow Beigh to transcend time and space and appropriate the identity of Hannah's friend and servant, Bhagmati. The competing narrative structures in this novel raise questions not just about colonial relationships and experience but also how they are signified.

This novel illustrates Homi Bhabha's observation that the postcolonial project, theoretically speaking, has forced the readers to rethink the discourse of cultural difference. *Holder* also rewrites the Raj narrative popular in British literature. These colonial narratives often tell tales of forbidden relationships between white women and native men, which the English characters perceive as rape, and such alleged rape of the English woman is a central trope of these narratives.

In *Holder* Mukherjee rewrites the Raj narrative by making the English woman (Hannah is seen as English in India) an agent in her sexual life rather than a passive subject. Hannah's interracial liaison with Jadav Singh is initiated by her, and when she is abducted by Aurangzebe as his prisoner of war, she argues with him about his militant policies and then manages to escape. She is not raped by either. The chaos and war in which she finds herself are not the result of her sexual liaison but of her relationship with Jadav Singh. The rape trope is transformed in this novel into the woman's choice of sexual relationships that is enabling rather than imprisoning. she spins an absorbing story, full of the drama and spectacle of the seventeenth century being lustily colonized and raided, amidst racial and religious tensions. As an American writer of Indian origin, Mukherjee has written an account of the colonial experience from a western perspective.

In an essay on colonialism and the postcolonial condition, Satya Mohanty argues that location is more than personal, geographical, or sociological facts; the consequences of location are to be found in the "epistemic role our location plays in our lives" (109). He posits that location is not an objective feature of the world one lives in. Location does not simply constitute various positions of power or powerlessness but "our location is causally significant; it shapes our experiences and our ways of knowing. It can limit the possibilities available to us, since it helps frame our choices by organizing the habitual patterns through which we perceive ourselves and our world" (110).

In an essay on being an Indian woman in the United States, Chandra Talpade Mohanty observes that "the very process of constructing a narrative for oneself—of telling a story—imposes a certain linearity and coherence that is never entirely there [...] home, community and identity all fall somewhere between the histories and experiences we inherit and the political choices we make through alliances, solidarities and friendships" (*Our Feet Walk the Sky 357*). Such a relationship between narrative and the construction of identity and how the location of the immigrant woman circumscribes her way of knowing as well as the framing of her narrative is what Mukherjee explores in her writing. Her fiction has sought various narrative frames for the immigrant woman's experiences from a third person realist narrative in *Wife* to Hindu myth in *Jasmine,* and more recently to virtual reality in *Holder*.

Mukherjee's "A Father" is the story of Mr.Bhownick, narrated, tongue-in-cheek, from his point of view by an omniscient narrator, a middle-aged, middle-class Bengali from Ranchi. Where "A Father" is about Indian immigrants in the United States, "A Wife's Story", told in the first person and the present tense by the wife herself, is about a woman who has won a brief respite from wifehood in India through her two-year Ph.D. course in special Education in America. Moreover, "A Father" is a story of an immigrant and "A Wife's Story" that of an expatriate. Urbashi Barrel in "Expatriate Indian or Immigrant American? A Study of 'A Father' and 'A Wife's Story' " says that "the former uses the irony and the omniscient narration which Mukherjee regards as being the hallmark of the British tradition, and therefore by extension that of Indian writing in English; and the latter uses the subjective mode and the present tense so characteristic of the American tradition, as seen for example, in the *Rabbit* series" (123).

In technique, very often expatriation is expressed through irony and an omniscient narrative with occasional shifts in perspective and also authorial comments. The immigrants often appear in first person narratives and reveal author's supple voice which can enter varied immigrant sensibilities. Mukherjee's *Middleman* deals with Asian immigrants. Eight of the 11 stories are in the first person narrative. Of the 11, four stories are in first person narratives by immigrants, four are first person narratives by native Americans whose lives have been affected by immigrants, and three are third person narratives with Indian immigrants as protagonists.

In *Middleman* Mukherjee is straightforward and sentimental. In it, she has been becoming more Americanized. In *Middleman* each character and story suggests a different style. She does not write a story with a pre-determined point of view. She writes some stories from a very authoritative third – person point of view; with others she uses an intimate, textured style and first person point of view. The style of writing in *Middleman* is in conformity with the themes and atmosphere in the stories. It is bare, functional, and self-consciously unemotional.

Similarly, as found in *Middleman,* Sidhwa's *Bride* shows a lack of unity. Indeed, its narrative structure is curious. It tells several independent stories. The main one is Zaitoon's story. A foil to that is Carol's story which develops side by side without much interaction. Before that is Nikka's story of how he rises from mere panwalla in a refugee camp to the leading strongman of Lahore. Even earlier are the smaller, self-contained stories of Sikander and Zohra and of Qasim's earlier life. It is evident that Sidhwa intends to tell not one, but many stories and all of them form a cluster of the novel; usually, in the West episodic novel consists of the adventures of one main character, loosely strung together. However, in her novel, even the protagonist is not central. The various events convey a sense of the multiplicity and complexity of the human experience. It is life that becomes important not the fortunes of the individual. It has three different inbuilt structures, according to Jasbir Jain in "The Male Presence in the 'Purdah' 'Novel'": "One of the tribal world, the other located in Lahore, the third the foreign world of Carol which is there through inference. All these three worlds are defined by men: Qasim and Nikka define the world in Lahore, Farukh and Mushtaq define Carol's world, and Sakhi and his brother the tribal world" (222-223). As *Bride* tells about Zaitoon's story in an open form, Mukherjee's *Daughter,* with the structure of an open-ending novel, tells about the dangling personality of Tara who is torn between the American and Indian selves. Commenting on the structure of *Daughter,* Jasbir Jain in "Foreignness of Spirit: The World of Bharati Mukherjee's Novels" says:

> The four-part division of the novel moves in a circle. Beginning with her arrival the novel ends with her proposed exit, rejecting India and her Indianness unable to grasp its meaning, and equally unable to understand the America she plans to go back to. The first part is brief and deals with her responses to India; the second moves into her ancestral past, which both Tara and her father have tried to reject, a past which is overwhelmed and pushed aside by Westernization; the third section of the novel is concerned with Tara's early experiences in America, her loneliness, her attempt to stick to Indian ways and the gradual acculturisation leading to her marriage to David Cartwright; the fourth brings us back to India and Tara's move from Calcutta to Darjeeling with its own peculiar brand of foreigners. Here in Darjeeling she is seduced and this act of seduction is symbolic of her foreignness which is an experience which cannot be undone.
>
> (15)

This four part division is identical to three different structures of Sidhwa's *Bride*. It has a very complex and mysterious plot shuffling between cultures and continents. In it, she has created a tale both magical and mysterious resounding with spiritual healing for both the living and the dead. In *Darkness,* Mukherjee's success lies in her technical virtuosity. A.V. Krishna Rao in "From Expatriation to Immigration: The Case of Bharati Mukherjee" says:

> She deftly dovetails into her apparently explosive plot about racial harmony and disharmony in Canada, the primordial elements of ancient geology and geography, modern history and politics, illustrated and symbolized by the scientific account of Hsu about the formation of the earth and the environment at one level and the political volatility and violence in former French colony, at another. Once again, it is her ability to use the ironic juxtaposition as an effective creative tool that Mukherjee succeeds in developing and resolving the problem of racial encounters and cultural collisions. In this story, Toronto and Montreal become the metaphors for possible racial tension and harmony, respectively.
>
> (100)

Daughters encompasses a large span of time. It is scattered over twelve decades. The chronicle moves through reminiscences and directs narration and the action of the narrative circumventing Calcutta, Bombay and America. The title of the novel is ironic. The daughters are not desired. The plot of *Daughters* is conceived in a tone of defiance as the three sisters Padma, Parvati and Tara are bent upon breaking traditions and to live their own lives. In *Wife,* Dimple wishes to begin a journey from midpoint and thus the nihilistic undertones of her situation. The sense of time is more important for the understanding of her life. The present and past do not interact in *Wife.* In *Daughter* they do interact but the interaction is non-productive. In both these novels, there is the significance of the authorial point of view. The heroines are the focus and both the episodes and the characters are seen through their responses and relationships. At *Holder* Mukherjee uses two timeframes – the twentieth and seventeenth centuries. In the end of the narrative, two time frames collapse into one as Beigh relates herself to the lineage of Hannah. The erasure of time allows Mukherjee to explore cultural identity as a function of space / location. It involves translation. Nalini Iyer in "American/Indian: Metaphors of the Self in Bharati Mukherjee's *The Holder of the World*" elaborates:

> The pun on the word translation is significant here. On one level, the word refers to linguistic transformation, or literally changing an expression from one language to another. On another level, it refers to the ability to convey a person, place or condition to another condition. In the seventeenth century, the word was commonly used to describe physical transportation. But in this novel, it is used simultaneously in the dominant seventeenth and twentieth century meanings, thereby suggesting that Hannah has been translated linguistically by Beigh's narrative into a simultaneous existence in the seventeenth and the twentieth centuries. Similarly, Venn's computer-assisted time reconstruction also provides time on a scale of 1:1, with a new concept of real time. He won't call it time-travel. Neither we, nor time, will have traveled an inch, or a millisecond (138). The suspension of time in both Venn and Beigh's reconstruction of Hannah's experience allows Mukherjee to reduce the significance of time in narrative and to translate culture, thereby interrogating the discourse of cultural difference.
>
> (34-35)

Time is usually related to the phenomenon called 'existence' Sidhwa relates time to existential despair as is seen is *Bride*. Dipika Sahai in "Culture-Consciousness and Gender Bias in Bapsi Sidhwa's *The Pakistani Bride:* A Post-Colonial Approach" says: "*The Pakistani Bride* is a woman's lyric cry in prose against the existential fate and societal abuse. Sidhwa has fashioned complex metaphors to orchestrate the multiple agonies of a woman, a successful portrayal of pain and suffering in the character of Zaitoon." (85).

Sidhwa and Mukherjee use images to cover an idea or a feeling. Mukherjee's *Wife* abounds with repulsive, revolting images of disease, crime and death. In *Middleman* imagery reinforces the lonely, bleak sombre and violence atmosphere and disintegrating relationships. Subash Chandra in "Americanness of the Immigrants in 'The Middleman and Other Stories'" highlights:

> Human beings have become 'locusts' to survive, the chandelier is broken, the steps, the path, the house are falling apart, afternoons are 'pure dynamite,' Miami is 'jungle' and human beings are compared to gutters: a 'laugh leaks out of him' [Auguste], Marshall is 'burned out', and the test of his manliness is whether he can 'fuck' a whore; America has gone 'down the rabbit hole,' it is to the 'Zoo' that Marshall goes in London. The sight he sees in the Zoo is symbolic: 'The twenty-eight feet long python, squeezing out Jaguars and crocodiles like dishrags'; the smell that emanates from hot-water ports like Florida, Bangkok, Manila and Bombay is like that of the 'snakeshit,' Renata's world needs to be 'healed'; instead of the baby, a cat is held on the hip; love has become a destructive force, a tornado which leaves behind 'debris', a room in a house looks 'impersonal as a room in a Holiday Inn,' and flowers in New York have no fragrance.
>
> (135)

However, at a deeper level, *Daughters* throws fresh perspective on the collision and synthesis of multicultural strands—New world sensitivity and tradition, mythology and old world values. Mukherjee's use of the cracking and splitting of earthquake as a metaphor is effective. She has skilfully used the metaphor of fault lines to describe human relationships. After a heated exchange of words between Tara and Rabi, Rabi leaves home in a huff. Referring to that Andy says:

> He's on the edge, babe. All the fighting is just pifle and pufle. That's what thirty years working construction has taught me: It's pifle and pufle. I fix the pifles and I look for the pufles. "A PIFL is a Previously Identified Fault Line" [...] A PUFL, a Previously Unidentified Fault Line, is a Killer.
>
> (*DD* 92)

In another context, Tara makes a reference to the "invisible fault lines" (*DD*: 180) that run between her and Didi. Talking about the sudden appearance of Christopher Dey and the subsequent dislocation in the peaceful household of Tara, Andy says, "[...] you guys are like those plates pushing against each other" (*DD*: 127). Referring to her perspective of Didi's lifestyle, Tara says:

> Didi, was sitting just inches away, a firm identity resisting all change, at least from a distance, on a brief inspection. But under scrutiny, fractured, like cracks under old glaze. Up close, I didn't recognize her. I didn't know who she was. I was following the cracks, fascinated by their complexity, not the simple, shining face. "Pufles and Pifles," Andy once called them, but I never thought that previously unidentified fault lines could refer to my sister, or to me.
> (*DD*: 196)

Thus Mukherjee has effectively used the metaphor of earthquake to refer to personal relationships as *Daughters*, as the blurb claims, is a stirring novel of three women of two continents and a hazardous journey from the old world to the new world. When she uses images to show human relationships, Sidhwa uses symbols to highlight the bond of human relationship. In *Bride,* river and the gorge become symbols by representing the partitioned and dislocated relations between the Kohistanis and the Army. Furrukh Khan in "Women, Identity, Dis-Location in *The Bride*" points out: "It is a fast moving, tumultuous body of water which has cut the mountain into two, and its speed is perhaps the true indication of the hostile relation between Kohistanis and the Army" (142).

The bridge is the symbol on the influence of 'outsiders' which has been built to encroach on the Kohistanis' separate and unique way of life. The very fact that the bridge is there reveals the chasm which has been in place not only to sever links but to maintain the status quo of fervent hostilities between two ways of life on either side of the river / bridge. It is rather ironic that the bridge, which under normal circumstances may have resulted in fostering a more understanding and conciliatory fashion on Kohistan, is guarded by the Army and each side displays a barely hidden fear and hostility towards the other. So the bridge is nothing more than a construction of concrete and cement, serving as a mere and persistent symbol of division rather than a tool of unification. Zaitoon in *Bride* has to reach the bridge by following the river. It is only after she experienced the trauma of travelling along the true division that she can cross over the architectural form of the bridge. Furrukh Khan in "Women, Identity and Dislocation in *The Bride*" affirms: "Her journey assumes the role of 'a rite of passage', which Zaitoon has to pass through successfully, not only to gain a new identity for herself but to literally survive" (142).

The novelist has used the bridge symbolic of the divide between the two cultures as also extending the helping hand to Zaitoon. The bridge is the presence of the modern technological power, so also the helping hand of civilization. Zaitoon of the plains awakens the tribal women to comprehend their plight which is crystallized in Hamida whose sympathies are with Zaitoon and who does not want Zaitoon to be caught and killed by her own men. She feels, "Any way, this would teach the menfolk a lesson" (*PB* 216). Silently but forcefully Zaitoon has established her individuality.

One is tempted to consider Sidhwa's portrayal of the women a feminist one, but she doesn't present any feminist philosophy nor any craze for individuality. But with powerful Dickensian details she portrays the social environment of the mountains which are as cruel and suffocating as they are attractive and romantic. One has the picture of Zaitoon moving from passivity to active assertion of her will against the imprisoning, cold and cruel men and mountains, from the exclusive masculine brutality and rigid patterns of existence. She escapes to the powerful intimidating and terrifying mountains, and ultimately defying her fate. She crosses over to free and normal life of civilization.

What is adventure for both Carol and Zaitoon into the romantic rosy world of fantasy turns out to be a voyage into dark and cruel layers of humanity. Both the women do not wish to become simply the victims of trends and traditions of culture they do not understand nor belong to. What the novelist presents is the consciousness of these women of their victimization at the hands of the age-old cultural, social and environmental forces of a different culture.

The novel presents the collapse of negativity into the positivity that the two women characters display. In a broader sense, the initial thrill is followed by a seizure of panic at the realities of life and the women rebel and try to break off the shackles of another culture and attain freedom, their own individual self. It is a struggle to seek freedom from negation of life and freedom to attain one's identity.

Though the novel remains a series of pictures to begin with and is loosely structured, once the journey begins, it gets its central focus. The novelist gives a glimpse into the dark inner recesses of man and brings into sharp focus the characters of Zaitoon and Carol and the theme of the novel; the early part serves as a contrasting backdrop against which the drama of life and death is enacted in the natural surroundings of white, beautiful yet challenging and hostile mountains. Sidhwa attempts not only the social and cultural responses but also presents the states of being and quest for survival. It is a struggle to cross the deep and unbridgeable abyss of the changeless and stagnant social order of the Muslim male and to become a whole person.

In *Wife*, the word Dimple is symbolic. It suggests 'beauty', particularly 'flawed beauty'. Lexicographically it means 'any slight surface depression'. This depression on the surface is again symbolic of the depression within her psyche. It is described throughout the novel. Looking at the lakes with an annoyed countenance she "hated the lakes, thought of them as death" (*W* 29). Her name "Just does not suit" (*W* 18) her. Her flat is "horrid" (*W* 18). She hates Amit talking to Kwatily. Her craze for an ideal man carved out of "a forehead from an aspirin ad, the lips, eyes and chin from a body-builder and shoulders ad, the stomach and legs from a trousers ad" (*W* 23) points to her abnormal self-longing for the man of her vision. All these may be taken as a manifestation of her self-assertion and ego fulfillment issuing out of her syndrome depression.

Sidhwa and Mukherjee are similar in using humour and comedy to satirise the human follies and foibles. In *Brat*, the comic mode is used. Sidhwa also uses irony, parody, and slang to create humour. In *Brat* the most humorous sections are the contrast between the polite Feroza and the brash Americans in usage of words. Novy Kapadia in "Expatriate Experience and Theme of Marriage in *An American Brat*" says:

> Seemingly this novel is a humorous portrayal of alternately funny and terrifying perceptions of an upper middle class Parsi family about the USA, but the novel functions on two levels. The expatriate experience in which the novelist cleverly juxtaposes first and third world perceptions provides humour. At a serious level, the problem of inter-community marriage and adjustment of a migrant to a different culture is carefully and ironically delineated.
>
> (187-188)

In *Brat* Sidhwa's humour is both situational and a result of astute characterization. There are situations, when the nuances of language, the usage of Americanisms which Feroza is unable to fathom, cause humorous situations and misunderstandings. There is a situation at a drug store, when Feroza's polite use of expressions like "May I [...]" leads to a dispute with an acerbic shop keeper who mistakes politeness an appeal for charity. It is Jo, her room-mate who teaches Feroza various Americanisms, so that she does not feel a misfit. *Crow Eaters* is a novel that may shock, offend and dismay due to its inclusion of Indian and Pakistani history and politics. It is a rumbunctious mixture of gentle perceptiveness and wild barnyard humour.

In *Crow Eaters,* the overall mode of the novel is comic. It is not a social comedy like that of Jane Austen or a satirical comedy of Swift or a comedy of manners / humorous but is a genial comedy. Human foibles and follies are treated with much tolerance and mild corrective irony. The comic aspect is brought out when Junglewalla resorts to dubious practices like Ganesh of V.S. Naipaul's *The Mystic Masseur* like setting his shop deliberately on fire, after hiding his goods in a hired godown, to claim insurance money. *Crow Eaters* derives its humour from a blend of fantasy, scatology, physical and verbal incongruity and caricature. Sidhwa uses a mixture of farce and irony which arouses laughter.

Crow Eaters truly belong to a comic mode. It emanates originally from a rich network of details of Parsi life. The world view is quintessentially Zoroastrian in its celebration of the values of charity and Asha. The narrative depicts the meteoric rise of Freddie, the Parsi protagonist and his prosperity. In capturing the Parsi ethos, she strikes an unexpectedly rich vein of humour (Why Do I Write? 33). The narrative employs comic and ironic modes at the levels of realization of Zoroastrian values in the lives of Freddie and his two sons, Billy and Yazdi. Structurally the narrative employs the shifting locale of central India where Freddy's journey starts to Lahore, Karachi, Bombay and London. The narrative employs the dynamics of change as integral to the materialistic and spiritual compulsions of Freddie. Lahore becomes an ultimate metaphor for his fulfilment in mercantile activity as much a locale for practising the Zoroastrian virtues in the society.

Crow Eaters has a somewhat loose, episodic structure. Much of its comic energy and exuberance is derived from a string of gags or comic episodes. Most of these episodes have a self-contained unity, a recognizable beginning, middle and end. Besides, they have other common comic features. Each has an element of the ridiculous or incongruous. There is a good deal of physical comedy involved. There is some reference to sex. Sometimes, verbal humour accompanies physical humour. A good example of a typical comic episode is the incident of the troublesome rooster. Freddy's cock enters the bullockcart when Freddy is making love to his wife. Sidhwa portrays:

> One momentous evening, the rooster happened to chance into the shelter. Locking his head to one side, he observed Freddy's curious exertions with curious interest. Combining a shrewd sense of timing with humour, he suddenly hopped up and with a minimum of flap or fuss planted himself firmly upon Freddy's amorous buttocks. Deep in his passion, subconsciously thinking the pressure was from his wife's rapturous fingers, Freddy gave the cock the ride to his life. Eyes as sparkle, wings stretched out for balance, the cock held on to his rocking perch like an

> experienced rodeo rider. It was only after Freddy sagged into a sated stupor, nerves uncurled with languous (sic), that the cock, raising both his tail and his neck, crowed, "coo-ka-moo-cooo!".
>
> (*CE* 6-7)

The last touch of the cock's triumphant crowing is called 'milking the gag', or extracting that last bit of extra mileage from a comic situation. Throughout the passage, the double meaning of the word 'cock' is exploited. This incident is an example of verbal humour to physical. An accent on the ridiculous, the frank and funny use of sex, the reliance on physical clumsiness is found in other comic passages. Another example of this technique is the consummation of Billy's marriage with Tanya. After their wedding, Billy and Tanya are packed off to Simla on their honeymoon in a first class coupe. When Billy tries to kiss Tanya, she bites his tongue: "You are a filthy sweeper fellow! Haven't you studied hygiene? Poking your germs into my mouth!" (*CE* 224). Billy realizes to his horror that Tanya is completely innocent of sex and that their consummation will have to wait. It finally takes place when they have gone trekking to Jacco Hill, a famous monkey sanctuary. The silly complications, absurd situations and clumsy physical comedy is seen in the novel. The language is frankly colloquial, but not coarse or vulgar. *Crow Eaters* explores both the superficial and the more profound dimensions of the comic mode, as Paranjape in "The Early Novels of Bapsi Sidhwa" admits:

> Not only is it an entertaining satire and farce on the foibles of its main characters, but it also embodies a larger vision of the world, a vision which is best described as broad, tolerant, and sympathetic. This vision is comic in the same sense as Chaucer's vision or Shakespeare's is comic, for it tries to convey the variety, diversity, vitality and validity of life at all points.
>
> (94)

In *Crow Eaters* the most successful comedy, however, is found in chapters 42-43, which concern the Junglewalla's visit to England. Jerbanoo is a complete misfit, first in the home of their hosts, the Allens, and then in the hotel. With true comic energy, she disrupts with calculated impunity all the social conventions around her. She revenges herself on the exasperated Mrs. Allen by defecating on a newspaper in the centre of the landing. Once ejected out of Allen's residence, she proceeds to make herself at home in the Junglewallas' hotel rooms on Oxford Street. Being a good Indian lady who cannot do without her daily baths, she decides to improvise when she finds that their rooms do not have attached baths. She uses walled balcony for this purpose. It slopes away into the street. She is unconcerned about drainage. That is, until she hears this from below: "Blimey! God, we're being flooded!" (*CE* 266) What follows is a rip-roaring exchange between "brown, fuzz-haired," (towel-wrapped), Jerbanoo, and the "red, wet and choleric face of a bull-necked Englishman":

> "Come on, what's going on up here? You washing clothes or something?"
>
> Jerbanoo glowered. "You not poke your nose into me, mister, I not poke my nose into you!" [...]
>
> "You want to know?" She asked, and her voice despite its malice rang with authenticity. "I tell you! I wash my bottom I no dry-clean like you dirty Englishmen. I wash my bottom!"
>
> (*CE* 267)

Here verbal incongruity arising out of Jerbanoo's pidgin and the Englishman's cockney, in addition to physical humour, the element of the ridiculous, scatology, and the climax make this perhaps the funniest of the scenes in the book.

Sidhwa uses irony to expose fundamentalism which is shown as characterized by parochialism, ignorance, a drive to conformity and a sense of security threatened by what is visibly different. Her mode of perception is ironic: In *Crow Eaters* she shows that Faredoon's charity does not make him a paragon of virtue but is tinged with self-promotion. In characteristic ambivalent and ironic tone she shows that Faredoon developed his philanthropic image to increase his business contacts and to appear selfless and counter the impression being a toady of the British. She uses irony to create humour and to present the ambivalent attitude towards charity of Freddy. Here irony is a mode of acceptance, a type of philosophy, highlighting the Parsi paradox.

There is an underlying irony in *Brat* but the story line of *Brat* is simple, lucy and pacy. In it, Sidhwa chronicles the adventures of a young Pakistani Parsi girl, Feroza, in America. Her Lahore—based family sends her to the USA for a three month vacation to broaden her outlook on life. They are concerned at Feroza's conservative attitudes which stem from Pakistan's rising tide of fundamentalism. Novy Kapadia in "Expatriate Experience and Theme of Marriage in *An American Brat*" points out:

> The paradox here, of course, is self-evident. It adds to the irony that exists throughout the novel. The Gingwallas fail to realize that the journey to the USA (the New World) will broaden Feroza's thinking and open up further avenues for her. She will become 'modern' in the truest sense of the word. By thinking for herself she will challenge traditional views, static orthodoxy and grow beyond the confines of communality and the norms of a patriarchal society. Bapsi Sidhwa shows that the journey to the USA was supposedly a learning process but instead it makes her 'too modern' for her patriarchal and seemingly liberal family. So in this novel of self-realization, the self-awareness that Feroza Ginwalla acquires ironically isolates her from her Parsi heritage. (188)

In *Brat*, there is an ironic exposure of the Parsi attitude to inter-faith marriages. The mother Zareen realizes that she is being as fundamentalist as the orthodox mullahs in Pakistan, by opposing her daughter's marriage. Still the tradition of community and desires for cultural purity prevail and such insights remain only a flash in Zareen's mind. By hinting such thinking, Sidhwa indicates the turmoil and acrimonious debate that the contentious issue of inter-community marriages causes amongst Parsis.

Mukherjee also uses irony like Sidhwa to poke fun at the way in which immigrants live in America. While talking about expatriates and immigrants Mukherjee makes a statement:

> Expatriates, on the other hand, knew all too well who and what they were; and what foul had befallen them. Like V.S. Naipaul in whom I imagined a model, I tried to explore state-of-the-art expatriation. Like Naipaul, I used a mordant and self-protective irony in describing my characters' pain. Irony promised both detachment from, and superiority over, those well-bread post-colonials much like myself, adrift in the new world, wondering if they would ever belong [...] If you wait—surrendering little bits of self every year, clutching the souvenirs of an ever—retreating past you'll never belong, anywhere.
>
> (*D* 2)

Tara's journey to India, her own native land, ironically proves to be frustrating and slowly leading her to illusion, alienation and depression and finally her tragic end. The greatest irony hidden in the story of Tara is that she survived of the racial hardships of survival in a foreign country. She becomes a victim of her tragic end in her native land. Her desire to find a place to live and security which she missed in New York end ironically in frustration. The irony with which the readers are left is that Tara, an Indian born young woman, feels greater love and security in the arms of her American husband. The irony is that the immigrant's return to her own country proves frustrating both physically and metaphysically. In *Wife* the irony is that all the premeditation that has gone into Dimple's planning of nine ways of suicide finally ends in her murder of her husband, Amit. In *Middleman* irony is used as an important device to probe the hypocrisy of the self and others, while, simultaneously functioning as a protective cover for insulating the self from hurts and pain.

Mukherjee's narrative method is best described as social satire, if one applies Northrop Frye's definition that "satire is irony which is structurally close to the comic: the comic struggle of two societies, one normal and the other absurd, is reflected in its double focus of morality and fantasy" (224). Mukherjee's diasporic Indians struggle with the cultural codes of their old and new countries indulging in behaviours that border on the absurd. In Mukherjee's short fiction, the satiric narrative contrasts interior monologues with public actions as the principal device by which characters confront their own concealed desires. By this process, Mukherjee's protagonists discover the new, at times fragile, identities that they have fashioned in the new country.

The satire of Sidhwa though sharp in *Crow Eaters* is never castigating and censorious like that of Swift and Naipaul but is a genial tolerance of the foibles of a community. It is full of paradoxes with an identity crisis caused by Parsi minority status and ideas of loyalty to the ruling authorities – the British. *Crow Eaters* purports to be a succinct and satirical account of the success of Junglewalla, the central figure, whose rise to fortune and social stardom is conveyed in good-natured humour and drollery. In *Crow Eaters* Parsi alienation from mainstream Indian culture and fascination with things western is satirized in Junglewalla's hilarious attempts at quoting English proverbs. This alienation is underlined in the Junglewalla's family horror when their son Yazdi wants to marry an Indo-Anglian girl. The Parsi fascination is stained in Faredoon's visit to Britain. *Crow Eaters*, describes itself as the hilarious saga of a Parsi family, had been attacked by a section of the Parsi community, because the novel was a controversial one. Their attack is on Sidhwa's unfair portrayal of Parsi community. Sidhwa herself acknowledges the basis for the controversy, as Paranjape in, "The Early Novels of Bapsi Sidhwa" quotes:

> Because of a deep-rooted admiration for my community- and an enormous affection for its few eccentricities – this work of satirical fiction has been a labour of love. The nature of satire being to exaggerate, the incidents in the book do not reflect at all upon the integrity of a community whose scrupulous honesty and sense of honour are renowned.
>
> (89-90)

The protagonist, Faredoon Junglewalla and all the major characters of the book are Parsees. Parsi life and their rituals like Navajot ceremony, a wedding, death rites and the aspects of Zoroastrian religion are minutely described in the novel. Yet, these factors do not make the book an indictment or even an attack on the community. Rather, the characters and their tendencies are satirized, exploiting those ethnic features that are conducive to such satire.

Sidhwa in *Crow Eaters* accurately depicts historical facts interwoven with satirical fiction and lampoon which aptly recreate the Parsi milieu. In the novel, her description of the exploits of Faredoon Junglewalla and his family is not just historical fiction but has a strong autobiographical element too as Sidhwa belonged to the third generation of Parsi settlers in North Indian cities whose family, the Bhandaras of Lahore, migrated into India in the last century. In this novel, *Crow Eaters,* Sidhwa turns autobiography into art by her clever use of irony which prevents the novel from becoming either laudatory or disparaging, an inherent danger when writer writes about her community. In it, she mode of perception is ironic. It becomes protective irony balancing personal inadequacies against the contradiction of life itself. It becomes a mode of acceptance—a type of philosophy which emphasizes on the need to exist. Faredoon asks:

> And where, If I may ask, does the sun rise?
>
> No, not in the East. For us it rises – and sets – in the Englishman's arse. They are our sovereigns! Where do you think we'd be if we did not carry favour? Next to the nawabs, rajas and princelings, we are the greatest toadies of the British Empire! These are not ugly words, mind you. They are the sweet dictates of our delicious need to exist, to live and prosper in peace. Otherwise, where would we Parsis be? Cleaning out gutters with the untouchables – a disbursed pinch of snuff sneezed from the heterogeneous nostrib of India!.
>
> (*CE* 12)

Mukherjee's novels are representative of the expatriate sensibility. Jasbir Jain in "Foreignness of Spirit: The World of Mukherjee's Novel's" comments: "This alone offers an understanding of the ambivalent present not only in the psychology of the protagonists but also that of the author; this helps us understand the satiric interludes, the ironic juxtapositions, the shifting point of view and also the final disintegration" (162). Further, there are a number of satiric interludes in *Daughter* and *Wife*. In *Daughter* it is the marriage arrangement, the bargaining over dowry and the sacrificial marriage ceremony. In *Wife* it is marriage, man-woman relationships, the little India in America, the pseudo-westernization of the Indians, the immigrant lifestyle and so on.

Allegory is another literary device used by Sidhwa to depict the trauma of partition. The child-narrator Lenny is also affected by the violence at Lahore: "The whole world is burning. The air clothes will catch fire. I start screaming: hysterically sobbing." (*ICM* 137) Her age is directed at her collection of dolls. In frenzy she acts: "I pick out a big, bloated celluloid doll. I turn it upside down and pull its legs apart. The elastic that holds them together stretches easily. I let one leg go and it snaps back, attaching itself to the brittle torso" (*ICM* 138). The destructive urge overcomes Lenny and she is not satisfied till assisted by her brother Adi. She wrenches out the legs of the doll and examines the spilled insides. This violent act by Lenny is an apt allegory on the mind-less violence of Partition.

Thus both Sidhwa and Mukherjee use caustic wit, racy style, genial comedy and shrewd observations of human behaviour to fix all the follies and foibles of the society with humour, wit and satire.

Works Cited

Appadurai, Arjun. *Modernity at Large: Cultural Dimensions of Globalization.* Minneapolis: University of Minneapolis Press, 1996.

Chandra, Subash. "Americanness of 14 Immigrants in *The Middlemen and Other Stories*". *The Fiction of Bharati Mukherjee: A Critical Symposium:* 130-136.

Crane, Ralph. J. "'A Passion for History and for Truth Telling': The Early Novels of Bapsi Sidhwa" *The Novels of Bapsi Sidhwa:* 48-60.

Didur, Jill. "Cracking the Nations: Gender, Minorities, and Agency in Bapsi Sidhwa's *Cracking India*" *ARIEL.* Vol.29. No.3 (July, 1998), 43-64.

Fowler, Roger. ed. *Essays on Style and Language.* London: Routledge and Kegan Paul, 1966.

Ghose, Amitav. *The Calcutta Chromosome*. Delhi: Ravi Dayal Publishers, 1996.

Grewal, Gurleen. "Born Again American: The Immigrant Consciousness in *Jasmine*". *Bharati Mukherjee: Critical Perspectives:* 181-196.

Iyer, Nalini. "American/Indian". Metaphors of the Self in Bharati Mukherjee's *The Holder of the World. ARIEL*. Vol.27. No.4 (October, 1996): 29-44.

Jaidka, Manju. "Hyphenated Perspectives on the Cracking of India: Bapsi Sidhwa's *Ice Candy Man*". *South Asian Review*. Vol. 25. No.2 (2004): 43-50.

Jain, Jasbir. "Foreignness of Spirit: The World of Bharati Mukherjee's Novels". *Journal of Indian Writing in English*. Vol. 13. No. 2 (July, 1985), 12-19.

________. "The Male Presence in the "Purdah" Novel". *Margins of Erasure: Purdah in the Subcontinental Novel in English*. Eds. Jasbir Jain and Amina Amin. New Delhi: Sterling Publishers, 1995, 216-230.

Kapadia, Novy. "Expatriate Experience and Theme of Marriage in *An American Brat*". *The Novels of Bapsi Sidhwa,* 187-199.

Khan, Farukh. "Women. Identity and Dis-location in *The Bride*". *The Novels of Bapsi Sidhwa:* 140-151.

Mohanty, Chandra Talpade. "Defining Genologies: Feminist Reflections on Being South Asian". *Our Feet Walk The Sky: Women of South Asian Diaspora*. Ed. Women of South Asian Collective. San Francisco: Aunt Lute Press, 1993: 351-358.

Mohanty, Satya. P. "Epilogue, Colonial Legacies, Multicultural Features: Relativism, Objectivity, and the Challenge of Otherness". *PMLA*. 110 (1995), 108-118.

Mukherjee, Bharati. *The Tiger's Daughter*. 1971. New Delhi: Penguin, 1971.

________. *Wife*. 1975. New Delhi; Sterling Publishers, 1976.

Mukherjee, Bharati. *Darkness*. Canada: Penguin, 1985.

________. *The Middle Man and Other Stories*. 1988. New Delhi: Prestige, 1989.

________. *Jasmine*. 1989. New Delhi: Viking, 1990.

________. *The Holder of the World*. 1993. New York: Fawcott Books, 1993.

________. *Leave It To Me*. 1997. New York: The Ballantine Publishing Group, 1999.

________. *Desirable Daughters*. 2002. New Delhi: Rekha Printers Pvt. Ltd., 2004.

Naipaul, V.S. *The Mystic Masseur*. London: Andre Deutsch, 1957.

Nair, Hema. "'A Puritan in a Mughal Court'. Rev. of *The Holder of the World*". *The Toronto Review of Contemporary Writing Abroad*. Vol. 12. No.2 (Winter, Spring, 1994), 104-107.

Paranjape, R. Makarand. "The Novels of Bapsi Sidhwa". *Commonwealth Fiction*. Ed. R.K. Dhawan. New Delhi: Classical Publishing

Company, 1988: 80-103, also as "The Early Novels of Bapsi Sidhwa" in *The Novels of Bapsi Sidhwa*: 88-106.

Parekh, Pushpa N. "Telling her Tale Narrative Voice and Gender Roles in Bharati Mukherjee's *Jasmine*". *Bharati Mukherjee: Critical Perspectives:* 109-126.

Rao, A.V. Krishna. "From Expatriation to Immigration: The Case of Bharati Mukherjee". *Indian Women Novelists:* Set III. Vol. 3, 88-102.

Sahai, Dipika, "Culture-Consciousness and Gender Bias in Bapsi Sidhwa's *The Pakistani Bride*: A Post Colonial Approach". *The Commonwealth Review.* Vol.15. No.1 (2004), 78-86.

Sampat, Manju."Bharati Mukherjee: Some Essential Conclusions". *Critical Practice.* Vol. Vii. No.1 (January, 2001), 71-81.

Schorer, Mark. "Technique As Discovery". *Sons and Lovers.* Ed. Gamini Salgado. London: Macmillan, 1969, 106-111.

Sidhwa, Bapsi. *The Crow Eaters.* 1980. New Delhi: Penguin, 1990.

________. *The Pakistani Bride.* 1983. New Delhi: Penguin, 1989.

________. *Ice-Candy-Man.* 1988. New Delhi: Penguin, 1989.

________. *An American Brat.* 1994. New Delhi: Penguin, 1994.

________. "Why Do I Write?" *The Novels of Bapsi Sidhwa:* 27-34.

St. Andrews. "Co-Wanderers Kogawa and Mukherjee: New Immigrant Writers". *World Literature Today.* 66.1 (1992), 56-58.

6
Summation

> Any new thing must find a new shape,
> then afterwards one can call it 'art'
>
> (Frieda Lawrence)

The aim of this study, *Bapsi Sidhwa and Bharati Mukherjee: A Comparative Study* is to see how Sidhwa and Mukherjee construct their characters' expatriate and immigrant consciousness which is ever shifting and fluid. In inscribing the female subject, they foreground an identity-in-process, aspiring towards a matured artistic vision. In their developmental process their protagonists dismember the past, the self, sexual identity, male-female relationships and most importantly sexual violence and the conflicting self of an individual. Sometimes, as is the case with Feroza, Tara and Jasmine, the dismembering is followed by re-construction and re-membering, involving change in spatial and temporal perspectives of the subject – the evolution of the female subject from a self-divided, conflictual identity to a mature woman—Zaitoon, Carol, Ayah, Feroza, Tara, Jasmine, Hannah and so on.

In their writings, the retrospective autobiographical consciousness of the first person narrator is a split consciousness as is strongly evident in Mukherjee's *Wife*. In it, the subject is shown to be divided by time, by voice, by language and by male 'gaze' (on Zaitoon, Carol, Feroza, Jasmine particularly by tribesmen in Pakistan and Americans) in a way that constantly questions subjectivity/identity. The dis-membering and re-membering in their works/subject can be seen to be working on two levels: structured by the quest motif and by the narrating I's quest for a form to tell of that chaos. Their concern is to be the one leaving, going away, not the one left, rejected.

Sidhwa's and Mukherjee's women characters are mainly expatriates, geographically as well as in mind and spirit. They share the expatriate characteristic of being ill at ease both in the native culture and in the alien one. They represent the dilemma faced by expatriates. Their novels are representative of the expatriate sensibility. Both Sidhwa and Mukherjee in their novels, present some of the more violent and grotesque aspects of cultural collisions. A close examination of their fiction reveals that the Western and Pakistani, and Western and Indian worlds give them an authentic and objective perspective with a combination of malice, charm, irony, and sympathy. They push both their protagonists to the edges of their worlds and liberate them for a new world order.

Focusing on the lives of characters migrating to North America, Sidhwa and Mukherjee produced mediations on cultural displacement on the pleasures and regrets of exile and on what Eleke Boehmer terms "the exuberant clash of immigrant cultures" (240). Their writings trace the location and exploration of the contingent, fluid forms of identity that are the inevitable concomitant of geographical displacement. They probe the processes of transculturation, the tragedies, misunderstandings and comedies that define the contact zone and the disruptive effect that migrancy can have on the individual.

The female subject of their novels is preoccupied at the roots of women's psyche with the banalities of either cultures or a desperate attempt to deny and subvert either cultural codes and is caught in the nauseating dilemma of their essential rootlessness. Thus where home becomes a matter of perspective, of displacement, adaptation and identification, they become essentially homeless. Disjunction and dislocation become both a psychic pathology and an objective reality.

Sidhwa and Mukherjee look at Pakistan and India respectively from the perspective of third world writers, expatriates and immigrants. Their countries figure in their narratives as a part of memory, as a Third World place, as a fragment of nostalgia. In their works they depict a liquid society, a society in flux. Their protagonists cross geographical and psychological boundaries in an assay to search their roots remembering / re-remembering / dis-membering their ancestral ties with their homelands—be it Pakistan or India. They show the awakening of the female heroine into political awareness and consciousness of their bodies and how they relate to the culture. Mukherjee paid importance to the condition of the Indian woman immigrants in America. In an Interview she admitted that her stories are about psychological transformation, especially among women immigrants from Asia. Her attitude to expatriation, immigration and exile has changed over years. She had first felt herself an exile or an expatriate and then she felt that America's melting-pot approach to imagination was better than Canada's stance on multi-culturalism. She is obsessed by the experience of expatriation and also by immigration. Her *Daughter* is a story of an expatriate returning to her home country, *Wife* is a novel about immigration and psychological crises, *Days and Nights* poses questions of identity, [illegible] *Darkness* is about South Asian immigrants, *Middleman* has a tone of affirmation of belonging, *Jasmine* is about an immigrant girl, *Holder* [illegible] is about an immigrant from the Puritan world, *Bride* is about Tara, an immigrant in both India and America and *Daughters* is about an immigrant called Tara.

In her novels, Sidhwa portrays people from all walks of life and from all communities. They are Hindus, Muslims, Christians, Sikhs and Parsees. The event of Partition has been depicted through the painful experiences of these ethnic groups. The theme of inter-community marriage is at the core of her novels. Her handling of the theme of inter-community marriage is relevant and contemporary. Kapadia in "The Theme of Marriage in Parsi Fiction" shows that, "marriage outside the community can be self-damaging, thereby seemingly endorsing the traditional Parsis construct of prohibition of inter-community marriages" (114). This sensitive issue arouses acrimonious debates in Parsi community. In Parsi faith, it is believed that a Parsi could be one only by birth. In mixed marriages, the children lose their right to be members of Parsi community. The Parsees have a patriarchal society. While dealing with the theme of marriage, Sidhwa maintains a balance without revolting against rigid social codes as is revealed in the case of Feroza. *Brat* succeeds in defining the American experience first as Feroza views it, than as her mother reacts to it. Like Tara, Feroza realizes that "There would be no going back for her, but she could go back at will" (*PB* 317). In a sense, like Mukherjee's Jasmine and Tara, and like so many immigrants, she is between communities, unable to go back fully and to go forward fully, until she discovers herself fully. In contrast, Zareen needs to return to her secure community in order to regain balance, thinking that all would be well "once she was with her family and friends [....] She needed desperately to be with them, to be assured she had done the right thing" (*PB* 308). Sidhwa's *Bride* challenges the patriarchal culture and values of India–Pakistani society. The novel's ideological stance is to set free the female life that has remained marginalized within its own system.

Zaitoon is a symbol not only of woman fighting oppression in Pakistan but of the human spirit struggling against all physical odds to survive and maintain its integrity. Zaitoon represents Khudi or the mental and spiritual strength of human kind, indefatigable, indomitable, and irrepressible. She represents the triumph of mind over matter and of spirit over flesh. Considering Zaitoon's triumph Makarand R.Paranjabe in "The Novels of Bapsi Sidhwa" says:

> Zaitoon's triumph can be appreciated properly only when she is compared with the prominent images of the other women in the novel: Afshan, married to Qasim, a boy often, in lieu of a loan; Miriam, matronly and domesticated, always in Purdah; the grotesque, misshapen prostitute and Shahna is the high-class courtesan; Hamidu, a woman broken by the hard life in the hills, beaten by her own son; Carol, the American wife of Farukh, sexually exploited by Major Mushtaq; the unknown tribal girl, decapitated, head floating in a dirty pond; and the crazy beggar woman of Lawrence Gardens, a plaything of her rapists. Against these images Zaitoon's choice of freedom over slavery, her rejection of the

> oppressive and brutal society, her courageous and heroic struggle for survival against impossible odds- all these are a testimony to the fighting spirit of the weak and the crushed.
>
> (100-101 also in Dhawan R.K. and Novy Kapadia 104)

In *Brat*, Sidhwa shows the complex love- hate relationship that exists between the land and migrants. Feroza's nostalgia with the passage of time is typical of an exile. She stays as a marginal being, unable to discard the old and equally unable to find solace in the chosen land. *Brat* deals with the inter-cultural theme. In this narrative the west is described as a set of values in conflict with the value system of the East. The conflict between the two cultures is discernible not only on the social plane but also on the personal level leading to a quest for identity. The Zoroastrian mode of life of Feroza clashes with the modern American way of life with its emphasis on material prosperity. The resultant friction compels her to make a moral choice in life as Feroza is caught between conservatism, which is the result of the rising wave of fundamentalism in Pakistan, and progressive liberalism for which her mother stands. She lacks interest in religion. In her, a valid and active sense of self is eroded by displacement.

Sidhwa's *Bride* provides an incisive look into the treatment of women. It is most critical towards unjust traditions that undermine the structure of community. The novel relates how Zaitoon, trained as an obedient Muslim girl, is captivated by the fantasies of her protector-father's visions of the lost mountain paradise. Married eventually to a tribal man in the north-west regions of Pakistan, she rapidly discovers that reality is harsh and her romantic dreams erroneous. She rebels at the cruel treatment, the beating, mistrust, and realizes that her imagined ideal community is no longer a region where heroic, proud and incorruptible, ruled by a code of honour that banned all injustice and evil. *Bride* reflects not only the conflict between man and man / woman / nature and the tension generated by differing cultures, but also the clash between people who simultaneously inhabit different eons.

Sidhwa in *Crow Eaters* talks about serious issues like national policies, fraud, death-dealing of mother-in-law, Parsi superstitions, faiths, marriages, rites of death, romance, birth, multi-faceted activities and forays to London.

Most Parsees in *Crow Eaters* are shown as cultural hybrids, living and sharing intimately in the cultural life, traditions, languages, moral codes and political loyalties of two distinct peoples, which never completely inter-penetrated and fused. In *Crow Eaters* Freddy's fame and wealth are shown to have dubious roots. The maintenance of identity, in spite of being a microscopic minority, is shown as mere public relations, bordering on sycophancy. Sycophancy is shown as a need to exist.

Crow Eaters describes the social mobility of a Parsi family. The description of Faredoon's exploits has a strong autobiographical element. Sidhwa belongs to a pioneering family, the Bhandaras of Parsi settlers in north Indian cities. The use of irony, caricature or buffoonery prevents the novel from becoming either excessively laudatory or too disparaging. Sidhwa's mode of perception is ironic. Faredoon's acts of charity are not virtuous. He has developed a philanthropic image to increase his business contacts and appear selfless. He has amassed capital by the dubious practice of setting his shop on fire, after hiding his goods in a hired godown, to claim insurance money. He has prospered in Lahore because of sycophancy towards the British officials in the guise of public relations. In all such incidents, Sidhwa's tone is not moralistic but ironic. The irony in the novel balances personal inadequacies against the contradictions of life itself.

Sidhwa's *Crow Eaters* and *Bride* are remarkably different from each other, in both subject and treatment. *Crow Eaters* certainly belongs to the comic mode. It deals with the lives and fortunes of the Junglewallas, a Parsi family in British India. Though it has serious touches here and there, farce and satire pervade the whole work. The novel derives its humour from a blend of fantasy, scatology, physical and verbal incongruity, and caricature.

Bride, on the other hand, is serious, almost tragic, though it has its lighter moments. The novel shows the struggle of an orphaned girl for survival in the brutal society in the mountains of Pakistan. Both novels cover wide sweeps of time and place. It portrays accurately and astutely the societies that they are set in. *Crow Eaters* is as much of Parsi life and manners as it is about individuals. The second is about the inter-action of two cultures, the mountain tribe and the urban plain.

Crow Eaters portrays the potential destroyer of community that is Partition. The inhabitants of this cozy Parsi world, Anglicized to a greater degree than most of their neighbours, fear that Independence and the subsequent departure of the British might leave them in an alien setting. The instinct for community remains so strong. They appreciate its fluidity and try to stabilize it once again. At the end, one of the characters in *Crow Eaters* asks: "But where will we go? What will happen to us?" Faredoon replies: "We will stay where we are [...] let Hindus, Muslims, Sikhs, or whoever, rule. What does it matter? The sun will continue to rise – and the Sun continues to set – in their asses [...] !" (*CE* 282)

Zaitoon and Carol in *Bride*, Feroza in *Brat*, Dimple in *Wife*, Jasmine in *Jasmine*, Hannah and Bhagmati in *Holder* recurrently defy estrangement in the society they live in and get the answer in rejecting cultural stereotypes. They develop a life of their own outside the home. The more they learn about themselves, the more individualistic they become. Like Hannah all are self-possessed, intelligent and desirable as far as their sense of assimilation is concerned. Zaitoon and Hannah are dissimilar to all the rest. They remain inadaptable to the new environment. Jasmine is initially unable to adopt the American culture but soon adjusts herself to the new way of life. Dimple is perturbed and her migration to USA proves disastrous to her hyper-sensitive nature. Zaitoon and Hannah prove to be a pure product of time and place. Sidhwa's *Candy-Man* deals with the theme of Pakistan by a non–partition writer, a Parsi, who does not belong to either of the two communities which perpetrated mayhem on each other.

Subash Chandra in "Bapsi Sidhwa's *Ice-Candy-Man:* A Feminist Perspective" observes "Therefore it is more likely to be a more neutral and objective account of the traumatic event of partition which caused divisiveness, disharmony, mutual suspicion, hardening and then turning into hostility of feelings of friendliness and good-neighbourliness and the eventual holocaust" (118).

The theme of separation caused by Partition is also revealed in a simple but vividly poignant observation by Lenny. During her romps at the Queen's garden she notices the absence of the cosmopolitan gathering:

> The garden scene has depressingly altered. Muslim families who added colour when scattered among Hindus and Sikhs now monopolize the garden, depriving it of colour. The absence of the brown skin that showed through the fine veils of Hindu and Sikh women and beneath the dhoties and shorts of the men, has changed the complexion of the queenless garden.
>
> (*ICM* 236)

The uprootedness of Partition is revealed as Lenny drifts through the Queen's garden searching in vain for familiar faces and acquaintances. Through the wondering eyes of the precocious Lenny, the novelist shows the disruption of a settled order and traumatic separation of friends, the legacy of Partition. Freddie has an unflinching loyalty to the British to ensure him social prestige and security. His loyalty to the British has no religious character. It merely acts as a means of self-promotion. His identification with the wiser is strong. After settling down in Lahore, he wears his finest clothes and visits the Government House to sign his name in the Visitors' Book. The sitting of Freddie's loyalty is a survival strategy which the Parsi community adopted since they were exiled 1,300 years ago. For example, when Partition becomes imminent, Freddie assures his Parsi community that they could stay on. Sidhwa by providing insights about the Parsi faith in antiquity, their culture and tolerance of other beliefs, creates a better understanding about her community. Sidhwa fulfils the concept of the essential role of the writer as a preserver of the collective tradition, a folk historian and myth maker.

Sidhwa in her novels portrays the Purdah society. In *Bride* she portrays a purdah–dominated Muslim society. In *Crow Eaters* and *Candy-Man* she focuses on her own Parsi milieu.

In fact, she reveals how the purdah system embraces even those outside its purview. Niaz Zaman in "Images of Purdah in Bapsi Sidhwa's Novels" says: "Thus what she succeeds in portraying is a system that penetrates and permeates all layers of society and all religions so that relationship between the sexes as well as the attitude of women towards themselves is dominated by purdah and its mores" (156). Sidhwa's *Bride*, as a social document, gives a detailed glimpse into a society where the segregation of the sexes gives rise to spatial divisions. On its positive side, purdah gives rise to a certain type of mystery, romance and excitement.

Sidhwa uses themes such as the Partition crisis, expatriate experience, the Parsi milieu, and social idiosyncrasies of the small Parsi community, the theme of marriage, women's problems, patterns of migration, the complexities of language and art of story telling. In Sidhwa's novels, societies collapse due to colonialism. Pakistan's perspective of partition is evident in the *Candy-Man,* tribal customs, their treatment of women, and the concept of honour in contrast with the values of people of the plain as shown in *Bride*, and the fundamentalist ethos as depicted in *Brat*.

In Sidhwa's work, borders act as important agents for the actions of her texts. These borders are not only the physical borders between countries and neighbourhoods, but also the invisible borders placed between religious groups, between classes, between stages of development, and between women and men. These physical and psychic borders often represent limitations placed on the characters in their struggle for entry into the dominant social structure. They are limits that insure the marginalized stay marginalized, and sometimes they are limits.

Mukherjee's novels show the change in her work from a primary concern with the Indian expatriates' experience in the new society to a situation where the expatriate becomes an immigrant. The expatriate is slowly assimilated into the host society—at all levels, psychological, sociological and linguistic. Her protagonists break the umbilical cord with the homeland. In *Daughter*, Mukherjee sets about exposing how it feels for a fifteen-year-old girl to leave a sheltered home hedged by class privilege and wealth, come back to it grown to young womanhood—to come home after breaking all the social taboos by marrying a foreigner—and see whether she can find her place at home again. Mukherjee's *Wife* takes up a more complex dimension on the theme of immigrant experience. It centres round the life of a middle class Bengali woman who migrates from Calcutta to New York. In *Wife* Mukherjee dramatizes the opposition between two cultures, the despair of prejudice and the pre-consciousness of immigrant status; but the psychological fragmentation, alienation, and insanity that her protagonists experience are viewed not only in terms of culture shock but also as an "intense experience of female biological, sexual and cultural castration, and a doomed search for potency" (Chestler 31).

In *Daughter,* Mukherjee presents the decay of Calcutta and the decadent life of its upper class. The city seems to be coming apart at it seems because of a number of factors: endemic violence, chronic political unrest, economic stagnation and poverty, disease, over population and class conflicts.

Mukherjee's *Daughter* and *Wife* concentrate on the cultural conflict of the East and West. These novels are an imaginative rendering of Mukherjee's personal experience in going west and the after effects of the culture—shock felt by her personally. Tara reacts mentally and physically to the changed scenario of riot-torn Calcutta on returning to the city of her birth and Dimple takes it as a nightmarish experience. Both Tara and Dimple are projected as middle women between two cultures and both are shown as experiencing culture shock in a diametrically opposed situations. Their disillusionment with India and America is not sudden but gradual. They take drastic steps at the end to get away from the cultural maladjustment that enmeshes them.

Mukherjee in *Jasmine* and *Daughter* presents a dual cultural shock as Jasmine and Tara leave their respective countries in search of their dreams. This migration or cultural transplant leads to a crisis of identity and a final reconciliation to the choice. Jasmine's every moment is a calculated one to assimilate America and its experience in Americanization. Her flight to Iowa and her renaming as Jane is indicative of a slow but steady immersion into the mainstream American culture. She willingly embraces the company of an American without—marriage and also is carrying his child in her womb. Unlike Zaitoon, Jasmine is an adaptor and a survivor with a sheer will to exist. In it, she resembles Mukherjee and her life in Canada, as Mukherjee admits in an interview with Michael Connell:

> I have been murdered and reborn at least three times, the very correct young woman I was trained to be, and was very happy being, is very difficult from the politicized, shrill, civil rights activist I was in Canada, and from the urgent writer that I have become in the last few years in the United States.
>
> (18)

This is strikingly similar of what Jasmine says: "There are no harmless, compassionate ways to remake oneself. We murder who we were so we can rebirth ourselves – in the images of dreams" (*J* 29). Nagendra Kumar in *The Fiction of Bharati Mukherjee: A Cultural Perspective* is of the view that in *Jasmine* Mukherjee "tries to unravel the complicated layers of cross–cultural reality through a series of adventures which the heroine undertakes during her odyssey from Punjab to California via Florida, New York and Iowa. Her struggle symbolises the restless quest of a rootless person piqued by a depressing sense of isolation all around" (107). From Jyoti to Jasmine, Kali to Jazzy and Jase to Jane is a long and arduous journey "hustle through time tunnels" (*J* 240), surviving the worst in life. From the special and unique nature of her evolving 'Jasmine' self, Jane becomes, as her name implies, a nonentity, been a conscienceless 'gold digger' in Karin's words (*J* 195). From the Sati goodess 'Jyoti (*J* 176) to the Kali–Jasmine to "adventurous Jase" (*J* 186) to "Plain Jane" (*J* 26) has been an eventful and uneven odyssey. The protagonist's name changes as well as her shifts in places of residence become metaphors for an immigrant woman's process of uprooting and rerooting.

Tara, Zaitoon and Jasmine are rebels. They protest against vigorous culture. They protest against conservative attitude towards women who are treated like non–entities. They rebuke the male-dominating society which discourages self-reliance in women. Their grudge is against the artificially maintained ghetto-like life which bars the women from identifying themselves. Zaitoon and Jasmine are love goddesses and life-forces. Their morality is their own way of looking at life. They are the path finders and pierce their way through the dense jungle of problems. Every movement adds to their self-confidence and their experience guide their future course of action.

Mukherjee's novels deal with nostalgia for a lost home, disillusionment of 'expatriation', fragmentation of the self, exuberance of immigration, assimilation, cultural translation and negotiation. Her *Daughters* marks a new trend in her writings. In her earlier novels, leaving one's own native country for an alien land meant liberating oneself from the clutches of a convention-bound society. In the same manner, clinging on to one's own native culture while living in an alien land was presented as something to be shunned and total assimilation into the host culture was hailed. But, in *Daughters* Mukherjee acknowledges the alternate ways to belong. In addition to that, Mukherjee focuses on cultural hybridity, simultaneity and the third space of enunciation which are markers of the post-colonial condition of existence.

In *Daughters*, Mukherjee interrogates cultural essentialism and celebrates cultural hybridity. She also challenges the stereotypical notions of national identity. Tara is a cultural hybrid, who is at home in both the cultures. She has 'affiliation' with the host culture but that does not in any way hinder her 'filation' with her homeland and native culture. Padma is an Indo-American who believes in hyphenation. She is an Indian cultural ambassador in the United States. Parvati is a western educated Indian woman of the conventional mould. She is contended with her role as the woman of the household. These are the three distinct and different ways to belong in the new world.

Holder has the theme of sexual awakening through another lover. This theme can be seen in *Wife,* "The Lady from

Lucknow" and in "A Wife's Story". It is conveyed in *Holder* through Hannah Easton's relationship with the Raja of Devghat. *Holder* criticizes canonical American literature's white centredness, by forcing the recognition of the immigrant experience and the multicultural aspects to American history. Hannah, who returns to America as Hester, brings with her Black Pearl, the daughter of Hannah and Jadav Singh. Black Pearl is Indo-American; her very existence signifies the merging of cultures. Hawthorne's Pearl is white, and in creating Black Pearl, *Holder* inserts immigrant culture and history into the American canon. In it, Mukherjee is claiming a place within the canon of American literature for immigrant writers like herself. It is in this sense that she sees herself as an American writer; by calling herself American. She is not naively adopting an alien identity but is refusing a hyphenated existence as an Indo-American writer.

Pandit in "Woman as Protagonist: Self in Margaret Lawrence's *The Diviners* and Bharati Mukherjee's *The Tiger's Daughter*" says: "Bharati Mukherjee projects the self in *The Tiger's Daughter* as someone who encounters a double culture shock – the first on going abroad to the USA for higher education and the second on return to India as the bride of a Canadian writer" (34).

Beginning with her first novel, *Daughter* to her latest *Daughters*, it becomes obvious to her readers that Mukherjee's fiction has traversed a full one hundred and eighty degrees as it has moved gradually from the 'Aloofness of Expatriation', to the 'Exuberance of Immigration'.

Mukherjee repeatedly differentiates between the expatriate and the immigrant. The former, she believes, are still rooted in their pasts and maintain their ethnicity, while the latter look to the present and the future and are open to being influenced by their host country. On the road to becoming 'immigrants', she feels her protagonists have to try out new identities and this often necessitates the death of their former selves. This is her artistic way of showing the psychic damage that often takes place as immigrants change and adapt. In her earlier novels, especially in *Jasmine* this change was brought about through violence since her immigrant characters often suffer dislocation as they grab at the change to reinvent themselves in the new world. This phenomenon is connected to the diaspora, and the transplanting of a people from one nation to another. However, in *Daughters*, this diasporic violence is absent as by now the concept of the immigrant protagonist has already matured, and Mukherjee no longer finds it necessary to portray the angst of the transplanted individual. There is more restraint, and the style too is more leisurely and controlled.

Some ethnic and gender stereotyping remain in Mukherjee's characterization. Mukherjee's sympathetic Indians are largely female. Her Indian men are unromantic, overwhelmingly acquisitive, and slightly ridiculous. Their rejection by their romantic, sensual, and sensitive women in Mukherjee's short fiction emphasizes the crumbling masculine power structure in the South Asian immigrant community in the United States. However, Mukherjee's social critique remains politically oblique in that her satire bypasses the feminist emphasis on women's anger.

The immigrants who seek to refashion themselves materialistically and romantically are predominantly educated professionals. Among the male characters, the physicians Vinny Menezies ("Angela"). Manny Patel ("Nostalgia"), Ashoke Mehta ("The Tenant"), the physicist Rabindra Chatterjee ("The Tenant"), and the engineer Bhowmic ("A Father") typify Mukherjee's immigrant Indian men in that the orderliness, success, and prosperity of their public lives contrast sharply with the self-division, deprivation and turmoil of their emotional lives.

Sidhwa's novels reveal that the female characters pulsate with a will and life of their own. They are unselfconscious of the biological essentialism of their sex. They cut loose the constraints imposed by the gender which is a social construct—a biased, motivated and calculated orchestration of the aggressive patriarchal postulates.

Mukherjee's presentations of her situations and people are characteristically American. She places her immigrant characters in real American settings. Her characters are real, modern, and life-like. They are typical representatives of men and women, particularly of the Third World countries who cherish the dream of emigrating to America. Their situations and the difficulties they face are realistically portrayed.

Mukherjee's protagonists have to go through deep suffering in order to realize their ambitions and to experience a sense of liberation. They have to shed all their inherited racial, religious and cultural heritages. Consequently, new relationships between characters of the opposite sex from different countries are forged.

In *Middleman,* Panna feels emotional stability in the company of her Hungarian friend Imre or before her Chinese friend, Charity's uncle (who too was shot at during the Wuchang Uprising). These relationships give Panna confidence and a new knowledge: "If I hadn't left home, I'd never have heard of the Wuchang Uprising. I've broadened my horizons." "(A Wife's Story," 31) The North Italian-American girl, Renata, falls in love with Ro from Afghanistan. She makes up her mind to teach him how to walk like an American, how to dress like Brent but better, how to fill up a room as Dad does instead of melting and blending but sticking out in the Afghan way.

The American Griff falls in love with a sales-lady Maura but his Philippine wife Blanquita would not like to lose her husband to the new lady with her silvery blonde hair. New relationships may perhaps continue alongside old ones, though she would not also allow Griff to be jealous of her professional contacts ("Fighting for the Rebound").

Maya Sanyal, an elitist Bengali from India, marries an American John Hadwen, divorces him after two years, and looks forward to developing a new friendship, this time with an Indian American settled at Hartford, Ashoke Mehta.

Although Maya would not disclose her various abortive relationships she had had, yet Mehta knows that like himself she was not free from problems. The story of her marriage outside the Brahminic caste, the quick divorce, the chequered career of sleeping with married men and many men—these details do not hinder her welcome to Hartford extended by Mehta ("The Tenant").

Jasmine the Trinidad-born Indian immigrant makes love to Bill Moffitt, a married biology teacher, when his wife Lara is away on a two-week tour for performance rehearsals ("Jasmine").

Roashan flees from persecution at home in the trouble-torn Kabul in Afghanistan to New Jersey where he will get an opportunity to pursue higher studies at NJIT and become an electrical engineer ("Orbiting," 64).

Panna leaves Ahmedabad for the States on a scholarship for two years to do her Ph.D. in Education but it is only a pretext for escaping from her dominating mother-in-law and an indifferent husband. She is scared to think of Indian husbands who turn into wife-beaters or of households which bum young brides for not getting adequate dowry ("A Wife's Story"). Maya Sanyal ("The Tenant") wants to stay independently in America and become an emancipated woman. She wants to experience absolute freedom in her free associations with men.

Jasmine is 'a girl with ambitions.' She believes that she could do much better than many other Trinidad girls in the States. She is fascinated by Ann Arbor which has a famous university. Obviously, she too has an eye on opportunities for advancement. Her emigration to America is motivated by her higher goal which she wishes to fulfill both physically and intellectually. She dreams of becoming the "flower" of Ann Arbor rather than of Trinidad. Her sexual adventure with her American host Bill Moffitt gives her a hope of getting rooted in the American soil.

Likewise, both Sidhwa and Mukherjee uniformly show how the ethnic minorities try to retain their cultural moorings and identity even while assimilating modern ideas. The multiple codes of their novels expose both the paradoxical energy and emptiness of American society as well as the antithetical combination of flexibility and adherence to tradition displayed by immigrants to the United States.

Sidhwa and Mukherjee seek to contribute through their novels to the process of change that has started all over the world. They radically reconstruct the social thought. They depict the determined women for whom the traditional role is inadequate. Their women wish to affirm their independence and autonomy. They are perfectly capable of assuming new roles and responsibilities. They wish to build a world which is free of dominance and hierarchy, a world that rests on the principles of justice and equality and is truly human.

Sidhwa and Mukherjee chartered a path for their own concerns for acquiring space and place for their women protagonists in life and society. They attempt to trace the development of the protagonists trying to find a place of their own in the world at large either through rebellion or acceptance of realities.

Sidhwa and Mukherjee by portraying Zaitoon, Feroza, Jasmine, Tara, and Hannah Easton suggest, by subjecting them to multiple codes of society and geographical locales, that if one has to assimilate oneself to the mainstream culture of the adopted land, one should forget one's past. But Zaitoon and Tara are not able to forget their past. They share similar feelings of what is true to Jasmine as Puspha N. Parekh observes in "Telling Her Tale: Narrative Voice and Gender Roles in Mukherjee's *Jasmine*". "Fear, anger, pain, bitterness, confusion, silence, irony, humour, as well as pathos underline her observations as she discovers for herself the undefined median between the presentation of the old world and the assimilation into the new one" (117). Mukherjee admits:

> It was not right to describe the American experience as one of the melting pot but a more appropriate word would be 'fusion' because immigrants in America did not melt into or were forged into something like their white counterpart but immigration was a two-way process and both the whites and immigrants were growing into a third thing by this interchange and experience.
>
> (*The Hindustan Times* 3)

Feroza and Jasmine move from place to place with a mixture of frustrations, anger and humour. Sidhwa and Mukherjee humorously delineate their characters adapting to an alien culture and the stress that accrues when colliding cultures clash. As Adrienne Rich says, "to assimilate means to give up not only your history but your body" (142). Sidhwa's Feroza, Carol, and Mukherjee's Jasmine, Tara and Hannah are ready to give up both. They make much of the fact that Third world immigrants are able to love and compress in one lifetime, the development of centuries. Hurtling through time, they move from a feudal village to the global metropolis.

Sidhwa's and Mukherjee's women made progress in their path to attain self-realization. Zaitoon runs away from the hills in search of a bridge to start anew in *Bride;* Feroza, though initially fearful of the American way of life, later chooses David, an American-Jew to liberate herself from the closed Parsi community way of life; Carol, an American in Pakistan seeks sexual congress with Mushtaq to realize her inner longing in *Bride;* Tara of *Daughter* marries an American but on returning to India she feels alienated among the filth of Calcutta; Dimple in *Wife* blunders her way toward liberations by having an affair with a white American man but ends up in madness and stabbing her husband to death; in *Jasmine,* Jasmine deserts her common-law husband and opts for freedom and an open relationship with another white American man; in *Holder* Beigh Master and Hannah seek superficial relationships to a meaningful encounter with Indian men that allow them to be fully themselves and in *Tree Bride* and *Daughters* Tara seeks a new life by having an affair with Andy. Such is the common and comparable themes operate in Sidhwa's and Mukherjee's novels with an intention to portray / effect changes that take place among south Asian women in the old/new world.

In Sidhwa's *Crow Eaters* like that of Mukherjee's *Jasmine* and *Wife* one can find that the interaction of two cultures produces tension. In *Crow Eaters* Putli, the wife of Freddy, resists changes. In fact, "what revolted Putli most was the demand that she, a dutiful and God-fearing wife, must walk a step ahead of her husband. She considered this hypocritical and pretentious, and most barbarous" (*CE* 188). Putli adapts to new fangled customs. When she and her husband are invited to formal tea parties on the gracious lawns of the Government House, it is an opportunity for advancing contacts and consolidating friendship for Freddy. The Parsee milieu of Putli have a different value system. Sidhwa writes: "Deep-rooted in the tradition of wife walking three paces behind her husband, their deportment was as painful to Putli as being marched naked in public" (*CE* 188).

Crow Eaters like most of Mukherjee's later fiction like *Daughters, Tree Bride* and *Holder* shows the gradual assimilation of British value systems in the Parsee milieu like that of Banerjee's from Bengal into America who try to assimilate American cultural values and customs. Even *Crow Eaters* breaks the age-old conventions. While Putli prefers to walk behind her husband, her daughter Yasmin after marriage ignores such notions as old fashioned and vehemently protests at the servile attitude of woman saying: "Anyway it's stupid to walk behind your husband like an animal on a leash – Oh Molher! Hasn't Papa been able to modernize you yet? (*CE* 190-91).

Both Sidhwa and Mukherjee portray the changing generations in their societies. In *Crow Eaters* Billy's scrap iron deal becomes increasingly westernized like that of Tara's husband, Bish's business in Silicon valley. Sidhwa writes:

> They made friends with modern couples equally determined to break with tradition. It amounted to no more than a fanatical faith in the way of English society in India, and a disciple's knack at initiation. They were not of the masses, their young crowd. If their wealth did not set them apart, their ability to converse in English certainly did. They were utterly ashamed of traditional habits and considered British customs, however superficially observed, however trivial and exemplary.
> (*CE* 245)

In Sidhwa's novel *Crow Eaters* Behram Junglewalla known as Billy also compromises with the value systems and social codes of his community. Billy and his wife Tanya belong to the generation of Parsees who have assimilated British value systems in the Parsi milieu. They become increasingly westernized. Billy and Tanya represent the urbanized, fashionably cosmopolitan section of Parsees who experience the trappings of ostensibly liberal Western culture. Similarly Jasmine, Dimple, and Tara assert the autonomy of their self through violence. They find vision in their life by voicing the voiceless. In *Jasmine*, Mukherjee does not probe into the inner consciousness of Jasmine but makes the novel examine the American life from immigrant's point of view leaving aside the American experience of the immigrants.

Asian males in Sidhwa's and Mukherjee's view tend to be too preoccupied with economic transformation. Thus, they are less interesting as fictional subjects. Their women run the whole gamut of emotions in their bid to adjust and immerse themselves in to a new world.

As Sidhwa and Mukherjee have been compared to so many writers, their works may be compared to any expatriate, immigrant, third world writers of considerable repute. In Tamil literature, both they can be compared to women writers like Lakshmi, Sivasankari, and Vasanthi as these writers raise questions related to women and their position in and outside their societies with the changing cultural, societal, religious, and economic perspectives.

Works Cited

Blaise, Clark and Bharati Mukherjee. *Days and Nights in Calcutta*. 1977. USA: First Hungry Mind Press Printing, 1995.

Chandra, Subash. "Bapsi Sidhwa's *Ice-Candy-Man*: A Feminist Perspective." *The Commonwealth Review*. Vol. V. No.1 (1994-95), 118-126.

Chestler, Phyllis. *Women and Madness*. New York: Avon, 1977.

Connell, Michael, Jessia Grearson and Tom Grimes. "An Interview with Bharati Mukherjee". *Iowa Review*. 20. No.3 (Spring, 1990), 7-32.

Kapadia, Novy. ed. "The Theme of Marriage in Parsi Fiction". *Parsi Fiction*. Vol. 1, 100-120.

_______. *Parsi Fiction*. Vol. 2. New Delhi: Prestige Books, 2001.

Kumar, Nagendra. *The Fiction of Bharati Mukherjee: A Cultural Perspective*. New Delhi: Atlantic Publishers, 2001.

Mukherjee, Bharati. *The Tiger's Daughter*. 1971. New Delhi: Penguin, 1971.

_______. *Wife*. 1975. New Delhi; Sterling Publishers, 1976.

_______. *Darkness*. Canada: Penguin, 1985.

_______. *The Middle Man and Other Stories*. 1988. New Delhi: Prestige, 1989.

_______. *Jasmine*. 1989. New Delhi: Viking, 1990.

________. *The Hindustan Times*. 9. Feb., 1990, 3.

________. *The Holder of the World*. 1993. New York: Fawcott Books, 1993.

________. *Desirable Daughters*. 2002. New Delhi: Rekha Printers Pvt. Ltd., 2004.

Pandit, M.L. "Woman as Protagonist: Self in Margaret Lawrence's *The Diviners* and Bharati Mukherjee's *The Tiger's Daughter*". *New Commonwealth Writing: A Critical Response*. New Delhi: Prestige Books, 1996, 31-34.

Paranjape, R. Makarand. "The Novels of Bapsi Sidhwa". *Commonwealth Fiction*: 80-103, also as "The Early Novels of Bapsi Sidhwa" in *The Novels of Bapsi Sidhwa:* 88-106.

Parekh, Pushpa N. "Telling her Tale Narrative Voice and Gender Roles in Bharati Mukherjee's *Jasmine*". *Bharati Mukherjee: Critical Perspectives:* 109-126.

Rich, Adrienne. "Resisting Amnesia: History and Personal life". *Blood, Bread and Poetry*. New York: W.W. Norton, 1986, 136-155.

Sidhwa, Bapsi. *The Crow Eaters*. 1980. New Delhi: Penguine, 1990.

________. *The Pakistani Bride*. 1983. New Delhi: Penguin, 1989.

________. *Ice-Candy-Man*. 1988. New Delhi: Penguin, 1989.

________. *An American Brat*. 1994. New Delhi: Penguin, 1994.

Bibliography

Primary Sources

Mukherjee, Bharati. *The Tiger's Daughter*. 1971. New Delhi: Penguin, 1971.

_______. *Wife*. 1975. New Delhi; Sterling Publishers, 1976.

_______. *The Middle Man and Other Stories*. 1988. New Delhi: Prestige, 1989.

_______. *Jasmine*. 1989. New Delhi: Viking, 1990.

_______. *The Holder of the World*. 1993. New York: Fawcott Books, 1993.

_______. *Leave It To Me*. 1997. New York: The Ballantine Publishing Group, 1999.

_______. *Desirable Daughters*. 2002. New Delhi: Rekha Printers Pvt. Ltd., 2004.

_______. *The Tree Bride*. 2004. New York: Hyberian Books, 2004.

Sidhwa, Bapsi. *The Crow Eaters*. 1980. New Delhi: Penguin, 1990.

_______. *The Pakistani Bride*. 1983. New Delhi: Penguin, 1989.

_______. *Ice-Candy-Man*. 1988. New Delhi: Penguin, 1989.

_______. *An American Brat*. 1994. New Delhi: Penguin, 1994.

Secondary Sources

Adhikari, Madhumalati, "An Angle of Seeing Gender Politics: Margaret Atwood's *The Handmaid's Tale*, Alice Walker's *The Color Purple* and Bapsi Sidhwa's *An American Brat*". *The Indo-American Review*. No.7 (1999), 9-24.

Afzal-Khan, Fawiza. "Women's in History". *International Literature in English: Essays on Major Writers*. Ed. Robert L. Ross. New York: Garland Publishing, 1991, 272-281.

_______. "Indian Sub-Continent: Pakistani Writing in English: 1947 to the present: A Survey. *Wasafri*. No.21 (September, 1995), 58-61.

Agarwal, Beena. "Cross-Cultural Dilemma in Bharati Mukherjee's *Desirable Daughters*". *New Perspectives on Indian English Writing.* Ed. Malti Agarwal. New Delhi: Atlantic Publishers, 2007, 217-280.

Agarwal, Malti. ed. *New Perspectives on Indian English Writing.* New Delhi: Atlantic Publishers, 2007

Agarwal, Ramlal. "Rev. of *Desirable Daughters*" *World Literature Today.* Vol.77. No. 3-4 (Oct-Dec., 2003), 86-87.

Alam, Fakrul. *Bharati Mukherjee.* New York: Twayne Publishers, 1996.

________. "Migration and Settlement in North America in Bharati Mukherjee's Fiction". *Asian–American Writing.* Vol. 2. New Delhi, Prestige Books, 2000, 61-82.

Allen, Diane. S. "Reading the Body Politic in Bapsi Sidhwa's Novels: *The Crow Eaters, Ice-Candy Man* and *An American Brat*". *South Asian Review.* Vol. 18. No. 15 (December, 1994), 69-80.

Anand, Usha. "*Jasmine*: A Study". *Women in Indo-Anglian Fiction: Tradition and Modernity.* Ed. Naresh Jain. New Delhi: Manohar Publishers and Distributors, 1988, 214-218.

Appadurai, Arjun. *Modernity at Large: Cultural Dimensions of Globalization.* Minneapolis: University of Minneapolis Press, 1996.

Ashcroft B. ed. *The Empire Writes Back: Theory and Practice in Post-Colonial Literatures.* London and New York: Routledge, 1989.

Asnani, Shyam M. "Identity Crisis in *The Nowhere Man* and *Wife*". *Quest for Identity in Indian English Writing.* Ed. R.S.Pathak. New Delhi: Bahri Publications, 1992: 38-47.

Asnani, Shyam M. and Rajpal, Deepika. "Identity Crisis in *The Nowhere Man* and *Wife*". *Language Forum.* 1-2 (January–December, 1992), 38-47.

Bapsi Sidhwa's Home Page. 2000-2002. 20 Feb. 2004. <http://members.aol. com/ht a/bsidhwa/?mtbrand=Aol.vs.>

Barat, Urbashi. "Expatriate Indian or Immigrant American? A Study of 'A Father' and 'A Wife's Story'. *The Fiction of Bharati Mukherjee: A Critical Symposium.* Ed. R.K. Dhawan. New Delhi:Prestige Books, 1996. 116-124.

Barche, G D. "Feroza in Bapsi Sidhwa's *An American Brat* and Olivia in Jhabvala's *Heat and Dust*: A Psychological Study". *Parsi Fiction.* Vol. 2. Ed. Novy Kapadia. New Delhi: Prestige Books, 2001, 46-55.

Bassnett, Susan. *Comparative Literature: A Critical Introduction.* Oxford: Blackwell Publishers Ltd., 1993.

Bhabha, Homi. *The Location of Culture.* London: Routledge, 1994.

Bhargava, Raju. ed. *Indian Writing in English: The Last Decade.* New Delhi: Rawat Publications, 2002.

Bharucha, E. Nilufer. "Reflections in Broken Mirrors: Diverse Diasporas in Recent Parsi Fiction". *Wasafiri.* No. 21 (September, 1995), 32-35.

________. Vilas Sarang. eds. *Indian English Fiction 1980-90: An Assessment*. Delhi. B.R. Publishing Corporation, 1994

________. Vrinda Nabar. eds. *Mapping Cultural Spaces: Postcolonial Indian Literature in English*. New Delhi: Vision Books Pvt. Ltd., 1998.

Bharvani, Shakuntala. "*Jasmine*: An Immigrant's Experience". *Indian Women Novelists*. Set I. Vol.V. Ed. R.K. Dhawan. New Delhi: Prestige Books, 1991, 197-201.

________. "Bharati Mukherjee's *The Holder of the World*". *Indian Women Novelists*. Set III. Vol. 3. Ed. R.K. Dhawan. New Delhi: Prestige Books, 1995, 190-192.

Bhatt, Indira. "Bharati Mukherjee's *Jasmine*: An Immigrant's Attempt at Assimilation". *Indian Women Novelists*. Set III. Vol.3. Ed. R.K. Dhawan. New Delhi: Prestige Books, 1995, 184-189.

Bhattacharya, Bhabani. *Music for Mohini*. Delhi: Orient Paperbacks, 1984.

Blaise, Clark and Bharati Mukherjee. *Days and Nights in Calcutta*. 1977. USA: First Hungry Mind Press Printing, 1995.

Boehmer, Elleke. *Colonial and Postcolonial Literature: Migrant Metaphors*. Oxford: Oxford University Press, 1995.

Bose, Brinda. "A Question of Identity: Where Gender, Race and America Meet in Bharati Mukherjee". *Bharati Mukherjee: Critical Perspectives*. Ed. Emmanuel S Nelson. New York & London: Garland Publishing, 1993: 47-63.

Bromley, Roger. *Narratives for a New Belonging: Diasporic Cultural Fictions*. Edinburgh: Edinburgh UP, 2000.

Budholia, O.P. "Dialectis of Culture / Acculturation in Bharati Mukherjee's *Jasmine* and Anita Desai's *Journey to Ithaca*." *The Quest*. Vol.20. No. 1 (June, 2006), 20-29.

Carb. B. Alison. An Interview with Bharati Mukherjee under the title "Bharati Mukherjee: The Immigrant Sensibility". *Span*. Vol.xxxi. No. 6 (June, 1990), 35.

Carchidi, Victoria. "Orbiting: Bharati Mukherjee's Kaleidoscopic Vision". *MELUS*. 20.4 (Winter, 1995), 91-101.

Carter-Sanborn, Kristin. "We Murder Who We Were: *Jasmine* and the Violence of Identity". *American Literature*. Vol.66. No.3 (September, 1994), 573-593.

Celly, Anu. "Stuck in Dead Space: The Sense and Sensibility of the Indian American in Bharati Mukherjee's Short Stories". *The Indo-American Review*. Vol.12, 153-167.

Chandra, Subash. "Bapsi Sidhwa's *Ice-Candy-Man*: A Feminist Perspective." *The Commonwealth Review*. Vol. V. No.1 (1994-95), 118-126.

________. "Americanness of 14 Immigrants in *The Middlemen and Other Stories*". *The Fiction of Bharati Mukherjee: A Critical Symposium*. Ed. R.K. Dhawan. New Delhi: Prestige Books, 1996, 130-136.

Chestler, Phyllis. *Women and Madness*. New York: Avon, 1977.

Chowdhury, Enakshi. "Images of Woman in Bharati Mukherjee's Novels". *Literary Voice*. No.2 (Oct., 1995), 81-87.

Chowdhury, Neel. "'Not for the Mature Reader'. Rev. of *The Holder of the World*". *The Book Review*. Vol.18. No.2&3 (Feb-Mar., 1994), 67-69.

Chua, C.L. "Passage from India: Migrating to America in the Fiction of V.S.Naipaul and Bharati Mukherjee". *Reworlding - The Literature of the Indian Diaspora*. Ed. Emmanuel S. Nelson. West Port: Greenwood Press, 1992, 51-61.

Connell, Michael, Jessia Grearson and Tom Grimes. "An Interview with Bharati Mukherjee". *Iowa Review*. 20. NO.3 (Spring, 1990), 7-32.

Crane, Ralph. J. "'A Passion for History and for Truth Telling': The Early Novels of Bapsi Sidhwa" *The Novels of Bapsi Sidhwa,* 48-60.

Daiches, David. *The Novel and the Modern World*. Chicago: Chicago University Press, 1960.

Dass, Veena Noble and R.K. Dhawan. eds. *Fiction of the Nineties*. New Delhi: Prestige Books, 1994.

Dass, Veena. ed. *Violence and Subjectivity*. New Delhi: Oxford University Press, 2000.

Dayal Samir. "Creating, Preserving, Destroying: Violence in Bharati Mukherjee's *Jasmine*". *Bharati Mukherjee: Critical Perspectives*. Ed. Emmanuel S.Nelson. New York: Garland Publishing, 1993, 65-88.

Desai, Anita. *Cry, the Peacock*. Calcutta: Ruba and Co., 1980.

Devi, Itishree. "Negotiating the Gap: Cross-Cultural Tensions in Bharati Mukherjee's Short Fiction" *Revaluations*. Vol. 2. No.3 (Winter, 1996), 21-29.

Dhaliwal, Amarpal K. "Other Subjects: Identity, Immigration, and Representations of Difference in *Jasmine*". *South Asian Review*. Vol.18. No.15 (December, 1994), 15-25.

Dhawan. R.K. ed. *Commonwealth Fiction*. New Delhi: Classical Publishing Company, 1988.

________. *Indian Women Novelists* Set. I Vol. V. New Delhi: Prestige Books, 1991.

________. *Indian Women Novelists* Set. III Vol. 3. New Delhi: Prestige Books, 1995.

________ and Novy Kapadia. eds. *The Novels of Bapsi Sidhwa*. New Delhi: Prestige Books, 1996.

________. "Entree: The Fiction of Bapsi Sidhwa". *The Novels of Bapsi Sidhwa,* 9-26.

Didur, Jill. "Cracking the Nations: Gender, Minorities, and Agency in Bapsi Sidhwa's *Cracking India*" *ARIEL*. Vol.29. No.3 (July, 1998), 43-64.

Dimri, Jaiwanti. "From Marriage to Murder: A Comparative Study of Bharati Mukherjee's *Wife* and *Jasmine*". *American Literature*

Today. Ed. Suman Bala. New Delhi: Intellectual Publishing House, 1994, 170-175.

D'Souza, Florence. "Bharati Mukherjee". *A Companion to Indian Fiction in English*. Ed. Pier Paolo Piciucco. New Delhi: Atlantic Publishers, 2004, 179-209.

________. "The Americanisation of an Immigrant Writer: Bharati Mukherjee". *Journal of Literature & Aesthetics*. Vol. 2. No. 2 (July–December, 2002), 7-15.

Eliot. T.S. *Notes Towards the Definition of Culture*. London: Faber and Faber, 1948.

Emmanuel. S. Nelson. ed. *Writers of the Indian Diaspora: A Bio-Bibliographical Critical Source*. Connectiant: Greenwood Press, 1993.

en. Wikipedia.org/wiki/cultureshock.

Fowler, Roger. ed. *Essays on Style and Language*. London: Routledge and Kegan Paul, 1966.

Frye, Northrop. *Anatomy of Criticism: Four Essays*. Princeton, N.J.: Princeton University Press, 1957.

Gabriel, Sharmani Patricia. "Tedium Aspiring to Literature." Rev. of. *The Holder of the World CRNLE Reviews Journal*. No. 1 & 2 (1995), 225-228.

________. "'Immigrant' or 'Postcolonial'? Towards a Poetics for Reading the Nation in Bharati Mukherjee's *The Tiger's Daughter*". *The Journal of Commonwealth Literature*. Vol.39. No.1 (2004), 85-103.

Gaur, Rashmi. "Gender Relations and Cross-Cultural Transactions in Bharati Mukherjee's *Desirable Daughters*". *Indian Journal of English Studies*.Vol. XLI. 2003-2004.

Ghanshyam, G.A. and Vasumati Nadig. "Bharati Mukherjee's *The Holder of the World:* A Bridge Between the Past and the Present". *Indian English Literature*. Ed. Basavaraj Naikar. New Delhi: Atlantic, 1984, 149-155.

Ghose, Amitav. *The Calcutta Chromosome*. Delhi: Ravi Dayal Publishers, 1996.

Gibaldi, Joseph. *MLA Handbook for Writers of Research Papers*. New Delhi: Affiliated East-West Press Pvt. Ltd., 2004.

Gomez, Christine. "The On-Going Quest of Bharati Mukherjee from Expatriation to Immigration". *Indian Women Novelists*. Set III, Vol.3. Ed. R.K.Dhawan. New Delhi: Prestige Books, 1995, 71-87.

Gravley – Novello, Lori. "Dangerous Crossings in Bapsi Sidhwa's *Ice-Candy Man* (*Cracking India*) and *An American Brat*". *South Asian Review*. Vol. 18. No.15 (December, 1994), 81-93.

Grewal, Gurleen. "Born Again American: The Immigrant Consciousness in *Jasmine*". *Bharati Mukherjee: Critical Perspectives*. Emmanuel. S. Nelson. New York & London: Garland Publishing, 1993, 181-196.

Hammond, Andrew. "Cultural Perspectivism in Bharati Mukherjee's Short Stories". *The Atlantic Literary Review*. Vol.5. No.3-4 (July-Sep & Oct-Dec., 2004), 120-136.

Hancock, Geoff. "An Interview with Bharati Mukherjee". *Canadian Fiction Magazine*. 59 (1987), 30-44.

Harvey, David. *The Condition of Postmodernity*. Oxford: Basil Blackwell, 1989.

Hashmi, Alamgir. "Prolegomena to the Study of Pakistani English and Pakistani Literature in English." *New Literatures Review*. No.25 (Summer, 1993), 1-21.

Havely, Cicely. "Patterns of Migration in the Work of Bapsi Sidhwa". *The Novels of Bapsi Sidhwa*. Ed. R.K. Dhawan and Novy Kapadia. New Delhi: Prestige Books, 1996, 61-70.

Holmes, Martha Stoddard. "Literature Annotations: Sidhwa, Bapsi: *Cracking India*." 2001. *Literature, Arts and Medicine Database*, 52nd ed., 2004. New York University, 20 Feb. 2004.

<http://endeavor.med.nyu.edu/litmed/lit-med-db/webdocs/webdescrips/sidhwa/1864-des-html>.

Holoway, John. *Narrative and Structure: Exploratory Essays*. Cambridge: Cambridge University Press, 1979.

Horney, Karen. *The Neurotic Personality of Our Time*. New York: W.W.Norton, 1937.

<http://web.cocc.edu/cagatucci/classes/hum 210/tml/India TML/India tml4.htm>

<http://web.cocc.edu/cagatucci/classes/hum 210/tml/asian TML.htm>. *India Timeline 3: The British Raj* (late 17th – early 20th centuries).

http://web.cocc.edu/cagatucci/classes/hum 210/tml/India TML/India tml3.htm India Timeline 4: Independence of India and Pakistan (20th century).

http://voices.cla.umn.edu/vg/Bios/entries/Mukherjee bharati. Bharati Mukherjee html.

http://en.wikipedia.org/wiki/Immigration.

Husain, Shahrukh. "Indian Women Writers in Britain and America – Novels of the Asian Experience: Journeys to the Promised Land". *Aspects of Commonwealth Literature*. (Collected Seminar Papers). Vol.2. London: University of London, 1992, 19-37.

Inamdar. F.A. "Immigrant Lives: Protagonists in Bharati Mukherjee's *The Tiger's Daughter* and *Wife*". *Indian Women Novelists*. Set I. Vol. V. Ed. R.K. Dhawan. New Delhi: Prestige Books, 1991, 187-196, also in *The Fiction of Bharati Mukherjee: A Critical Symposium*. Ed. R.K. Dhawan. New Delhi: Prestige Books, 1996, 39-52.

________. "Man-Woman Relationship in *The Tiger's Daughter* and *Wife*". *Contemporary Indian English Fiction: An Anthology of Essays*. Ed. Awasthi Kamal. Jalandhar: ABS Publications, 1993, 65-73.

Indira, S. "Exploration of Inner space: Anita Desai's *Cry, the Peacock* and Bharati Mukherjee's *Wife.*" *The Fiction of Bharati Mukherjee: A Critical Symposium.* Ed. R.K. Dhawan. New Delhi: Prestige Books, 1996, 59-65.

_______. "*Jasmine:* An Odyssey of Unhousement and Enhousement". *Commonwealth Writing: A Study in Expatriate Experience.* Eds. R.K.Dhawan and L.S.R. Krishna Sastry. New Delhi: Prestige Books, 1994. 86-90.

_______. "Splintered Self: An Approach to Bharati Mukherjee's *Wife*". *Commonwealth Writing: A Study in Expatriate Experience.* Eds. R.K.Dhawan and L.S.R. Krishna Sastry. New Delhi: Prestige Books, 1994, 72-76.

Itwaru, Arnold Harichand. "Who Jane?." Rev. of *Jasmine. The Toronto South Asian Review.* Vol.8. No.2 (Winter, 1990), 70-77.

Iyer, Nalini. "American/Indian". Metaphors of the Self in Bharati Mukherjee's *The Holder of the World. ARIEL.* Vol.27. No.4 (October, 1996), 29-44.

Jaidka, Manju. "Hyphenated Perspectives on the Cracking of India: Bapsi Sidhwa's *Ice Candy Man*". *South Asian Review.* Vol. 25. No.2 (2004), 43-50.

Jain, Jasbir and Amina Amin. eds. *Margins of Erasure: Purdah in the Subcontinental Novel in English.* New Delhi: Sterling Publishers, 1995.

Jain, Jasbir. "Foreignness of Spirit: The World of Bharati Mukherjee's Novels". *Journal of Indian Writing in English.* Vol. 13. No. 2 (July, 1985), 12-19.

_______. "The Male Presence in the "Purdah" Novel". *Margins of Erasure: Purdah in the Subcontinental Novel in English.* Eds. Jasbir Jain and Amina Amin. New Delhi: Sterling Publishers, 1995, 216-230.

Jain, Naresh. K. ed. *Women in Indo-Anglian Fiction: Tradition and Modernity.* New Delhi: Manohar Publishers and Distributors, 1998.

Jameson, Frederic. *Post-Modernism or The Cultural Logic of Late Capitalism.* London: Verson, 1991.

Joshi, Arun. *The Foreigner.* Delhi: Hind Pocket Books, 1968.

Juneja, Anita. "The Theme of Immigration and Transformation in *Jasmine*". *Poetcrit.* Vol.14. No.2 (July, 2001), 14-19.

_______. "Bharati Mukherjee at Sixty-Three". *Poetcrit.* Vol. 16. No. 2 (July, 2003), 72-78.

Jussawalla, Feroza. "Navjote Ceremonies: The Location Bapsi Sidhwa's Culture." *The Novels of Bapsi Sidhwa*: 80-87.

_______ and Reed Desenbrock. *Interviews with Writers of the Postcolonial World.* Jackson: University Press of Mississippi, 1993.

Kalpana, Wandrekar. *The Ailing Aliens: A Study of the Immigrant Psyche in Six Indian English Novels.* Gulbarga: JIWE Publications, 1996.

Kamal, Awasthi.N ed. *Contemporary Indian English Fiction: An Anthology of Essays.* Jalandhar: ABS Publications, 1993.

Kapadia, Novy. ed. *Parsi Fiction.* Vol. I. New Delhi: Prestige Books, 2001.

_______. "The Theme of Marriage in Parsi Fiction". *Parsi Fiction.* Vol. 1, 100-120.

_______. "Ethnic Identity in Rudy Wiebe's *Peace Shall Destroy Many* and Bapsi Sidhwa's *The Crow Eaters*". *Perspectives on Canadian Fiction.* Ed. Sudhakar Pandey. New Delhi: Prestige Books, 1994, 121-133.

_______. "The Parsee Paradox in Bapsi Sidhwa's '*The Crow Eaters*". Ed. R.K. Dhawan. *Commonwealth Fiction.* New Delhi: Classical Publishing Company, 1988 also in *The Novels of Bapsi Sidhwa* Eds. R.K. Dhawan and Novy Kapadia. New Delhi: Prestige Books, 1996, 125-135.

_______. "Expatriate Experience and Theme of Marriage in *An American Brat*". *The Novels of Bapsi Sidhwa,* 187-199.

_______. *Parsi Fiction.* Vol. 2. New Delhi: Prestige Books, 2001.

Khan, Farukh. "Women. Identity and Dis-location in *The Bride*". *The Novels of Bapsi Sidhwa.* Eds. R.K. Dhawan and Novy Kapadia. New Delhi: Prestige Books, 1996, 140-151.

King, Russell, John Connell and Paul White. eds. *Writing Across Worlds: Literature and Migration.* London: Rout ledge, 1995.

Kirpal, Viney *The Third World Novel of Expatriation: A Study of Émigré Fiction by Indian, West African and Caribbean Writers.* New Delhi: Sterling Publishers, 1989.

Kumar. Gajendra eds. *Indian English Fiction: Readings and Reflections.* New Delhi: Sarup & Sons, 2003.

Kumar, Nagendra. *The Fiction of Bharati Mukherjee: A Cultural Perspective.* New Delhi: Atlantic Publishers, 2001.

Kumar, Narendra V.L.V.N. "The Sword and the Needle: Protest in Bapsi Sidhwa's *The Pakistani Bride*". *The Feminist Mode in Commonwealth Literature.* Ed. R.A. Singh. Bareilly: Prakash Book Depot, 2001. 84-89.

_______. "Parsi Writing a Note". *Parsee Novel.* Ed. V.L.V.N. Kumar Nagendra. New Delhi: Prestige Books, 2002, 27-33.

_______. "The Twain Shall Meet: Bapsi Sidhwa's Novels". *Parsee Novel,* 34-75.

_______. *Parsee Novel.* New Delhi: Prestige Books, 2002.

Leech, Geoffrey. N. *A Linguistic Guide to English Poetry.* England, Longman, 1969.

Luo, Shao Pin. "Rewriting Travel: Acdaf Souief's *The Map of Love* and Bharati Mukherjee's *The Holder of the World.*" *Journal of Commonwealth Literature.* Vol. 38. No. 2 (2003) 77-104.

Malmberg, Jacob Lee. "Bapsi Sidhwa, b.1939". 2001. *Voices From the Gaps: Women Writers of Color.* Dept. of English, write, of Minnesota 2002.

20 Feb. 2004. <http://voices.cla.umn.edu/newsite/authors/SIDHWA Bapsi. htm>

Mandal, Somdatta, ed. *Asian American Writing*. Vol.2. New Delhi: Prestige Books, 2000.

Mangayarkarasi, R. "Parsi Identity in Boman Desai's *The Memory of Elephants* and Bapsi Sidhwa's *The Crow Eaters* and *Ice-Candy-Man*". *Some Perspectives in Indian Writing in English.* Chennai: The Dept. of English, SDNBV College for Women, 2005, 177-190.

Manju, Kak. "Travelling in Time." Rev. of *The Holder of the World." Indian Review of Books*. Vol.3. No.5 (Feb 16-Mar.,1994), 24-25.

Manju Sharma, Maya. "The Inner World of Bharati Mukherjee: From Expatriate to Immigrant". *Bharati Mukherjee: Critical Perspectives*. Ed. Emmanuel. S Nelson, New York & London: Garland Publishing, 1993, 3-22.

Manvi, Meera, "Rereading Indian Womanhood: A Note on the Narrative Structure of *Wife*". *Osmania Journal of English Studies*. Vol.25 (1989), 140-150.

Mehta, Sandhya. "The Utmost Coasts Abroad. Hannah Easton's Quest in *The Holder of the World." Indian Women Novelists*. set III. Vol. 3. Ed. R.K.Dhawan. New Delhi: Prestige Books, 1995, 193-198.

Minh-ha, Trinh. T. *Woman, Native, Other*. Bloomington: Indiana University Press, 1989.

Mohanty, Chandra Talpade. "Defining Genologies: Feminist Reflections on Being South Asian". *Our Feet Walk The Sky: Women of South Asian Diaspora.* Ed. Women of South Asian Collective. San Francisco: Aunt Lute Press, 1993, 351-358.

Mohanty, Satya. P. "Epilogue, Colonial Legacies, Multicultural Features: Relativism, Objectivity, and the Challenge of Otherness". *PMLA.* 110 (1995), 108-118.

Mukherjee, Bharati. "Beyond Multiculturalism: Surviving the Nineties". *Journal of Modern Literature.* Vol. 20. No.1 (Summer, 1996), 29-34.

________. *Darkness.* Canada: Penguin, 1985.

________. "Interviewed. "*The Times of India*". October 1, 1989.

________. <http://www.english.emory.edu/Bahri/Mukherjee.html>

________. *The Hindustan Times.* 9. Feb., 1990, 3.

________. "BANGLA: The Way Back". *The Genius of Language: Fifteen Writers Reflect on Their Mother Tongues*. Ed. Wendy Lesser. New York: Pantheon Books, 2004, 11-24.

Myles, Anita. "Bharati Mukherjee". *Feminism and the Post-Modern Indian Women Novelists in English.* New Delhi: Sarrup & Sons, 2006, 107-123.

Naikar, Basavaraj. ed. *Indian English Literature.* New Delhi: Atlantic Publishers, 1984.

———. *Indian English Literature.* Vol. III. New Delhi: Atlantic Publishers and Distributors, 2002, 247.

Naipaul, V.S. *The Mystic Masseur.* London: Andre Deutsch, 1957.

Nair, Hema. "'A Puritan in a Mughal Court'. Rev. of *The Holder of the World*". *The Toronto Review of Contemporary Writing Abroad.* Vol. 12. No.2 (Winter, Spring, 1994), 104-107.

Nayak, Bhagabat. "Quest for Identity in Immigrant Sensibility: A Study of Bharati Mukherjee's *Desirable Daughters*". *Studies in Women Writers in English.* Volume IV. Eds. Mohit K. Roy and Rama Kundu. New Delhi: Atlantic Publishers and Distributors, 2005, 250-265.

Nelson, Emmanuel. S. *Bharati Mukherjee: Critical Perspectives.* New York & London: Garland Publishing, 1993.

———. "Kamala Markandaya, Bharati Mukherjee and the Indian Immigrant Experience". *Toronto South Asian Review.* 9. No. 2 (Winter, 1991), 1-9.

———. *Reworlding – The Literature of the Indian Diaspora.* Westport: Greenwood Press, 1992.

———. "Introduction". *Bharati Mukherjee: Critical Perspectives:* ix-xvii.

Nithyanandam, Indira and Reena Kothari. eds. *Indo-English Fiction: The Last Decade.* New Delhi: Creative Books, 2002.

———. "Language and Style. Bharati Mukherjee's *Leave It To Me* and *Jasmine* – A Comparative Study". *Indo-English Fiction: The Last Decade.* Eds. Indira Nithyanandam and Reena Kothari. New Delhi: Creative Books, 2002, 79-84.

Niven, Alastair. ed. *The Commonwealth Writer Overseas: Themes of Exile and Expatriation.* Brussels: M. Didier, 1976.

"Oh Calcutta! Bharati Mukherjee's *The Tiger's Daughter*". *Times Literary Supplement.* 29 (June, 1973), 736

Pabby, D.K. "Portrayal of the Diasporic Experience in Bharati Mukherjee's *Desirable Daughters*". Paper presented at the MELUS conference. 4-5 April 2003, Panjab Univ. Chandigarh.

Padma, T. "From Accultaration to Self-Actualization: Diasporal Dream in Bharati Mukherjee's *Jasmine*". *Indian Women Novelists.* Set III. Vol. 3. Ed. R.K.Dhawan. New Delhi: Prestige Books, 1995, 161-168.

Pandey, Mithilesh. ed. *Recent Indian Literature in English: A Cultural Perspective.* New Delhi: Anmol Publications, 1999.

Pandey, Sudhakar. ed. *Perspectives on Canadian Fiction.* New Delhi: Prestige Books, 1994.

Pandit, M.L. *New Commonwealth Writing: A Critical Response.* New Delhi: Prestige Books, 1996.

———. "Woman as Protagonist: Self in Margaret Lawrence's *The Diviners* and Bharati Mukherjee's *The Tiger's Daughter*". *New Commonwealth Writing: A Critical Response.* New Delhi: Prestige Books, 1996, 31-34.

Pandit, M.L. "The Indian Middle-Woman in America. Cross-Cultural Concerns in Bharati Mukherjee's *The Tiger's Daughter* and *Wife*". *New Commonwealth Writing: A Critical Response*. New Delhi: Prestige Books, 1996, 35-40.

Parameswaran, Uma. "What Price Expatriation?". *The Commonwealth Writer Overseas: Themes of Exile and Expatriation*. Ed. Alaistair Niven. Brussels: M. Didier, 1976, 41-52.

________. "Rev. of *The Holder of The World*". *World Literature Today*. Vol.68. No.3 (Summer, 1994), 636-637.

Paranjape, R. Makarand. "The Novels of Bapsi Sidhwa". *Commonwealth Fiction*. Ed. R.K. Dhawan. New Delhi: Classical Publishing Company, 1988, 80-103, also as "The Early Novels of Bapsi Sidhwa" in *The Novels of Bapsi Sidhwa*. Ed. R.K. Dhawan and Novy Kapadia. New Delhi: Prestige Books, 1996, 88-106.

Parasuram, Laxmi. "Holding the Colliding Walls: Cross-Cultural Perception in *The Holder of the World*". *The Fiction of Bharati Mukherjee: A Critical Symposium*. Ed. R.K. Dhawan. New Delhi: Prestige Books, 1996, 196-201.

Parekh, Bhiku. "Multiculturalism". 24 July 2005, http://google.com/.

Parekh, Pushpa N. "Telling her Tale Narrative Voice and Gender Roles in Bharati Mukherjee's *Jasmine*". *Bharati Mukherjee: Critical Perspectives*. Ed. Emmanuel S. Nelson. New York & London: Garland Publishing Inc, 1993, 109-126.

Pathak. R.S. "Problematising the Minority Discourse: Inlets to the Parsi Sensibility". *Parsi Fiction*. Vol. I. Ed. Novy Kapadia. New Delhi: Prestige Books, 2001, 88-99.

________. *Quest for Identity in Indian English Writing*. New Delhi: Bahri Publications, 1992.

________. *Recent Indian Fiction*. New Delhi: Prestige Books, 1994.

Patil, Mallikarjun "Bharati Mukherjee's *Wife*: A Post Modernist Novel". *Indian English Fiction: Readings and Reflections*. Eds. Gajendra Kumar and Uday Shankar O'sha. New Delhi: Sarup & Sons, 2003, 116-123.

Patricia Gabriel, Sharmani. "Tedium Aspiring to Literature". *CRNLE Review Journal*. RJ. 182 (1995), 225-228.

________. "'Routes of Identity': In Conversation with Bharati Mukherjee". *Ariel*. Vol. 34. No.4 (October, 2003), 125-138.

________. "'Immigrant' or 'Post-Colonial'? Towards a Poetic for Reading The Nation in Bharati Mukherjee's *The Tiger's Daughter*". *The Journal of Commonwealth Literature*. Vol.39. No.1 (2004), 85-103.

Pennebakar, Mattie Katherine. "The Will of Men: Victimization of Women During India's Partition". *Agora*. No.1. Issue 1 (Summer, 2003) <http://www.tamu. edu/chr/agora/summeroo/pennebaker.pdf>

Piciucco, Pier Paolo. ed. *A Companion to Indian Fiction in English*. New Delhi: Atlantic Publishers, 2004.

Ponzanesi, Sandra. "Bharati Mukherjee's *Jasmine*: The Exuberance of Immigration, Feminist Strategies and Multi Cultural Negotiations". *Studies in Indian Writing in English.* Vol.11. Ed. Mittapalli Rajeshwar and Pier Paolo Piciucco. New Delhi: Atlantic Publishers, 2001, 77-107.

Prabha Barat, Ananda. "Bharati Mukherjee and the Immigrant Psyche: *The Tiger's Daughter*". *The Fiction of Bharati Mukherjee: A Critical Symposium.* Ed. R.K. Dhawan. New Delhi: Prestige Books, 1996, 53-58.

Prabhu, M. "Plagiarised Pap Alienated work. Rev. of *The Holder of the World*". *Indian Book Chronicle* Vol. 20. No. 2 (Feb., 1995), 7-8.

Prasad, Madhusudan. ed. *Indian English Novelists: An Anthology of Critical Essays.* New Delhi: Sterling Publishers, 1982.

Pratab Singh, Randir. *Bapsi Sidhwa.* New Delhi: Ivy Publishing House, 2005.

Rajan, Gita. "Bharati Mukherjee (1940 -)". *Writers of the Indian Diaspora: A Bio-Bibilographical Critical Source.* Ed. Nelson Immanuel. Connecticut: Greenwood Press, 1993, 235-242.

Rajan, Julie. "Cracking Sidhwa: Interview with Bapsi Sidhwa". *Monsoon Magazine.* 3 (2000). 21 Feb. 2004. http://www.monsoonmag.com/interviews/i3inter-sidhwa.html

Rajeshwar, M. "Sado-Masochism as a Literary Device in Bharati Mukherjee's *Wife*". *Indian Women Novelists.* Set III: Vol.3 Ed. R.K. Dhawan. New Delhi: Prestige Books, 1995: 127-139 also in *The Fiction of Bharati Mukherjee: A Critical Symposium.* Ed. M. Rajeshwar. New Delhi: Prestige Books, 1996, 90-99 and also in *Indian Women Novelists and Psychoanalysis: A Study of the Neurotic Characters.* Ed. M. Rajeshwar New Delhi: Atlantic Publishers and Distributors, 2001, 34-44.

Rajeshwar, Mittapalli and Pier Paolo Piciucco eds. *Studies in Indian Writing in English.* Vol. II. New Delhi: Atlantic Publishers, 2001.

Ramachandra, Ragini. "Bharati Mukherjee's *Wife:* An Assessment". *The Literary Criterion.* Vol. 26, No. 3 (1991), 56-67.

Ramamurthy. K.S. *The Rise of the Indian Novel in English.* 6th ed. New Delhi: Sterling Publishers, 1987.

Rani, Nirupa. K. "Gender and Imagination in Bapsi Sidhwa's Fiction". *The Novels of Bapsi Sidhwa.* Eds. R.K. Dhawan and Novy Kapadia. New Delhi: Prestige Books, 1996, 118-124.

Rao, A.V. Krishna. "From Expatriation to Immigration: The Case of Bharati Mukherjee". *Indian Women Novelists:* Set III. Vol. 3. Ed. R.K. Dhawan. New Delhi: Prestige, 1995, 88-102.

Rao, P. Mallikarjuna. "Between Expatriation and Assimilation: A Study of Bharati Mukherjee's *Jasmine*". *Indian Fiction in English.* Eds. P. Mallikarjuna Rao and M. Rajeshwar. New Delhi: Atlantic Publishers, 1999, 270-278.

________ and M. Rajeshwar. eds. *Indian Fiction in English*. New Delhi: Atlantic Publishers, 1999.

Rathod, Pradip Singh B. "The Psycho/Cross-Cultural Patterns in the Protagonist of Bharati Mukherjee's *Wife*". *POETCRIT*. Vol.17.No.2 (July, 2004), 32-38.

Ray. K. Mohit and Rama Kundu. eds. *Studies in Women Writers in English.* New Delhi: Atlantic Publishers, 2005.

Remak, Henry, H.H. *Comparative Literature: Method and Perspective.* Carbondale: Southern Illinois Press, 1961.

Rich, Adrienne. "Resisting Amnesia: History and Personal life". *Blood, Bread and Poetry*. New York: W.W. Norton, 1986, 136-155.

Richler, Mordecai. *Son of a Smaller Hero.* Toronto: McClelland & Stewart, 1965.

Ross, L. Robert. "*The Bride*: The Treatment of Women". *The Novels of Bapsi Sidhwa*, Eds. R.K Dhawan and Novy Kapadia. New Delhi: Prestige Books, 1996, 162-165.

________. *International Literature in English: Essays on Major Writers.* New York: Garland Publishing, 1991.

Roy, Sumita. "*Jasmine:* Exile as Spiritual Quest". *Indian Women Novelists.* Set III. Vol.V. Ed. R.K. Dhawan. New Delhi: Prestige Books, 1991, 202-209.

Rushdie, Salman. *Imaginary Homelands: Essays and Criticism 1981-1991.* London: Granta Books, 1991.

Rustomji-Kerns, Roshni. "Expatriates, Immigrants, and Literature: Three South Asian Women Writers". *The Massachusetts Review.* 29. No. 4 (Winter, 1988-1989), 655-665.

Sachdeva Mann, Harveen. "*Cracking India*': Minority Women Writers and the Contentious Margins of Indian Novelists Discourse". *The Journal of Commonwealth Literature.* Vol. 29. No. 2 (1994), 71-94.

Sahai, Dipika, "Culture-Consciousness and Gender Bias in Bapsi Sidhwa's *The Pakistani Bride*: A Post Colonial Approach". *The Commonwealth Review.* Vol.15. No.1 (2004), 78-86.

Said, Edward. *Culture and Imperialism.* New York: Knopf, 1993.

Sampat, Manju. "Bharati Mukherjee: The Fiction of Alienation and Identification". *Indian English Fiction 1980-90: An Assessment*. Eds. Nilufer E Bharucha and Vilas Sarang. Delhi: B.R. Publishing Corporation, 1994, 139-150.

________. "Bharati Mukherjee: Some Essential Conclusions". *Critical Practice.* Vol. Vii. No.1 (January, 2001), 71-81.

________. "'Expatriate Exuberance' Rev. of *Desirable Daughters*". *A Review of Books.* Vol. 7. No. 7 & 8 (July-August, 2002), 15

Sandler, Linda. "Review of *Wife*". *Saturday Night* (October, 1975), 75-76.

________. "Violence as a Device of Problem Solving". *Saturday Night.* 90.5 (October, 1975), 75-76.

Sarada, T. "Marriage: A Boon or Bane? A Study of Bharati Mukherjee's *Wife* and Gita Hariharan's *The Thousand Faces of Night*". *Women's Writing in India: New Perspectives.* Ed. K.V. Surendra. New Delhi: Sarup & Sons, 2002, 57-64.

Sathupati, Prasanna Sree. "Psychotic Violence of Dimple in Bharati Mukherjee's *Wife*", *Indian Women Novelists.* Set III: Vol.3. Ed. R.K. Dhawan. New Delhi: Prestige Books, 1995, 110-116.

Sattar, Arshina. "Review of Bharati Mukherjee's *The Holder of the World.*" *The Sunday Times* (Sunday Review) (20 March, 1994), 6.

Saxena. O.P. *Glimpses of Indo-English Fiction.* Vol. 1. New Delhi: Jainsons Publications, 1995.

Schorer, Mark. "Technique As Discovery". *Sons and Lovers.* Ed. Gamini Salgado. London: Macmillan, 1969, 106-111.

Sengupta. C. "Asian Protagonists in Bharati Mukherjee's *The Middleman and Other Stories*". *Quest for Identity in Indian English Writing Part I: Fiction.* Ed. R.S. Pathak. New Delhi: Bahri Publications, 1992, 148-156.

________. "Feminine Mystique in Bharati Mukherjee's *Jasmine*". *Fiction of the Nineties.* Eds. Veena Noble Dass and R.K. Dhawan. New Delhi: Prestige Books, 1994, 197-204.

________. "Feminine Mystique in Bharati Mukherjee's *Jasmine*". *Indian Women Novelists.* Set III. Vol.3. Ed. R.K. Dhawan. New Delhi: Prestige Books, 1995, 159-168.

Shaffer. E.S. ed. "Editor's Note: Comparative Literature in Britain". *Comparative Criticism. A Year Book.* London: Cambridge University Press, 1979.

Shakespeare, William. *Sonnets.* New Delhi: Mac millan, 1983.

Sidhwa, Bapsi. "New Neighbors". 11 Aug. 1997. *Time* 20 Feb. 2004. <http://www.time.com/time/magazine/1997/int/970811/spl.neighbors.html>

________. "Sense of the City: Lahore" *BBC News* World ed., 29 July 2003. 20 Feb. 2004. <http://news.bbc.co.uk/2/hi/south-asia/3106541.stm>

________. "Why Do I Write?" *The Novels of Bapsi Sidhwa.* Eds. R.K. Dhawan and Novy Kapadia. New Delhi: Prestige Books, 1998, 27-34.

Singh, Amarjit, "Symbolism in Bharati Mukherjee's *Jasmine*". *Symbolism in Indian Fiction in English.* Ed. K. Ramesh Srivastava. Jalandhar: ABS Publications, 1997, 163-169.

Singh. R.A. ed. *The Feminist Move in Commonwealth Literature.* Bareilly: Prakash Book Depot, 2001.

Singh, Randhir Pratap. "Buoyant Woman". *Bapsi Sidhwa.* New Delhi: Ivy Publishing House, 2005, 22-36.

Sivaramakrishna, M. "Bharati Mukherjee". *Indian English Novelists: An Anthology of Critical Essays.* Ed. Madhusudan Prasad. New Delhi: Sterling Publishers, 1982, 71-86.

Sivaraman. S. "*Jasmine*: A Search for Alternate Realities". *Recent Indian Fiction*. Ed. R.S. Pathak. New Delhi: Prestige Books, 1994, 210-218.

Srivastava, Ramesh K. ed. *Symbolism in Indian Fiction in English.* Jalandar: ABS Publications, 1997.

St. Andrews. "Co-Wanderers Kogawa and Mukherjee: New Immigrant Writers". *World Literature Today.* 66.1 (1992), 56-58.

Steiner, George. *Extra-territorial: Papers on Language and Literature.* London: Faber and Faber, 1968.

Subramanian. N. ed. *Introduction to the Study of Comparative Literature: Theory and Practice*. India: Teesi Publications, 1997.

Sujatha, S. "The Theme of Disintegration: A Comparative Study of Anita Desai's *Cry, the Peacock* and Bharati Mukherjee's *Wife*". *The Commonwealth Review*. Vol. 4. No. 2 (1992-93), 45-49.

Suman Bala. ed. *American Literature Today.* New Delhi: Intellectual Publishing House, 1994.

Suneel, Seema. "Emergence of New Woman in Indian Fiction: A Study of Bharati Mukherjee's *Wife*, Shashi Deshpande's *That Long Silence* and R.W. Desai's *Frailty, Thy Name is (W)Oman*". *Feminism and Literature.* Ed. Noble Veena Dass. New Delhi: Prestige Books, 1995, 219-229.

Surendra. K.V. ed. *Women's Writing in India. New Perspectives.* New Delhi: Sarup & Sons, 2002.

Swain. S.P. "Dimple in Bharati Mukherjee's *Wife*: A Study of the Lacerated Self". *Indian Women Novelists.* Set III. Vol. 3. Ed. R.K. Dhawan. New Delhi: Prestige Books, 1995, 117-126, also as "Dimple in *Wife*: A Study of the Lacerated Self " in *The Fiction of Bharati Mukherjee: A Critical Symposium.* Ed. R.K. Dhawan. New Delhi: Prestige Books, 1996, 82-89.

________. "Problems of Identity: A Study of Bharati Mukherjee's *Desirable Daughters*". *Journal of Literature & Aesthetics* (Jan–Dec., 2003), 127-133.

________. "Anatomy of Change and the Problems of Self: A Study of Bharati Mukherjee's *The Tiger's Daughter*". *Studies in Women Writers in English.* Vol. IV. Eds. Mohit K. Ray and Rama. Kundu. New Delhi: Atlantic Publishers, 2005, 229-239.

Trikha, Pradeep, "Quest for Self and the Immigrant Experience in Bharati Mukherjee's Fiction". *Indian Writing in English: The Last Decade.* Ed. Raju Bhargava. New Delhi: Rawat Publications, 2002, 178-194.

Trivedi, Harish and Meenakshi Mukherjee. eds. *Interrogating Post-Colonial: Theory, Text and Practice.* Shimla: Indian Institute of Advanced Study, 1996.

Veena Das, Noble. eds. *Feminism and Literature.* New Delhi: Prestige Books, 1995.

Vijayasree. C. "The Politics and Poetics of Expatriation: The Indian Version(s)". *Interrogating Post-Colonialism: Theory, Text and*

Content. Eds. Harish Trivedi and Meenakshi Mukherjee. Shimla: Indian Institute of Advanced Study, 1996, 221-229.

Vishnu, A.K. "Bharati Mukherjee's *Wife*: A Critique." *Recent Indian Literature in English: A Cultural Perspective.* Ed. Mithilesh Pandey. New Delhi: Anmol Publications, 1999, 204-210.

Viswanath, Gita. "Modes of Resistance in the South – Asian Novel: A Study of the Fiction by Bapsi Sidhwa, Rohinton Mistry and Yasmine Gooneratne". *The Fiction of Rohinton Mistry: Critical Studies.* Ed. Jaydipsingh Dodiya, New Delhi: Prestige Books, 1988, 38-43.

Wandrekar, Kalpana. *The Ailing Aliens:* (A Study of 'the Immigrant Psyche' in Six Indian English Novels) Gulbarga: JIWE Publications, 1996, 63-77.

Watling, Gabrielle. "Hybridity as Agency for the Post – Colonial Migrant: Bharati Mukherjee's *Jasmine* and Sara Suleri's *Meatless Days*". *Kunapipi.* vol. 21. No. 1 (1999), 60-70.

Weisstein, Ulrich. *Comparative Literature and Theory: Survey and Introduction.* London: Indiana University Press, 1968.

Wickramangamage, Carmen. "Relocations Positive Act: The Immigrant Experience in Bharati Mukherjee." *Diaspora.* 2.2 (1992), 171-200.

Wilder, Jay. "Bapsi Sidhwa". 1998, 2001. *Post-Colonial Studies at Emory* English Dept., Emory Univ. 2002. 15 Feb. 2004. <http://www/emory.edu/ENGLISH/Bahri/Sidhwa.html>www.pbs.org/wgbh/cultureshock.

Zaman, Niaz. "Images of Purdah in Bapsi Sidhwa's Novels". *Margins of Erasure: Purdah in the Subcontinental Novel in English.* Eds. Jasbir Jain and Amina Amin. New Delhi: Sterling Publishers, 1995, 156-173.

Index